Gerald Howard-Smith and the 'Lost Generation' of Late Victorian and Edwardian England

Gerald Howard-Smith's life is intriguing both in its own right and as a vehicle for exploring the world in which he lived. Tall, boisterous and sometimes rather irascible, he was one of the so-called 'Lost Generation' whose lives were cut short by the First World War. Brought up in London, and educated at Eton and Cambridge, he excelled at both cricket and athletics. After qualifying as a solicitor he moved to Wolverhampton and threw himself into the local sporting scene, making a considerable name for himself in the years before the First World War. Volunteering for military service in 1914, he was decorated for bravery before being killed in action two years later. Reporting his death, the War History of the South Staffordshire Regiment claimed that, 'In his men's eyes he lived as a loose-limbed hero, and in him they lost a very humorous and a very gallant gentleman.'

As well as telling the fascinating story of Gerald Howard-Smith for the first time, this important new biography explores such complex and important issues as childhood and adolescence, class relations, sporting achievement, manliness and masculinity, metropolitan-provincial relationships and forms of commemoration. It will therefore be of interest to educationalists, sports historians, local and regional historians and those interested in class, gender and civilian-military relations – indeed all those seeking to understand the economic, social, and cultural life of late nineteenth- and early twentieth-century Britain.

John Benson is Emeritus Professor of History at the University of Wolverhampton. He has written widely on nineteenth- and twentieth-century history, has held visiting positions in Canada and Japan and has spoken on his work throughout Great Britain as well as in Australia, Canada, Germany, Japan, the Netherlands, New Zealand and the United States of America. His books include *British Coalminers in the Nineteenth Century: A Social History*, *The Working Class in Britain, 1850–1939*, *The Rise of Consumer Society in Britain, 1880–1980*, *Prime Time: A History of the Middle Aged in Twentieth-Century Britain*, *Affluence and Authority: A Social History of Twentieth-Century Britain* and *The Wolverhampton Tragedy: Death and the 'Respectable' Mr Lawrence*.

Gerald Howard-Smith and the 'Lost Generation' of Late Victorian and Edwardian England

John Benson

Routledge
Taylor & Francis Group

LONDON AND NEW YORK

First published 2017
by Routledge
2 Park Square, Milton Park, Abingdon, Oxon OX14 4RN

and by Routledge
711 Third Avenue, New York, NY 10017

First issued in paperback 2018

Routledge is an imprint of the Taylor & Francis Group, an informa business

© 2017 John Benson

The right of John Benson to be identified as author of this work has been asserted by him in accordance with sections 77 and 78 of the Copyright, Designs and Patents Act 1988.

All rights reserved. No part of this book may be reprinted or reproduced or utilised in any form or by any electronic, mechanical, or other means, now known or hereafter invented, including photocopying and recording, or in any information storage or retrieval system, without permission in writing from the publishers.

Trademark notice: Product or corporate names may be trademarks or registered trademarks, and are used only for identification and explanation without intent to infringe.

British Library Cataloguing in Publication Data
A catalogue record for this book is available from the British Library

Library of Congress Cataloging in Publication Data
Names: Benson, John, 1945 July 23- author.
Title: Gerald Howard-Smith and the "Lost Generation" of late Victorian and Edwardian England / John Benson.
Description: Milton Park, Abingdon, Oxon : Routledge, 2017. | Includes bibliographical references and index.
Identifiers: LCCN 2016005915 | ISBN 9781472435903 (hardback : alkaline paper) | ISBN 9781315584614 (ebook)
Subjects: LCSH: Howard-Smith, Gerald, 1880-1916. | Great Britain--History--Victoria, 1837-1901--Biography. | Great Britain--History--Edward VII, 1901-1910--Biography. | World War, 1914-1918--Great Britain--Biography. | Soldiers--England--Biography. | Young men--England--Biography. | Upper class--England--Biography. | Athletes--England--Biography. | Teachers--England--Biography.
Classification: LCC DA565.H758 B46 2017 | DDC 942.082/3092 [B] --dc23
LC record available at https://lccn.loc.gov/2016005915

ISBN 13: 978-1-138-32968-3 (pbk)
ISBN 13: 978-1-4724-3590-3 (hbk)

Typeset in Times New Roman
by Taylor & Francis Books

 Printed in the United Kingdom
by Henry Ling Limited

For Joel, Tom and Emma

CONTENTS

LIST OF FIGURES ix
ACKNOWLEDGEMENTS x
INTRODUCTION xi

PART I
PRIVILEGE 1

1 'A THOROLY SOUND HEALTHY MINDED GOOD FELLOW': HOME, SCHOOL AND SOCIALISATION 3

2 'AN UNASSAILABLE DISTINCTION THROUGH LIFE': UNIVERSITY, SPORT AND STATUS 31

PART II
CAREER 53

3 'GENTLEMANLY MANNERS AND REFINED HABITS': LONDON, THE HOME COUNTIES AND TEACHING 55

4 'A GENTLEMAN OF EXPERIENCE': WOLVERHAMPTON, THE LAW AND SPORT 73

PART III
SACRIFICE 95

5 'THE THING TO DO': CLASS, PATRIOTISM AND PREPARATION 97

6 'LARGE, GALLANT, AND LOOSE-LIMBED': CLASS, PATRIOTISM AND SACRIFICE 115

PART IV
COMMEMORATION 135

7 'IN LOVING MEMORY': CLASS AND COMMEMORATION, REPRESENTATION AND MISREPRESENTATION 137

BIBLIOGRAPHY 146
INDEX 151

FIGURES

I.1	Gerald Howard-Smith, c. 1902.	xvii
1.1	Gerald Howard-Smith (back row, far right) and the Eton Field XI, 1898.	20
2.1	Gerald Howard-Smith (back row, second from left) and a Trinity College Cricket XI, 1903.	45
6.1	Gerald Howard-Smith (far right) and fellow officers of the 6th Battalion, South Staffordshire Regiment, three miles southeast of Ypres, March 1915.	119

ACKNOWLEDGEMENTS

I am pleased to take this opportunity to acknowledge the help I have received in writing this book. I am grateful for the financial support of the British Academy and the University of Wolverhampton. I am grateful, too, for the support of friends and colleagues at the University of Wolverhampton: Lorella Baynes, John Bourne, John Buckley, Richard Hawkins, Lynn Leighton-Johnstone and Malcolm Wanklyn have provided me with a variety of advice, information and encouragement.

I have also received generous assistance from archivists, librarians and historians (many of whom I have never met and thus never had the opportunity to thank personally). George Bernard (University of Southampton), Philip Bye (East Sussex Record Office), Richard Croan, Adam Green (Cambridge University Library), Alan Jones, James Kirwan (Trinity College, Cambridge), Matthew Lucas, Anna Manthorpe (East Sussex Record Office), Joanne Peck (Lichfield Record Office), Peter Skidmore, Jonathan Smith (Cambridge University Library), Christine Vickers (Eton College Archives), Dave Walker (Kensington Central Library), Anthony Whitaker (in several ways over several years) and David Woods have all been extremely helpful.

However, my greatest debt is to friends, colleagues and fellow historians (two of whom I have again never met) who have taken a particular interest in the progress of the book. Jane Hamlett (Royal Holloway), Mike Huggins (University of Cumbria), Spencer Jones (University of Wolverhampton), Dilwyn Porter (formerly De Montfort University), Gary Sheffield (University of Wolverhampton), Laura Ugolini (University of Wolverhampton) and Harvey Woolf (formerly University of Wolverhampton) have all taken time from their own work to read and comment fully and helpfully on chapters from an earlier draft of the manuscript. I owe them a great deal.

INTRODUCTION

Privilege, power and status

There is no end, it seems, to the British public's fascination with the lives and loves of the aristocracy and the upper middle class. One has only to think of the popularity of the National Trust or of the television series *Downton Abbey* to appreciate the place that such elite groups have managed to retain in the national consciousness.[1] Despite recent attempts at diversification, the National Trust continues to market itself by urging potential visitors to connect with the lives of the celebrated and the privileged: 'From historic houses to castles, gardens to parklands, film locations to the homes of famous artists, authors, politicians and aristocracy, here are just a few suggestions of places you might like to discover with your pass.'[2]

Despite some carping on the sidelines, *Downton Abbey*, the Crawley family (and its servants) continue to attract both critical acclaim and viewing figures of 10 million or so.[3] Indeed, publishers have developed what amounts to a burgeoning mini-industry of *Downton Abbey* spin-offs, with books such as Jessica Fellowes's *The World of Downton Abbey*, Pamela Horn's *The Real Life Women of Downton Abbey* and the Countess of Carnarvon's *Lady Almina and the Real Downton Abbey: The Legacy of Highcleve*.[4] They are part of a broader phenomenon. 'For the past 10 years', explained Kathryn Hughes a few years ago with something of a shudder, 'publishers have been timidly churning out me-too versions of the last mega hit, Amanda Foreman's excellent *Georgina*, which had appeared a whole decade earlier. The bookshelves were full of biographies of vaguely naughty Duchesses with skyscraper hair and a bad gambling/drink/marriage habit.'[5]

The public's fascination with the goings-on of a tiny, privileged group who lived one hundred years and more ago and whose lives were so very different from their own needs some explaining. It has been fuelled in part, of course, by nostalgia for a world that has been lost, a world in which ladies were ladies, men were men and gentlemen were gentlemen, a world where Britain ruled the waves and everybody knew his place.[6] However, the fascination with the aristocracy and upper middle class can also be explained – to some extent at least – by the sense that remarkably little has changed since the late nineteenth and early twentieth centuries. There is a feeling that the privileged backgrounds of those responsible for the imposition of early twenty-first-century austerity mean either that they are ideally suited to take tough decisions or that they have no understanding of the lives of those in whose interests they claim to be governing. But whether the upper- and upper middle-class composition of the early twentieth-first-century Coalition and Conservative cabinets is welcomed as a reassertion of the natural order of things or castigated as a return to something approaching quasi-feudal rule, it now seems to be accepted that traditionally privileged groups retain power and status out of all proportion to their numbers.[7]

The revival of historical biography

The surge of interest in the aristocracy and upper middle class has coincided with, and become entwined with, the recent revival of historical biography. The change in attitudes towards biography has been truly remarkable. Criticised for years by literary scholars as theoretically naive, savaged by those on the left for prioritising the individual over underlying economic and social forces, and condemned by feminists for its concentration on dead white men, historical biography, one might think, had been dead and buried long ago.[8]

However, this is far from the case. Historical biography, as was seen above, has often been much more popular with commercial publishers and members of the general public than it has among either academic publishers or professional historians. But even this comparison is misleading. The fact that many, perhaps most, professional historians found so much to worry them in the biographical approach does not mean that they abandoned it. Far from it. With one eye on the individual and the other on the market, even historians working in those branches of the discipline most vociferous in their condemnation of biography continued to produce lives of the great and the good – and increasingly of the not so great and the not so good.

Labour history is a case in point. Although sometimes highly theorised and almost invariably distrustful of the role assigned to individual agency, biography has played a central role in the development of the discipline.[9] For many years, however, labour biography (and autobiography) tended to concentrate on the big beasts of the labour movement. Moreover, it was inclined towards hagiography, assuming one of two well-established genres: the man (almost always a man) who scaled the career ladder from 'pit to parliament'; or alternatively the activist (again almost always a man) whose life is best understood, it is suggested, as one of revolutionary 'struggle' against the powers that be. So it was, to take but a few examples, that Arthur Horner called his 1960 autobiography *Incorrigible Rebel*; that Kenneth Morgan entitled his 1975 study, *Keir Hardie: Radical and Socialist*; and that Tristram Hunt gave the title *The Frock-Coated Communist: The Revolutionary Life of Frederich Engels* to the highly successful biography that he published in 2010.[10]

Much, however, has changed in recent years. The growth of 'history from below', the surge of interest in family history, the expansion of self-publishing, and the example set by the multi-volume *Dictionary of Labour Biography* all had their effect. Labour history biographers have turned their attention increasingly towards the great majority of the workforce who neither achieved high office nor led lives of unremitting class struggle and/or industrial relations warfare.[11] Again, though, it is easy to be misled. Even now, we know much more about the leaders of the labour movement than we do about rank-and-file trade union and Labour party members, let alone about the many more who did not join a union, did not support the Labour party, preferring instead to acquiesce in the economic and social status quo.[12]

Women's history biography has developed in much the same way as labour history biography.[13] As might be expected, historians (both male and female) began by focusing their attention on the tiny minority of women who assumed national prominence, usually it must said in such stereotypically female activities as nursing, marrying well or (more pleasingly for activists) social reform and the women's emancipation movement. The result was that even before the growth of feminist politics in the 1970s, most historians (however blinkered) would have heard of, and had some awareness of, the contribution made by such pioneering and/or heroic women as Florence Nightingale, Emmeline Pankhurst and Grace Darling.[14]

Thereafter, women's biography, like labour history biography, took steps to modify its concentration on national leaders and exceptional individuals. Those interested in women's history continued, it is true, to publish lives of the great and the good.[15] However, feminist scholars in particular did their best to begin uncovering the lives both of lesser figures and of the anonymous majority of women who lived their lives in obscurity, their activities attracting little attention beyond their immediate circle of family and friends.[16]

The two strands came together, on occasion, in the form of 'dual' and/or 'collective' biographies. Claire Tomalin's 1990 study of Nelly Ternan (the actress and mistress of Charles Dickens), *The Invisible Woman*, is a case in point: it considers, *inter alia*, the way in which Ternan – and of course other women like her – have simply been written out of history.[17] Just over fifteen years later, Carolyn Steedman opened her 2007 monograph *Master and Servant: Love and Labour in the English Industrial Age* by making clear that, 'This is a book about one servant and one master.' Embracing, rather than rejecting, the particularity of Phoebe Batson and the Reverend John Murgatroyd, Steedman uses their relationship to 'explain how historical actors were able to buck so many of the trends that their historians have seen them – people like them – enacting.'[18]

From the inside out and the outside in

Historical biography, then, is alive and well. It is also more homogeneous than might at first be apparent. This is because whatever their particular interests, whatever their ideological preconceptions and whatever their methodological preferences, virtually all biographers share one thing in common. They are at one in wishing to produce 'internal' biography. They aspire, that is to say, to write from the inside out. Driven by the need to know what their subjects were 'really' like, their focus is on bringing the dead to life, getting into their heads, burrowing beneath their skin as well, very often, as seeking to understand the world in which they lived.[19]

Writing from the inside out is difficult. This is not quite the statement of the obvious that it sounds. If one is to write an 'internal' biography, if one is even to attempt to recapture what one's subject was thinking and feeling, one needs access, it is clear, to source material that he or she themselves created. One hopes for a journal perhaps, diaries, note books, personal and business correspondence, published and unpublished writings and even, if one is lucky, an interview, a memoir or an autobiography. For the biographer, there is nothing like tracking down, holding in one's hands and reading a letter written by the subject of one's interest, be it twenty, fifty, one hundred or two hundred years ago.

The trouble is that the survival of any such material is likely to depend on the selection of a particular type of subject. Probably only an individual (or family) of some importance – or self-importance – created such material, kept it, saved it from weeding and ensured that it was stored from when it was produced until such time as the biographer turns up looking for it. The problem is compounded by the fact that only individuals of some importance are likely to find that their correspondence or other papers have been preserved, incidentally as it were, by a library, archive or other institution without any direct, immediate interest in them. The fact that such records were amassed, let alone survive, is sufficient, it goes without saying, to mark out their creators as untypical. The result, not surprisingly, is that even those most critical of the great man or great woman approach to history find it difficult to deliver the sort of biography that they would like. However desirable writing from the inside out may be, it is just not always possible.

The alternative is 'external' biography, writing from the outside in. If one is to produce a biography of this type, one needs, of course, to trawl through the many, many sources that might possibly contain some reference to one's subject. If he or she (like Gerald Howard-Smith, the subject of this book) lived one hundred years or so ago, there will almost certainly be information about them in the census. There could be material hidden among baptismal and school records; if he or she worked outside the home, it would be worth searching through local business collections. If he or she was delinquent or dishonest, there might be a record of their doings among police and legal records or in the pages of the local press; if he or she was poor and destitute, something might turn up in the voluminous archives of the Poor Law and its successors. If the subject of the biography were rich and successful, legal records and the local press might again be useful, albeit for different, probably more elevating, reasons.

But 'external' biography too has its difficulties. It is an approach that is prone to the class and gender biases that labour history and feminist history have been seeking to overcome: it is likely to be more effective when dealing with a man than with a woman; with somebody from the upper and middle classes, rather than from the working class; with a person who attained some sort of public profile. Moreover, it is an approach that tends, in most cases, to reveal more about the active middle years of life than it does about childhood or about old age.

However, 'external' biography possesses one distinct advantage over 'internal' biography. It virtually forces the biographer to abandon his or her 'isolating microscope', and so escape the great man or great woman perspective that can so inhibit our understanding of the past. In broadening the biographer's focus, it encourages, in fact it almost demands, a serious consideration of the relationship between the individual and society, between the particular and the general.[20] 'As historians', concludes Judith M. Bennett, 'we work always on two levels; we seek to understand the particularities of past lives, but we also quite rightly seek to place those lives in broader context.'[21] This is crucial. 'In the end,' concludes Richard J. Evans, 'no one has managed to better Marx's dictum that people make their own history, but they do not do it under circumstances of their own choosing.'[22]

The lost generation

The generation that grew up during the late nineteenth century and died, many of them during the First World War, would attest all too readily, one would think, to the terrible truth of Marx's dictum. The young men who were born in Europe during the 1880s and 1890s suffered, and suffered horrendously, from national and international forces beyond their, and it often seemed anybody else's, control. Indeed, this so-called 'lost generation' is remembered to this day in terms of loss and sacrifice, of promise unfulfilled, of the brightest and the best mown down and slaughtered across the killing fields of the Western Front:[23]

> Although every war death was wasteful, the deaths of thousands of educated and privileged young men brought about what was called a 'Lost Generation' of future politicians, philosophers, and poets who never had the chance to fulfil their promise.[24]

Such stereotyping is always tempting, and never more than when dealing with social classes other than one's own. There is a tendency, however much we deny it or try to avoid it, to categorise, to generalise – and, of course, to pass judgement on those different from ourselves. It is a tendency that is compounded, it seems, when dealing with those living in the past, particularly when they appeared – for much of their lives – to enjoy economic, social, cultural and other advantages that that we are denied.

So it is that we homogenise the men of the late Victorian and Edwardian upper middle class, the so-called 'lost generation', which perished in the First World War. We are inclined to view men like Gerald Howard-Smith and the world in which he and his contemporaries lived before the war through a sepia-tinted prism, overlaid very often with 'Downtonesque' embellishments.[25] We picture large, well-off professional families, living in attractive, rambling houses, whose inconveniences were mitigated by the armies of domestic servants employed to ensure that they functioned smoothly. If the man of the house needed to earn a living, it would be in the city, in one of the older professions (or just occasionally in business). His wife, of course, did not work and, with the children cared for by a nanny in a separate, self-contained section of the house, she was free to devote herself to an endless round of needlework, piano practice, good works, socialising and supervising the staff. When Violet Markham took over the running of her family home, Tapton House, Chesterfield, in 1912, she discovered that her mother had not only kept scrupulous domestic accounts but had also drawn up a detailed timetable describing the work that each of the household's nine servants was required to carry out on a daily and weekly basis.[26]

We have a firm view, too, as to how late nineteenth- and early twentieth-century upper middle-class families brought up their children. They were tutored at home until the boys were sent off, while still very young, to prep school, to one of the better public schools and finally to Oxford or Cambridge. Enthusiastic sportsmen, they played hard and worked as much as they needed to. Clever, confident and conformist, the young gentlemen who graduated from university in their early twenties turned, like their parents before them, to the city, the professions (or perhaps the Empire).[27] Then a few years later, they took safe, socially acceptable young women as their wives, making their homes, most of them, in one of the more agreeable parts of the country. In such families, notes Jane Hamlett, master bedrooms often came with a dressing room attached, allowing husbands and wives to 'dress modestly hidden from the other's gaze, maintaining a sense of mystique between marital partners.'[28]

This comfortable, self-regarding, self-perpetuating cycle was shattered, it is commonly accepted, by the devastation of the First World War. The flower of the country's youth flocked to the flag, only to be mown down amid the carnage of the Western Front. Lions led by donkeys, it was Gerald Howard-Smith and his upper middle-class contemporaries, we are told, who suffered particularly severely.[29] A.J.P. Taylor puts it like this:

> Casualties were about three times heavier in proportion among junior officers than with common soldiers. This struck at the highest in the land. Asquith lost his eldest son; Law lost two sons. The roll of honour in every school and college bore witness to the talents which had perished – the men of promise born during the eighteen-nineties [in Gerald Howard-Smith's case the eighteen-eighties] whose promise was not fulfilled. Though the death roll was not large enough to create statistically a 'lost

Introduction xvii

generation', there may have been an exaggerated sense of loss among those who survived.[30]

Gerald Howard-Smith

Gerald Howard-Smith (1880–1916) was one of the so-called 'lost generation' and this is his story. It is an 'external', rather than an 'internal' biography. Like the overwhelming majority of his contemporaries, the subject of this book left no personal papers, no autobiographical snippets, no recorded interviews, no undiscovered personal archive for the biographer to plunder. This then is neither a cradle-to-grave account of Howard-Smith's life, nor an attempt to uncover his innermost hopes and fears; neither does it attempt to unearth his underlying views, assumptions and attitudes.

But Gerald Howard-Smith was male, upper middle-class, comfortably off (and a fine all-round sportsman). It was a combination that afforded him a standing denied the overwhelming majority of his contemporaries, a standing that provides the biographer with source material unlikely to be available to those studying women, the working class or those who made less of an impact outside the home. The aim of this book is therefore to put these advantage to good use, to employ Gerald Howard-Smith as a prism through which we may

Figure I.1 Gerald Howard-Smith, c. 1902.
(Reproduced by permission of the Provost and Fellows of Eton College)

xviii *Introduction*

view – and better understand – the world in which he lived.[31] His interest lies precisely in the fact that he was not one of the great and the good, that today he has absolutely no name recognition at all. Born in 1880 and killed in 1916, he was one of the more than one and a half million men and boys who were brought up in Britain's Victorian and Edwardian heyday, only to be killed, injured or reported missing on the First World War's Western Front.[32]

Howard-Smith's life provides, at first glance, a stereotypical example of privilege, power and status brought low by forces beyond individual, national – or even international – control. Educated at Eton and Cambridge, he excelled at cricket and athletics, played for the MCC, taught briefly in preparatory schools, qualified as a solicitor, became a junior partner in the firm, volunteered for military service and was decorated for bravery before being killed in action in northern France. Whatever sympathy one feels for a life cut short in this way, it is a story with which we all probably feel that we are reasonably familiar.

In fact, Gerald Howard-Smith's life was less stereotypical, less conventional – and less glittering – than it appears at first sight. Although well off, well connected and well thought of, he did not marry, he lived with his parents, moving with them from Kensington, perhaps the most fashionable district in London, to Wolverhampton, one of the least well-regarded towns in the whole of the country. There was more happening – and not happening – in Gerald's life than is immediately apparent.

It is believed therefore that Gerald Howard-Smith is interesting both in his own right and as a vehicle for exploring – and reassessing – issues such as childhood and child rearing, elite education, sporting achievement, metropolitan-provincial ties, class and class relations, military-civilian relationships, and post-war forms of commemoration. It is hoped therefore that this book will appeal not just to specialists in upper middle-class life, but to all those interested in the social, cultural and economic history of late nineteenth- and early twentieth-century England.

Notes

1 Lucy Delap, *Knowing their Place: Domestic Service in Twentieth-Century Britain* (Oxford: Oxford University Press, 2011), especially section 6: 'Heritage Nostalgia: Domestic Service Remembered and Performed'.
2 www.nationaltrust.org.uk [June 2015].
3 *Daily Mail*, December 26, 2012; September 22, 2014; *Sunday Times*, September 20, 2015.
4 Jessica Fellowes, *The World of Downton Abbey* (London: HarperCollins, 2011); Pamela Horn, *The Real Life Women of Downton Abbey* (Stroud: Amberley, 2012); Countess of Carnarvon, *Lady Almina and the Real Downton Abbey: The Legacy of Highcleve* (London: Hodder & Stoughton, 2011).
5 Kathryn Hughes, 'The Lives of Others', *Guardian*, February 16, 2013. See, for example, Natalie Livingstone, *The Mistresses of Cliveden: Three Centuries of Scandal, Power and Intrigue* (London: Hutchinson, 2015).
6 Robert Hewison, *The Heritage Industry: Britain in a Climate of Decline* (London: Methuen, 1987).

7 See, for instance, Ben Kirby, 'The Big Society: Power to the People?', *Political Quarterly*, 81, 4, 2010; Richard Seymour, 'The Tories: An Anatomy', *International Socialism*, 131, June 2011; Anthony King, *Who Governs Britain?* (London: Penguin, 2015).
8 Alun Munslow, 'History and Biography: An Editorial Comment', *Rethinking History*, 7, 1, 2003.
9 Harry Knowles, 'Voyeurs or Scholars? Biography's Role in Labour History', *Journal of Australian Studies*, 25, 69, 2001; Mark Hearn and Harry Knowles, 'Struggling for Recognition: Reading the Individual in Labour History', *Labour History*, 87, November 2004; Joan Allen and Malcolm Chase, 'Britain: 1750–1900', in Joan Allen, Alan Campbell and John McIlroy (eds), *Histories of Labour: National and International Perspectives* (Pontypool: Merlin Press, 2010).
10 Arthur Horner, *Incorrigible Rebel* (London: MacGibbon & Kee, 1960); Kenneth O. Morgan, *Keir Hardie: Radical and Socialist* (London: Weidenfeld & Nicolson, 1975); Tristram Hunt, *The Frock-Coated Communist: The Revolutionary Life of Frederich Engels* (London: Allen Lane, 2009).
11 For changes in coalmining biography, a key component of labour history biography, see, for example, Bill Williamson, *Class, Community and Culture: A Biographical Study of Social Change in Mining* (London: Routledge, Kegan Paul, 1982); Peter Ackers, 'West End Chapel, Back Street Bethel: Labour and Capital in the Wigan Churches of Christ c.1845–1945', *Journal of Ecclesiastical History*, 47, 2, 1996; Keith Gildart, 'Mining Memories: Reading Coalfield Autobiographies', *Labor History*, 50, 2, 2009.
12 John Benson, *The Working Class in Britain, 1850–1939* (London: Longman, 1989).
13 Kathleen Barry, 'Biography and the Search for Women's Subjectivity', *Women's Studies International Forum*, 12, 6, 1989; Susan Groag Bell and Marilyn Yalom (eds), *Revealing Lives: Autobiography, Biography and Gender* (New York: State University of New York Press, 1990); Barbara Caine, 'Feminist Biography and Feminist History', *Women's History Review*, 3, 2, 1994.
14 Cyril J. Davey, *Lady with a Lamp: The Story of Florence Nightingale* (Cambridge: Lutterworth, 1958); Harold Champion, *The True Book about Emmeline Pankhurst* (London: Frederick Muller,1963); Richard Armstrong, *Grace Darling: Maid and Myth* (London: Dent, 1965).
15 Paula Bartley, *Emmeline Pankhurst* (London: Routledge, 2002); Kathryn Hughes, *The Short Life and Long Times of Mrs Beeton* (London: HarperCollins, 2006); Alison Light, *Mrs Woolf and the Servants* (London: Fig Tree, 2007).
16 Caine, 'Feminist Biography'.
17 Claire Tomalin, *The Invisible Woman: The Story of Nelly Ternan and Charles Dickens* (London: Penguin, 1990).
18 Carolyn Steedman, *Master and Servant: Love and Labour in the Industrial Age* (Cambridge: Cambridge University Press, 2007), p. 1.
19 Glen Jeansonne, 'Personality, Biography and Psychobiography', *Biography*, 14, 3, 1991; J.M. Bennett, 'Women's History: A Study in Continuity and Change', *Women's History Review*, 2, 1993; S.G. Magnusson, 'The Singularisation of History: Social History and Microhistory within the Postmodern State of Knowledge', *Journal of Social History*, 36, 3, 2003; Barbara Caine, *Biography and History* (London: Palgrave Macmillan, 2010).
20 I owe the phrase 'isolating microscope' to Kathryn Hughes, 'The Lives of Others'.
21 Bennett, 'Women's History', p. 177.
22 Richard J. Evans, *In Defence of History* (London; Granta, 1997), p. 189.
23 The standard study remains J.M. Winter, *The Great War and the British People* (London: Macmillan, 1985). Valuable, too, is J.M. Winter, 'Britain's "Lost Generation" of the First World War', *Population Studies*, 31, 3, 1977.
24 Winter, 'Lost Generation', p. 449.

xx *Introduction*

25 Delap, *Knowing their Place*, section 6.
26 Jane Lewis, *Women in England 1870–1950: Sexual Divisions and Social Change* (Brighton: Wheatsheaf, 1984), p. 115.
27 Patrick Joyce, *The State of Freedom: A Social History of the British State since 1800* (Cambridge: Cambridge University Press, 2013), pp. 283–4.
28 Jane Hamlett, *Material Relations: Domestic Interiors and Middle-Class Families in England, 1850–1910* (Manchester: Manchester University Press, 2010), p. 212.
29 Alan Clark, *The Donkeys: A History of the British Expeditionary Force in 1915* (London: Pimlico, 1991).
30 A.J.P. Taylor, *English History 1914–1945* (London: Penguin, 1985), p. 166. See, much more recently, Anthony Seldon and David Walsh, *Public Schools and the Great War* (Barnsley: Pen & Sword, 2013).
31 David Cannadine, *G.M. Trevelyan: A Life in History* (London: Fontana, 1993), p. xiv.
32 Perhaps, agrees Tim Travers, one can use the Western Front 'as a model by which middle- and upper-class Edwardian society can be better understood'. Tim Travers, *The Killing Ground: The British Army, the Western Front and the Emergence of Modern Warfare 1900–1818* (London: Routledge, 1993), p.xxii.

Part I
PRIVILEGE

1 'A THOROLY SOUND HEALTHY MINDED GOOD FELLOW': HOME, SCHOOL AND SOCIALISATION

Upright, manly characters

We all have a picture in our minds of the late Victorian and Edwardian upper middle-class family. In fact, our view of home, school and socialisation – and the relationship between them – is so powerful and so deeply entrenched that it can border on caricature. One of the family's crucial features, we are led to believe, is the way in which it brought up its children. Upper middle-class parents, it is said, avoided intimacy, farmed out childcare as much as they could, and organised their households on strictly gendered lines. They had staff to look after their children when they were young; they kept their daughters at home to learn the genteel accomplishments expected of them and sent their sons away, at an absurdly young age, to be toughened up in the boarding establishments designed specifically for the purpose.

We have in mind a process whereby prep school was followed by public school, culminating in a place at one of the two ancient universities. Concentrating on sport, the classics and the cultivation of character, private schools knew exactly what was expected of them. The boys who started out along this educational conveyor belt at the age of eight or nine metamorphosed ten or fifteen years later into young gentlemen, strong, confident and conventional, albeit intellectually rigid and supposedly sexually maladroit. They were expected, claims Tim Travers, to display 'Group loyalty, deference, obedience to the accepted hierarchy, an aversion to political and intellectual discussion, and an emphasis on self-assurance and character'.[1] F.M.L. Thompson agrees. Upper middle-class parents, he argues, regarded the public schools to which they sent their sons as a vital element in the process of socialisation:

> they were instruments for conditioning their boys into becoming upright, manly characters who did not cheat, sneak, or whine, and who could lead without being needlessly cruel to animals or servants. That was largely successful, and the public-school type was pretty easily recognized by speech, manner, dress, and behaviour.[2]

But how accurate is such a picture? Were upper middle-class families really emotionally sterile? Is it true that the schools to which upper middle-class parents sent their sons away to be educated focused single-mindedly on turning out classical scholars, unthinking sportsmen and upright, manly gentlemen? And if they did try so hard to cultivate character of the approved type, were they as successful as we are led to believe? One cannot help wondering whether Gerald Howard-Smith and his contemporaries were quite as supine as this view of upper middle-class socialisation suggests, whether they emerged into adulthood the virtually identical, interchangeable clones that the existing consensus might lead one to suppose.

A Kensington childhood

Gerald Howard-Smith's childhood and schooling go a long way, it must be admitted, to support the conventional view of upper middle-class socialisation. Indeed, his experience appears, on the face of it, to conform almost exactly to what one would expect of a respectable, comfortably off upper middle-class family wishing to do its best for its son. Gerald's parents employed staff to look after him while he was young, sent him away to prep school when he was nine years old and then, four years later, moved him on to Eton. It was an environment in which he flourished, taking part in a range of sporting and other activities, playing in the prestigious Eton–Harrow cricket match at Lords, and receiving the school's ultimate accolade, election to 'Pop', the Eton Society. Howard-Smith, concluded his house master when he left for Cambridge at the age of eighteen, was 'a thoroly sound healthy minded good fellow: not a great scholar, but might get a 2nd, In the Trip.Hv much affn for him + hope he is going to do his family + House credit.'[3]

His house master knew the family, of course, and knew therefore that Gerald Howard-Smith had been born into metropolitan privilege. The Smith family was successful, well established and well regarded. Gerald's father, Philip Howard Smith, was the son of the classical and biblical scholar William (later Sir William) Smith. A self-made man, William was a lexicographer known best for his contributions to the *Penny Cyclopaedia* and for his editorship of the two-volume *Dictionary of Greek and Roman Geography* and the three-volume *Dictionary of the Bible Comprising its Antiquities, Biography, Geography and Natural History*. These works, together with his other activities and publications earned him both a knighthood and an appreciative obituary in the *Morning Post*.[4]

However modest Sir William's antecedents, he went on to head a household which reflected his achievements, and to bring up Philip and his other children in conventional, upper middle-class fashion. By 1861, when Philip, Gerald's father, was fifteen years old, Sir William, his wife, two daughters and four sons were living in the desirable Hampstead area of north London. His wife and daughters (who were in their early and mid-twenties) did not work, the seven members of the family looked after by no fewer than four servants: a cook, a nurse, a housemaid and – a sure sign of success, status and aspiration – a footman.[5]

William sent Philip to St Paul's School, from where he went on to Trinity College Cambridge, before studying at the Inner Temple and being called to the Bar in 1870.[6] Living at home and practising at King's Bench Walk in the Temple, Philip set about forging his career.[7] A revising barrister and member of the Oxford Circuit, he began appearing for the Board of Trade in cases which, locally at least, attracted considerable attention.[8] As Chief Commissioner appointed by the Board to conduct inquiries into the causes of boiler explosions, he dealt with a number of serious marine accidents.[9] Early in 1880, for example, he represented the Board of Trade when a formal investigation was held in South Wales at the Town Hall in Newport into a boiler explosion aboard the steamship *Jones Brothers*, an incident that resulted in the loss of three lives.[10] Three years later (just after the passing of the Boiler Explosions Act of 1882), he was in Newcastle-upon-Tyne, representing the Board at the inquiry into the stranding of another steamer, the *Cyanus*.[11]

As Philip's professional career took off, so, too, did his personal life. He met his future wife Mary Beaumont O'Shaughnessy and they married in 1879, the couple remaining together until Philip's death forty years later. Mary O'Shaughnessy had an interesting, perhaps slightly exotic, Anglo-Indian background. Born in Calcutta in 1851, her father Richard O'Shaughnessy (1812/13–89) had gone out from Ireland to India where he served as a surgeon in the Bengal Army. An authority on the diseases and surgery of the jaw, he became Professor of Surgery at Calcutta Medical College, the first such institution in Asia.[12] After retiring from the College in 1860, Richard, his wife and four daughters (including Mary) left India for England.[13] By the early 1870s, the family was living in Kensington which, like Hampstead, was one of the most sought after areas of the capital. It was noted, it has been said, for its 'privacy, seclusion, respectability and remoteness from business'.[14] It was noted too for the number of old Indian hands who lived there:

> Kensington, home of Kensington Palace, close to Hyde Park and Buckingham Palace, housed the grandest of London's residents – it became a royal borough in 1901. Together with Bayswater, it was also the home of imperial connection, of the affluent Anglo-Indian families, bankers and investors, who rubbed shoulders with the aristocracy and the ambassadorial class.[15]

Having met presumably some time during the 1870s, Philip and Mary married at St Augustine's, South Kensington on Tuesday 15 April 1879. Although it was unusual perhaps for a couple such as Philip and Mary to choose a Tuesday for their wedding, they publicised the event in conventional, upper middle-class fashion with an announcement in the *Pall Mall Gazette*. It was a telling choice. The *Pall Mall Gazette* was aptly named, suggests Stephen Koss, because it catered 'expressly to a clubland clientele': it was 'easily digested after a hearty lunch or at teatime'.[16]

Once married, Philip and Mary remained in Kensington – in fact, they moved less than half a mile from where Mary's family had set up home. 'For the upper-middle classes', observes Alison Light, 'Kensington was a village, "a little colony" of interconnected family and friends all within walking distance.'[17] The house that Philip and Mary chose was on West Cromwell Road, one of eighteen built as part of a development that had been put up a few years before on land owned formerly by the third Lord Kensington. The houses sold for between £1,200 and £1,500 each and were designed, it has been said, for 'a solidly middle-class market'.[18]

However, this does justice neither to the style of the housing nor to the exclusivity of the area. Number 10, West Cromwell Road had been built to impress. Although terraced, it contained three main floors, with a basement below and servants' quarters above. It boasted a striking entrance, with steps leading up to the front door, and over it an open porch supported by three imposing columns. It opened on to one of London's better streets. The 1881 census which was taken soon after Philip and Mary moved in (and a year or so after Gerald was born) confirms that the Howard-Smiths counted among their neighbours some well-to-do families with servant-heavy households. At number 7, there was a wine and spirit distiller, his wife (and a visitor) who were looked after by seven servants; at number 5, there lived a mine owner, his wife, daughter, (two others) and a staff of six servants.[19] Number 3, meanwhile, was home to the Honourable Lady Caroline Beauchamp, her two daughters and their eight servants.[20] West Cromwell Road was no ordinary middle-class street.

There was little, it seems, to distinguish the Smiths from many other London, upper middle-class couples. Philip was in his mid-thirties and Mary in her late twenties when they set out on their married life together. Philip had begun building a successful career, Mary did not work and, as was not uncommon at this time, he and Mary had their first child soon after getting married. Gerald Howard-Smith, the subject of this book, was born on January 21, 1880, virtually nine months to the day after his parents' wedding. It may – or may not – be telling that Philip and Mary announced Gerald's birth, not in the *Pall Mall Gazette*, but in the less prestigious *Standard*.[21]

It was to be another eight years before Gerald had a sibling and Philip and Mary their second son. By the time Charles Howard-Smith was born, Philip and Mary were in their early forties and late thirties, and Gerald, of course, was eight years old. It is tempting – although necessarily inconclusive – to speculate as to why there was such a long gap between the births of the two boys. Maybe Gerald's had been a difficult pregnancy and birth, maybe Mary found it hard to get pregnant again; perhaps Philip and Mary were not getting on, perhaps Philip suffered from impotence (temporary or otherwise) – perhaps the two boys had different fathers.

Whatever the reasons, the gap between the brothers meant, of course, that Gerald was brought up for eight years as an only child. However, this did not mean that he grew up alone. Like virtually all children of his class, Gerald was brought up with – and by – a number of live-in servants. Philip and Mary took care, as one would expect, both to run their home and to bring up their children in the ways that were regarded as normal by upper middle-class parents. Like all families with pretensions to gentility – and the wherewithal to pursue them – they modelled their domestic arrangements, so far as they could, on those of their social equals and social superiors.[22] Philip and Mary provided Gerald (and later Charles) with the sort of life, the sort of home, the sort of support and the sort of opportunities that the overwhelming majority of his contemporaries could scarcely even begin to contemplate.

Philip and Mary were well enough off to be able to afford to employ three resident servants to look after the three of them (the four of them when Charles was born in 1888). Mary had help both with the housework and with the care of her son. We know from the census of 1881, which was taken when Gerald was just over a year old, that Philip and Mary employed three unmarried, live-in members of domestic staff: a twenty-two year-old housemaid, Phoebe Statham; a twenty-one year-old nurse, Elizabeth Hill; and a thirty-six year-old cook, Olive Godden.[23] The size of the establishment is interesting not just for what it tells us about the Smiths' day-to-day lives together, but also for what it reveals about their financial situation and about the values that they transmitted, whether wittingly or unwittingly, to their two sons.

Philip and Mary's employment of Phoebe, Elizabeth and Olive (and their successors, Clara Bailey, Amy Frior and Florence Stone)[24] meant, most obviously, that their lives were much easier and more comfortable than they would have been had they not been in a position to pay for such help. Whatever the burdens of managing domestic staff, they were as nothing compared to the demands of cooking, childcare and day-to-day manual work which the servants undertook on their employers' behalf.[25] Most middle-class (and upper middle-class) homes, it must be remembered, were still lit by oil lamps and heated by open fires; most cooking was still done on a range, most cleaning still carried out without the aid of anything that we would recognise today as a useful labour-saving device.[26]

Philip and Mary's employment of their trio of domestic staff suggests, just as obviously, that they were very well off indeed compared to the overwhelming majority of their contemporaries. In fact, it confirms that they were part of a tiny, privileged minority. J.H. Walsh suggested in the 1873 edition of his *Manual of Domestic Economy* that it took a household income of around £750 a year to provide a family with the sort of three-servant establishment that the Smiths were able to afford.[27] Very few families, it goes without saying, enjoyed anything approaching such an income. With inequality particularly marked between 1880 and the First World War, it has been calculated that:

> the upper and middle classes, under 2 per cent of all families, with upwards of £300 a year per family (nearly three times the average family income), received well over a third (36.9 per cent) of the National Income – nearly as much as the whole manual working class (39.1 per cent) who constituted three-quarters of the population.[28]

Philip and Mary's hiring of domestic staff meant finally that Gerald (and later Charles) grew up living with, and being looked after by, women from different, and obviously far less privileged, economic, social and cultural backgrounds. Whatever the relationships that developed between Gerald and Charles, on the one hand, and Phoebe, Elizabeth and Olive (and their successors), on the other hand, there were boundaries that would almost certainly never be crossed. The result was that, however close they were to the servants, the Smith boys, like all those brought up in a similar way, were introduced from the earliest possible age to the fundamental tenets of contemporary gender, class (and age) hierarchies.[29]

These were lessons that can only have been reinforced by the boys' dealings with Philip and Mary's family, friends, neighbours, business contacts and other acquaintances. The boys' grandparents were certainly part of a metropolitan elite. Mary's father, Richard, had made his name – and his money – as a surgeon in India before moving to Kensington. Philip's father, William (later Sir William), was a scholar, professor and knight of the realm. By the time Gerald was born, William, his wife, two daughters and granddaughter had also moved to Kensington, where they employed a staff of seven: a butler, a cook, two housemaids, a kitchen maid, a lady's maid and a footman, a liveried servant whose role was almost entirely ceremonial and had degenerated, it has been said, into that of 'an ornamental parasite'.[30]

Philip and Mary did not – indeed probably could not afford to – resort to such ostentatious signifiers of their achievements and aspirations. But they, too, moved in indisputably upper middle-class circles. Philip became a member of two London clubs: Savile's and the New University.[31] He and Mary numbered among their friends and acquaintances men such as the High Sheriff of Cumberland, Samuel Porter Foster, who was staying with them at the time of the 1881 census.[32] Philip and Samuel had much in common. Born just a year apart, both had attended Trinity College Cambridge, both were keen on cricket and both had been called to the Bar (Foster in 1869 and Smith in 1870).[33]

Philip also kept in touch with members of his extended family. In the spring of 1891, for instance, he took Gerald to stay with his younger brother Henry (and his wife Emily) who lived on the Boland estate near Chippenham in Wiltshire. Working as agent to the Marquis of Lansdowne (then serving as the Viceroy of India) brought Henry both impressive accommodation in which to live and access, albeit in a subordinate capacity, to one of the country's leading Anglo-Irish landholding families.[34] When Philip took Gerald there, he was the same age as Henry and Emily's eldest child, Cyril, and a little older than their daughters, Dorothea (who was nine) and Violet (who was six). As befitted a family with Henry and Emily's impressive home and prominent position in local society, Gerald's aunt, uncle and cousins were looked after by a cook and a governess as well as a housemaid and a parlour maid.[35]

It is clear, then, that Gerald Howard-Smith was born into, and moved within, privileged economic and social circles. Gerald, like all of us, was socialised from the day he was born by the places he lived in, the people he met, the things he saw, the things he heard, the things he did – everything, in other words, that he must have come to regard as normal.[36] But his parents were taking no chances. We do not know what arrangements Philip and Mary made for Gerald's early education. The fact that he was born in 1880 (and his brother in 1889) unfortunately precludes the possibility of using the census to discover whether the Smiths employed tutors or governesses to teach the boys before the time came for them to be sent away to school.[37]

Temple Grove

What we do know is that when Gerald was just under ten years old, Philip and Mary sent him (and later Charles) to preparatory school and then on to public school. It was a system designed to instil not just the rudiments of learning but also qualities such as loyalty, teamwork, fair play, a love of country and an awareness – and acceptance – of the economic, social and cultural structure of contemporary British society. The decision to educate a child privately was a matter, as F.M.L. Thompson has pointed out, of 'an older generation imposing upon and moulding the younger in the cause of the self-perpetuation of class identity'.[38] So it was that Philip and Mary's decision to send Gerald away to prep school reflected not just the couple's status and achievements but also the aspirations that they had for their first-born child. It signalled, in a highly visible way, both their ability to pay for private education and their determination to embed their son in the upper middle-class world that the family inhabited.

The school that Philip and Mary chose for their son, Temple Grove, had been established at East Sheen in Surrey, some eight or nine miles southwest of central London in 1811, and by the time Gerald went there had developed into one of the largest and best regarded schools of its type in the country.[39] Taking both day boys and boarders, Temple Grove Preparatory School (or 'Mr Edgar's' as it was also known) epitomised, it was thought, all that was best in late nineteenth-century preparatory school education.[40]

Certainly Temple Grove did its best instil in its young charges a sense of upper and upper middle-class exclusivity and superiority. Indeed, its fees alone were sufficient to deter all but the very well off. It charged 100 guineas a year – with additional payments for everything from buying books and taking German lessons, to being allowed to have a cold, early morning bath. The basic cost of educating a boy at Temple Grove was much the same as a coalminer, and twice as much as an agricultural labourer, could expect to earn during the course of an entire year.[41]

One's first day at school was – and is – a milestone in any child's life. Gerald was just nine years, nine months old when Philip and Mary sent him to begin boarding at Temple Grove.[42] His maternal grandfather Richard O'Shaughnessy had died earlier in the year and he was leaving his parents at home with his new, fifteen-month old baby brother. As if all this was not enough, prep school staff were renowned for expecting both parents and children to display the legendary British stiff upper lip. It is said, for example, that the headmaster of St Andrew's Eastbourne discouraged an anxious mother from visiting her son during his first two weeks at the school by demanding, 'If you had a puppy, would you cut off its tail an inch at a time or do it all at once?' Asked by other parents how their son was getting on, he replied only by reporting on the progress of the boy's batting technique.[43]

However caring Temple Grove's staff tried to be, however much support his parents were able to offer and however resilient Gerald turned out to be, there was a great deal to get used to. He, along with his new classmates had to cope not only with starting a new school, but also with living away from home (which meant, of course, eating and sleeping for weeks on end with people they hardly knew). Temple Grove had over one hundred and twenty pupils on its books and, like any preparatory school, could be a chilling and intimidating place for a small boy.[44] Although Gerald was far from the youngest of the new boys (one of those starting with him was less than eight years old), he, like all newcomers, had good reason to be cautious.[45] There were any number of rules, written and unwritten, formal and informal, that had to be understood and adhered to. Preparatory schoolboys, claimed Robert Graves, 'live in a world completely dissociated from home life. They have a different vocabulary, a different moral system, even different voices'.[46]

The Temple Grove School rules published in 1880 stipulated, for example, that boys were expected to write a letter home every Sunday, and that 'Subject to particular exceptions, only one boy of each class should be allowed to visit the closets at a time.'[47] Then, too, the boys had their own beliefs, their own practices. Newcomers were told that if they went to the lavatory at night, they would be seized by Charles Peace, a notorious murderer who had been hanged in 1879.[48] They learned that, 'It was a terrible disgrace if anyone at school found out your Christian name', recalled a boy who started at Temple Grove a couple of years after Gerald. 'But it was the custom for great friends to reveal each other their Christian names under an oath of secrecy.'[49] They learned soon enough to face the depredations of boys further up the school who were older and stronger than they were. 'Outside the little room from which the sweets (3d worth) were distributed there was always a row of big boys holding out their hands and saying "Give me, I'm stopped".'[50]

Once in the classroom, the curriculum was resolutely academic. The boys were divided into six classes (each of which wore a different cap), with emphasis placed, during the morning and early evening, on the teaching of the classics.[51] Such was the importance that preparatory schools placed on the subject that when Temple Grove's headmaster, the Rev. J.H. Edgar, chaired the inaugural meeting of the Association of Headmasters of Preparatory Schools in 1892, the main item of business was whether or not Greek should be taught alongside Latin. It was a mistake, the heads conceded, 'to teach all boys Greek, and ... the Public School Headmasters should give facilities for boys who know no Greek to take their proper places in the Public Schools'.[52]

Temple Grove, however, persisted with both languages. 'The lower classes, those few which did no Greek, learnt writing under a master of inferior status.'[53] The school's intellectual hierarchy was clear and unbending. 'The bulk of the serious work', it has been said, 'consisted of Latin and Greek, both well taught throughout, and, towards the top of the school, with such accuracy as to leave an ineffaceable impression through life':

> In the middle of the school Latin verses were begun, and the chief Latin author was Cornelius Nepos. Caesar was taken in the second class, Virgil in the first. Greek began with the Eton Sertum (a collection of short extracts and humorous extracts), followed by Xenophon's Anabasis, Homer's Odyssey not being reached till the second class.[54]

Boys who came out top in the monthly honours list (the *Honoris Causa*) were awarded a number of special privileges. They were entitled to use the school library and the school hall any afternoon after two o'clock, they were allowed to walk in the woods before dinner and (if 'of fit age') to go for a walk on half-holidays without being accompanied by a master. It is a list that says, of course, as much about Temple Grove's day-to-day restrictions as it does about the privileges it afforded its highest achieving pupils.[55]

The school placed as much – if not more – emphasis on the cultivation of character as it did on the inculcation of the classics. Its atmosphere, like that of most of its contemporaries, was inclined towards the Spartan.[56] Although the school's one hundred and twenty or so boarders lodged either in 'a fine red brick William and Mary building' or in the homes of individual members of staff, neither the standard of hygiene nor the quality of food was necessarily of a high, or even a satisfactory, quality.[57] Dinner, it was said, was 'a turbulent ceremony lasting nearly an hour. The bread was stale, the meat roughly cooked, and still more roughly served, and the pudding often consisted of greasy suet with a little rhubarb or marmalade thrown in'.[58]

Temple Grove, along with its contemporaries, set great store on sport – a preliminary meeting of preparatory school masters in March 1892 was called ostensibly to discuss the size of cricket pitches and cricket balls suitable for boys under the age of fifteen.[59] 'For something like sixty years', notes Donald Leinster-Mackay, 'football and cricket were treated by many preparatory schools as if they were religious exercises.'[60] It was an ideology that had its effects, he believes, on virtually every aspect of school life. 'This cult of athleticism, as rampant eventually in the preparatory as in the public schools, filled school magazines with reports of matches and critical comment.'[61]

It is perhaps not surprising that Temple Grove's sporting curriculum was narrow, the school's encouragement of afternoon games revolving, as might be expected, around rugby in winter and cricket in summer.[62] What is surprising is that its provision of sporting facilities varied from the excellent to the seemingly very ordinary. On the one hand, a photograph of a game of cricket taken while Gerald was a pupil shows boys wearing flannels, using proper bats, pads and stumps and playing on a large, seemingly well-tended field, set against an impressive backdrop of mature trees and spacious grounds.[63] On the other hand, some contemporaries recalled things very differently: 'The Rugby goals were rather rotten and apt to fall suddenly with dire results. Except for the portion set apart for matches, the cricket ground, used for football also, was bumpy and the grass often rather long.'[64]

Whatever the facilities, the headmaster, the Rev. Edgar, was a keen cricketer, and by the time Gerald arrived at the school, the game was well established. Temple Grove selected its teams on merit, Gerald playing for the first eleven during the final summer he was there. The school arranged for team photographs to be taken, and organised a fixture list that included matches against local prep schools such as Eagle House, Tabor's and Hatrey's, and later Colet House, Elstree, Sandroyd and Stanmore Park.[65] As the *Temple Grove Magazine* explained in 1916, 'every English boy should show keenness for, and be proud to excel in his grand old national game.'[66]

Temple Grove's exclusivity, superiority and distance – both literally and metaphorically – from the majority of the population were epitomised by its royal connections. Its proximity to Richmond Park made it possible for the school to forge a close association with the 'White Lodge', the house that Queen Victoria had presented to the Duke and Duchess of Teck in 1869. The couple's two older sons, Prince Adolphus and Prince Francis, joined Temple Grove as day boys in 1879 and 'used to ride down every day from the White Lodge'.[67] The school maintained its royal (and aristocratic) connections. In the year that Gerald joined, for example, boys from the school sang at the wedding procession of the Duke of Fife and the Princess Louise (later the Princess Royal), and performed a 'somewhat antique' burlesque, 'Bombastes Furioso,' at the White Lodge for the Duke and Duchess of Teck.[68]

The Temple Grove Song, which almost certainly dates from around the time that Gerald was a pupil, encapsulates, in idealised form, the ethos of the school. The opening three verses, like those that follow, stress, not surprisingly, values such as patriotism, manliness, militarism and loyalty to the school:

1   Here's to the new boy of bashful eight years,

    Here's to the old one of forty,

    Here's to the boys who have always done well,

    And here's to the one who is naughty.

Chorus

    For whether they're bad or whether they're good,

    Or whether they shouldn't or whether they should,

    We hope for the best, and we find as a rule

    They some day do honour to Temple Grove School.

2 Here's to the boy who has always a smile

   Here's to the one who is glum, sir;

   Here's to the Pickle, whose tongue's never still,

   And here's to the one who is mum, sir.

3 Here's to the boy who a soldier would be,

   To follow Her Majesty's will, sir;

   He can't start too soon to prepare for the Line,

   And that's why he's always 'on drill', sir.[69]

There is no doubting then Temple Grove's efforts to inculcate its pupils with conventional, upper middle-class values. What is much more difficult to assess is what those on the receiving end made of such efforts at socialisation. And what is more difficult still is to gauge the effects that the school's efforts had on any particular pupil – let alone one like Gerald, who left, as we know, no diaries, no autobiography or any other kind of record of what he felt and thought. As F.M.L. Thompson pointed out many years ago when discussing middle-class attempts to instil middle-class *mores* into the children of working-class parents, it is one thing to ascribe motive, quite another to demonstrate success (or failure).[70]

It is impossible to get to the truth of the matter. Many of the ex-pupils who passed (and pass) judgement on the preparatory and public schools they attended tend to lapse either into bitter recrimination or into sentimental/self-satisfied apologia. The latter stance is certainly detectable in the two published recollections of late nineteenth-century Temple Grove. The first dates from the late 1860s and early 1870s, fifteen years or so before Gerald joined the school:

> So life was hard physically, and this, even if it did stunt the growth for a while, was good for the soul, and work, done under the constant dread of the Headmaster's wrath, rod and birch, was always thorough and often interesting. For this his pupils owe him and his school an everlasting debt.[71]

The second passage, which refers to the 1880s, appears, at first glance, to be less partial, more nuanced and thus considerably more useful. M.D. Hill was a new boy at Temple Grove in 1883, just a few years ahead of Gerald. When he looked back to his arrival as an eleven-year old, he avoided the stifling nostalgia of so many autobiographical accounts. 'The food was excellent', he remembered, although the boys avoided eating 'more than a minimum of what the school provided'. The teaching, by contrast, 'was not particularly good to say the most'. His first master 'was an incredibly bad teacher. He was never known to smile, he spoke so indistinctly and in such a low undertone that it was almost impossible to hear him except when now and then he bellowed like a bull of Bashan at our misdeeds!' The master of his next form took an instant dislike to him. 'He again was a very poor teacher, cold, cynical and conceited!' Yet eventually Hill, too, reverts to type: 'we throve more or less, and from being rather delicate I grew strong and sturdy for my age, and gained credit at football and athletic sports.'[72]

What, then, did Gerald learn at Temple Grove? The attribution of cause and effect with regard to socialisation is notoriously difficult. Even if it were possible to demonstrate, rather than merely assume, that the values and attitudes which the school taught were the same as those which Gerald adopted, it does not follow, of course, that it was the former which were the cause of the latter. Gerald was only at Temple Grove for five years, he was only there during term time and, by the time he arrived, he was already nearly ten years old.

That said, it can be suggested, and with some confidence, that Gerald, along with his fellow pupils, probably accepted a good deal of what he was taught at Temple Grove. There was always intense pressure in closed institutions like preparatory (and public) schools for pupils to conform to the ethos that the staff were attempting to inculcate. Indeed, one of the major reasons that Philip and Mary chose Temple Grove for their son was that presumably they believed it would reinforce the values and attitudes that they were attempting to instil in him at home.

Moreover, the years between the ages of ten and fourteen were – as they still are – crucial to the development of individual attitudes and beliefs. Thus R.D. Peace concludes from his study of the Eastbourne prep school St Cyprian's that even its most famously recalcitrant pupil Eric Blair (George Orwell) was not immune to the pressures to conform. The explanation, Peace believes, lies in the distinction between the emotional and the intellectual: 'emotional commitments are usually imbibed unconsciously at an early age, before the reasoning ego is able to discriminate: as a result, they often become part of the fabric of a human being.' The result, he concludes, was that prep school teaching which was 'accepted emotionally rather than intellectually, may often have been far more important than the more cerebral public school conditioning'.[73]

The suggestion that Gerald absorbed and accepted much of what he was taught at Temple Grove is reinforced, to some extent at least, by the fact that he secured a place at Eton.[74] Even before the introduction of the Common Entrance Examination in 1904, it was the primary purpose of preparatory schools – as, indeed, their name suggests – to prepare their pupils for entry to public school.[75] And Eton, of course, was by far the most prestigious of all public schools. As the Rev. Edgar remarked to a reluctant pupil, 'My boy, I feed Eton and Harrow and don't intend you to fail at a place like Marlborough.'[76] Gerald did not fail – and did not disappoint either the Rev. Edgar or his father and mother. In 1894, at the age of fourteen, Gerald Howard-Smith left Temple Grove for Eton.

Eton

Eton, that bastion of the British establishment was – and still is – known all over the world. That said, its function is not always fully understood. Eton's primary purpose, along with the rest of the so-called 'Sacred Seven' public schools (Rugby, Harrow, Shrewsbury, Westminster, Winchester and Charterhouse) was not to produce scholars but to turn out confident, rounded individuals who were fit to lead, whether in this country or in the wider Empire. The public school curriculum was designed, the Clarendon Commission explained in 1864, to develop in students 'the capacity to govern others and control themselves'.[77]

The schools' *raison d'être* did not change a great deal thereafter. Historians continue to stress the range of functions – both educational and non-educational – performed by late nineteenth- and early twentieth-century public schools. John Tosh claims, for example, that 'they offered an academic preparation for university and for entry into the professions; and in complete contrast to the atmosphere of home and family they offered a crash course in manliness.'[78] T.L. Chandler concludes that, 'The public schools continued to be conservative, performing a largely symbolic function with regard to education, but a very practical one where class and separateness were concerned.'[79] As one of Gerald's near-contemporaries explained after he left, 'Eton invests boys with a social stamp entitling them to enter the freemasonry of English gentlemen.'[80]

It is scarcely surprising therefore that Eton was – and still is – an institution that polarises opinion in the sharpest possible way. What the school's detractors condemn in Etonians and Old Etonians as privilege, arrogance and insouciance, its supporters acclaim as excellence, confidence and charisma. The debate on public school education in general – and Eton's impact in particular – raged fiercely during the late nineteenth and early twentieth centuries, culminating most notably in the controversy over national efficiency that erupted in the wake of British failings in the Boer War.[81]

Critics of the public schools pointed to what they regarded as their insularity, their outdated emphasis on the classics, their overemphasis on sport and their toleration of homosexuality.[82] Indeed, the schools exercised a malign influence, it was said, over the entire educational – economic, social and cultural – landscape. It was claimed at a conference on commercial education held in 1898, for example, that even the public schools' finest qualities were nothing but 'medieval armour, graceful and charming, but useless against the modern weapons of precision on the continent.'[83]

The supporters of private education were just as emphatic in their praise of the work done by the public schools. The *Eton College Chronicle*, as might be expected, was in no doubt as to the benefits that the school bestowed on those lucky enough to pass through it. In its report of a college dinner held (also) in 1898, it remarked that 'Eton is a little England; and at her best, as she was that evening, she bore witness to the best English traditions, love of our country's past and her long "island story", belief in her future, and the courageous spirit and high honour which makes her power the highest civilising influence moving in the world at the present hour.'[84]

What both supporters and critics of the public schools agreed on was that Eton was unique. When parents (guardians, grandparents and other interested parties) invested in an Eton College education, they knew what they were doing. The boys who went there would be educated in a particular way, in a particular type of environment, with a particular end in view.[85] Whether they conformed or rebelled, whether they were conscious of it or not, Etonians were shaped indelibly, it was believed, by their years at the school. Old Etonians, it was suggested, either had no desire, or found it particularly difficult, to shake themselves free of the values, attitudes and behaviour that they were taught during their adolescent years.[86]

Gerald Howard-Smith thrived at Eton. Although not particularly gifted academically, his schoolwork improved, he became a keen all-round sportsman (excelling at athletics and cricket) and he received the school's ultimate accolade when he was elected a member of the Eton Society ('Pop'). He appears, so far as one can judge, to have accepted the ethos that Eton inculcated and to have been popular both with fellow pupils and with members of the teaching staff. Certainly by the time he left for Cambridge in the summer of 1899, he cut a substantial figure in the life of the school.

In 1894, of course, Gerald was just one of many new boys. However assured he might seem and however many boys he knew from prep school, there was no escaping the uncertainty and insecurities that came with starting afresh. His paternal grandfather had died the previous year and his brother was still at home with his parents. His new school was more than eight times larger than Temple Grove.[87] With its own idiosyncratic language and customs, it was only too easy to say or do the wrong thing. How was Gerald supposed to wear his Eton suit and top hat? What was a Praeposter, and what on earth could a Tuglet be? Would he be birched by one of the older boys or maybe he would have to hold down one of the other boys while he was flogged? What would fagging be like, would he get enough to eat and would he be assaulted, sexually or otherwise, while he was asleep?[88]

Whatever his initial anxieties, Gerald seemed to settle in well. His new term-time home was Warre House, one of Eton's twenty-seven boarding houses, the majority of which accommodated between thirty and forty boys (each of whom had his own room, or at least his own space). The atmosphere in boarding houses, the extent to which they replicated the domestic environment varied, it has been stressed recently, both between schools and between individual housemasters.[89]

The head of Warre House, the Rev. S.A. Donaldson, was important, then, in creating the environment in which Gerald spent a good part of his adolescence. He is important, too, in providing most of what we know about Gerald's social, sporting and intellectual development during these crucial, formative years. Stuart Alexander Donaldson, like Gerald's maternal grandparents, was part of the imperial elite. The eldest son of Sir Stuart Alexander Donaldson, the first Premier of New South Wales, he was educated at Eton and Trinity College, Cambridge, before returning to Eton, where he taught for more than twenty-five years. Ordained a priest in 1885, he went on to become Master of Magdalene College, Cambridge and then briefly Vice-Chancellor of the University.[90]

Donaldson, it must be said, did not always find his housemaster's job easy or enjoyable. It was difficult, stressed those familiar with public school education, to combine teaching a subject with heading a house. Being in charge of Warre House, like any boarding house, involved a 'rush of general management, correspondence, visits from parents, and almost incessant association with boys on Sundays and weekdays alike'.[91] Donaldson found the year before Gerald arrived particularly demanding. It has been 'a very trying half to me', he wrote in the spring of 1893. There had been a number of complications and aggravations. On one occasion, he reported, fourteen boys were in bed with feverish colds and flu, while on another, two boys were 'whipped' for smoking in one of their rooms.[92]

Donaldson coped better with the disruptions that arose thereafter. Gerald and his thirty or forty fellow boarders posed, it seems, far fewer problems than their immediate predecessors. 'Boys all very well in the new House & on the whole remarkably good', Donaldson observed in the spring of 1894 (just before Gerald arrived). It was just as well: the starting date of Gerald's first term, in September 1894, had to be deferred a week ('on account of Drains'); seven weeks later, there was a flood which left behind over a foot of water; and this was followed by an epidemic of German measles.[93] But Donaldson was sanguine. The house was well run. (Jack Ramsden, he noted the following year, was an excellent Captain 'notwithstanding his want of real influence in the house, as being absolutely non athletic'.)[94] Indeed, by the end of 1896, Donaldson felt able to report with some pleasure that, 'We have a house of some Athletic distinction.'[95]

As Gerald's classical tutor as well as his house master during the whole of his Eton career,[96] Donaldson was well placed to observe his pupil's intellectual, physical and personal development. His reports suggest that, from his tutor/housemaster's point of view, Gerald's work, attitude and behaviour all improved substantially as he moved up through the school. He became a valued member of Warre House, took advantage of what the school had to offer, and went along, it appears, with what Eton – and no doubt his family and friends – thought to be important.

Insofar as his tutor/housemaster had concerns about Gerald, they centred on his untidiness, his lack of application and, as he grew older, his tendency – both literally and metaphorically – to throw his weight around. (By the time he was fifteen years old, he was five feet nine inches tall).[97] But Donaldson was never unduly worried. His early comments set the tone. Although Gerald was 'apt to be slack occasionally,' he was 'a good lad on the whole'. There was no cause for concern, he concluded at the end of Gerald's first year in the school: 'Howard Smith – very fair. – complaints of untidiness &c. – But shd. do well.'[98]

Donaldson's reports on Gerald's subsequent Eton career continued in much the same vein. He remained exasperated for several years both by the boy's attitude and by his spelling and handwriting. He was caught playing whist,[99] his 'handwriting was atrocious',[100] he 'writes and spells abominably'.[101] There was little immediate improvement. Howard-Smith 'only modtly inds.: villanous

18   *Privilege*

writing', noted Donaldson at the end of 1897 – and this when Gerald was getting on for eighteen years old.[102] Donaldson was aware, too, that Gerald had something of a temper, but again did not seem unduly perturbed – even when the anger was aimed in his direction. Howard-Smith 'still not bad, + a gd lad', he concluded in 1896, 'notwithstanding his having called me a liar on one occasn when he completely lost his temper!'[103]

Indeed, Donaldson came more and more to value Gerald's positive qualities and began to discern leadership potential in him. He must have been pleased when Gerald won the Holiday Task Prize at the end of 1895.[104] He would have been pleased, too, that Gerald was involving himself in many of the extracurricular activities that he, and the school, valued so highly. The choices that Gerald made, presumably with parental support, are highly revealing. They not only show his participation in, but also suggest his acceptance of, the military, religious and sporting ethos that lay at the core of Eton's late nineteenth- and early twentieth-century socialising mission.[105]

Within a few months of joining the school, Gerald enrolled in the Officer Training Corps (the Eton College Volunteer Battalion, the Oxfordshire Light Infantry, to give it its full title).[106] Although he was one of more than sixty boys to enlist in the summer of 1895, only two joined during the first term of 1896: 'There are several vacancies in the Corps', complained the *Eton College Chronicle*, 'and at a time when the air is full of rumours of war it behoves us to fill up our ranks'.[107] Donaldson was a former Commander of the Battalion, and a few months after Gerald joined, it was he who acted as the umpire at a Corps field day, involving two hundred and forty-five boys (of all ranks), which was held at Temple Park, near Marlow. The morning was given over to war games, the afternoon to training in drill.[108]

It is difficult to know how effectively the Corps promoted its particular brand of militarism – let alone what Gerald and his fellow cadets made of it all.[109] It is clear, however, that the emphasis, as might be expected, was placed on preparing the boys to take up positions in the officers' mess.[110] At a field day held a week or so before the one at which Donaldson acted as umpire, the two hundred and sixteen boys taking part had 'luncheon' before returning to Eton by special train. The Battalion placed less emphasis, perhaps, on the nuts and bolts of military life: it was reported early in 1897, for example, that, 'The Corps has not fully learnt to drill with the Magazine rifles which have been lately introduced.'[111] Certainly, some onlookers looked askance at the entire enterprise: 'young Eton volunteers go to Camp, and are supposed to be going to rough it, but yet, as I am told by a friend who was there, they have seven course dinners, and everything else on the same scale.'[112]

Early in 1896, Gerald took another step suggesting that he conformed – outwardly, at least – to the trinity of military, religious and sporting values that Eton was seeking to instil. Religion, of course, was crucial. But, as a general rule, explained the Rev. Donaldson, upper-class boys 'leave home and go to school with a lamentable want of definite religious knowledge; and by religious knowledge I mean the groundwork laid a more complete knowledge of doctrine hereafter, and for the application of doctrine to the ordinary duties of daily life'.[113] Whatever the impact his housemaster's views had on Gerald, it was during his second year at Eton that he was confirmed into the Church of England. The service, which was held in the Eton college chapel, was conducted by William Stubbs, the Bishop of Oxford. 'Blessed are the pure in heart', wrote Gerald, 'for they shall see God'.[114]

Whatever the difficulties of assessing Gerald's military and religious commitment, there is no doubting his enthusiasm for sport. It would be impossible to enjoy the wide-ranging and successful sporting career he did at Eton without demonstrating, accepting and, almost certainly, internalising the qualities that aristocratic and upper middle-class sport demanded. It is well known, of course, that Eton, like other public schools, embraced with enormous enthusiasm the cult of sport, the culture of muscular Christianity.[115] Sport was crucial, it was believed, both in defining and in distinguishing the public schools and the young men whom they produced. According to the *Eton College Chronicle*:

> Eton, with other public schools and universities, is the centre and mainstay of athletics, which we defend as being, upon the whole, the most laudable characteristic of a not very laudable age. By indulging in such manly – not in morbid or cruel – recreations, the upper classes set an example to the rest of the country, which they do not do ill in following.[116]

It would be difficult to exaggerate the part that sport played either in Gerald's Eton career or in the way that his life developed thereafter. A committed all-rounder, he took part both in team sports and individual sports; in those for which he had little or no aptitude, and those at which he excelled. So although he was no sprinter or middle-distance runner, he entered a number of races at these distances. In 1896, for instance, he ran both in the junior hundred yards (finishing fifth out of five in his heat)[117] and in the junior mile race (in which he did marginally better, finishing fifth out of six in his heat).[118] Although he went on to become a highly accomplished high jumper, he continued to turn out in events for which he had much less aptitude: he ran in the school half-mile in 1899, for instance, but was unable to make it into the first three of his heat.[119]

Gerald played, and played well, all four types of football that were on offer at Eton. He represented his house, the Oppidens (those who boarded out) and the school itself at the wall game, a sport whose rules, objectives and scrimmaging remain virtually impenetrable to non-Etonians.[120] But the game's own records and the *Eton College Chronicle* attest to Gerald's attainments in what was becoming an increasingly violent activity.[121] His play for his house was 'good', it was said in 1896;[122] and he made two 'nice kicks', it was reported, when playing for the School in a game against the Masters in 1898.[123] However, it was the match between the Oppidens and the Collegers (those who boarded in), on St Andrew's Day, which was the game of the year. Gerald played for

20 *Privilege*

the Oppidens in 1898, and reportedly 'did a lot of work' for his side.[124] The *Eton College Chronicle* was impressed. Howard-Smith was a 'very good and dashing "third". He plays with much determination, and is of the greatest possible use out of the calx (12st 3lbs).'[125] The staff, some of them at least, were in no doubt as to the benefits that ensued from participating in the wall game (and other strenuous physical activities):

> To struggle hard for an hour, bringing every muscle into action, to get covered with mud from head to foot, then two hot baths one after the after to fetch it off, followed by tea and a pipe, is a succession of simple pleasures rarely equalled.[126]

Gerald also took part in the other game unique to Eton, the field game (a version of football not dissimilar to rugby).[127] Those who played it seriously thought, not surprisingly, that it too offered many attractions. 'I feel sure', claimed one enthusiast, 'that there must be very few past or present Etonians who do not agree that the Field Game is the most suitable of all football for boys, and especially so for the younger boys at a public school'.[128] It seems, however, that Gerald did not begin to play the game seriously – or to a standard likely to receive recognition – until the autumn of 1898, his penultimate year at school.[129] 'Has plenty of strength', concluded the *Eton College Chronicle*, 'and some pace, and has been very useful on occasions, but he is rather clumsy in managing the ball'.[130]

Figure 1.1 Gerald Howard-Smith (back row, far right) and the Eton Field XI, 1898. (Reproduced by permission of the Provost and Fellows of Eton College)

Eton's wall game and field game were not the only forms of football to attract Gerald's interest. He also played rugby and soccer, representing Eton at both codes, when they were introduced to the school towards the end of the century.[131] As might be expected, the launch of a 'working-class' sport such as soccer provoked some controversy.[132] 'I have seen with much regret', observed 'An old Member of the Eton College Field Eleven' in 1896, 'how much way the Association game is making at Eton'.[133] The *Eton College Chronicle* did not share his discomfort: 'Those who ridiculed the introduction of the Association game at Eton in the Easter half must now see they were mistaken. The number of Etonians playing in the Freshers' Matches, and representing their Colleges has greatly increased.'[134] Gerald was one of those who took to the game. However, his involvement was not always as productive as it might have been. Playing on the left-wing for an Eton XI in February 1898, 'H.-Smith got away several times', it was reported, 'but failed to pass soon enough, but eventually scored from a good pass'.[135]

There were two sports at which Gerald did excel: athletics and cricket. It was a curious combination: although sport was so important at Eton, athletics, it seems, was treated almost flippantly: 'Hardly any coaching is ever given, and boys run and jump as and how they please.'[136] Although Gerald was no sprinter or middle-distance runner, he took the high jump seriously. And this even though he did not seem ideally suited to the event: he was heavy, weighing over twelve stones by 1898, and he had, apparently, 'a peculiar style of landing'.[137] But excel he did. He finished either first or second in the school competitions which he entered during 1897, 1898 and 1899, with jumps of five feet one and a half inches, and (on two occasions) five feet four inches. For a schoolboy, even an eighteen year-old schoolboy, five feet four inches was a remarkable achievement. It was a height which, if replicated, would have won him sixth place at the Paris Olympics of 1900.[138]

Cricket, unlike athletics, was regarded extremely highly. It was the game, it has been said, which 'in the opinion of the quality newspapers at least had an unchallenged claim to being the national games of the late Victorians'.[139] Insofar as this was the case, the public schools were at one with the rest of the country.[140] 'In this mania Eton is no exception to the rule of the general British public', concluded the *Eton College Chronicle*. 'It is hardly too much to say that the newspaper most – or at any rate first – read by the average present Etonian every morning is the *Sportsman*.'[141] Cricket, it was widely believed, embodied all that was best in the British, or at least the English, national character. When Lord Harris spoke in 1898 at a presentation to the school's retiring chief cricket adviser and coach, he referred to Edward Obert Hindley Wilkinson, the Eton captain of 1872, who died nine years later in the Zulu War, 'like a good cricketer and good Englishman, giving his life for his side'.[142]

Gerald rose steadily through the ranks of Eton cricket. As a sixteen year-old in 1896, he represented his house, Donaldson's, in the inter-house cup competition.[143] The following season, he played, primarily as a bowler, at 'second upper' level, just below the top tier of cricket in the school.[144] He performed well. Playing in the final of the house cup, he was his side's top scorer in the first innings with thirty-eight (out of a total of two hundred and sixteen). But he was unable to bowl to his usual standard: 'Howard Smith, a bowler on whom they relied to a considerable extent, strained himself early in the innings and could not do himself justice.'[145]

His progress continued. By the following season, he had forced his way into the first team and was playing for Eton in games against sides such as Winchester and the Household Brigade.[146] His success was epitomised by his selection to play in the most prestigious of all public school games and one that attracted wide public attention: the Eton vs. Harrow match at Lords.[147] The oldest fixture in the cricketing calendar, it drew crowds of 15,000 – middle- and upper-class – spectators. In fact, according to one Old Harrovian, it was 'the supreme rite when one identified oneself with every member of the side, suffered in their failures, exalted in their triumphs'.[148]

Eton lost the 1898 match by nine wickets, but Gerald played well. Possessed perhaps of a big-match temperament, he was Eton's second highest scorer with forty-nine runs (including ten fours), and the team's second most successful bowler, taking three wickets for sixty-one runs.[149] When the *Eton College Chronicle* looked back at his performances over the season, it was impressed, but in no doubt that there was room for improvement:

> Bowls straight and fast, and has often been most useful. A powerful hitter; with better defence he would be a dangerous batsman. Works hard in the field, and has done some brilliant things; but should not leave his place at short-slip before the ball is struck, unless it is obviously going to leg.[150]

Gerald's final season of cricket at Eton was crowned by another solid performance in the annual match against Harrow at Lords. It was 'the society cricket function of the year', enthused the *Daily Mail*, 'and despite the attractions of the Eclipse Stakes at Sandown, the crowd of well-dressed notabilities was as large as on any occasion during the past twenty years'.[151] Although he only scored eight runs, Gerald was again Eton's second most successful bowler, taking four wickets for sixty-four runs. He had enjoyed a good season: he was fifth (out of seven) in the school's bowling averages and third (out of seventeen) in the batting averages.[152] However, it was his attitude and commitment as much as his skill and accomplishments which impressed his contemporaries:

> Has fallen off in batting, and does not play as straight as he did, and besides, has developed a tendency to get l-b-w. His bowling has often been the means of breaking up a stand, and though erratic in length as a rule, he at times sends down a beautiful ball. His energy and keenness in the field have been most praiseworthy; he is excellent at short slip, and is able to field anywhere.[153]

Gerald was now well known and well thought of, making a positive impression on the staff as well as on his fellow pupils. Whether or not his sporting achievements were the catalyst, his housemaster's doubts about him had begun to dissolve. Gerald was 'full of football', Donaldson reported at the end of 1896, 'but is coming on: a gd fellow if bluff whom I look to help in house presently.'[154] Two years later, Donaldson's reservations were all but gone. Gerald, he found, was 'rather fond of answering in House but amenable on whole'.[155] His misgivings seem to have disappeared completely by the time Gerald came towards the end of his time at the school. He is 'doing thorog [sic] well both in work + play', Donaldson reported in 1898. He mixed well, he was a 'capital' captain of the football XI, and he was, in sum, 'a worthy fellow of whom I have a high opinion'.[156]

Gerald's Eton career was crowned by his selection in September 1898 to the best known and most exclusive of all Eton's clubs and societies, the Eton Society.[157] 'Pop', as it was commonly known, was small, exclusive and self-regarding. Deciding its membership by ballot, its members guarded admission jealously: when Gerald applied the previous summer, he had received the dreaded blackball.[158] But once elected, he became part of what was probably the most privileged group of young men in the whole of the country – if not the whole of the western world.

Clues to Pop's privilege and exclusivity crop up in unexpected places. Lanhydrock House, a National Trust estate in Cornwall, contains an 1899 photograph of the Eton Society which was given to it (along with the house and estate) by the Hon. Gerald Agar-Robartes, the 7th Viscount Clifden.[159] It shows the young men of Pop posing – languidly – on the steps into the College chapel. Alongside Gerald, records the stand below the photograph, are the Hon. T. Agar-Robartes, E.G. St Aubyn, the Hon. J. Bruce, J.S. Carter, J. Churchill, E.B. Denison, C.H. Ebden, W. Findlay, F. Grenfell, R.N. Grenfell, Lord Grimston, the Hon. W.E. Guinness, G. Hargreaves, L. Heathcoat-Amory, P.J.C. Huddleston, F.S. Kelly, P.L. Loraine, H.K. Longman, H.W.P. MacNaghten, E.G. Martin, C. Nicholl, W. Payne-Gallwey, F.A.W. Pickering, K. Rodwell, C.H. Taylor and A.A. Tod.

Gerald had joined the elite of the elite. The young men posing for the 1899 photograph of Pop included the scions of some of the best known and best connected families in the country. Thomas Charles Reginald Agar-Robartes was the son of Thomas Charles Agar-Robartes, the 6th Viscount Clifden of Gowran, and Walter Edward Guinness was the son on Edward Guinness, the 1st Earl of Iveagh. Ludovic Heathcoat-Amory was the son of Sir John Heathcoat-Amory, the 1st Baronet Heathcoat-Amory, while William Thomas Payne-Gallwey was the son of Sir Ralph William Frankland-Payne-Gallway, the 3rd Baronet Payne.

Once elected to 'Pop', Gerald played a full part in its activities. Indeed, it is his attendance at, and participation in, the society's debates that provide us with some of the few indications we have as to his interests and beliefs as he moved from adolescence into adulthood. The evidence needs to be handled, of course, with some care. Gerald's presence at a debate did not necessarily mean that he was interested in the subject under discussion. But it does mean that he was aware of, and must have learned something about, the topic being debated. During the winter of 1898–9, his first months as a member, he attended four debates – although he did not speak – on a range of topics. One meeting wondered, for example, 'Whether a belief in ghosts is compatible with Reason'. Another was narrowly parochial: 'That an Old Etonian colour is desirable'. But two at least of the motions under discussion were seriously political: 'That alien immigration ought to be checked by legislation', 'That canvassing at Parliamentary Elections should be declared illegal'.[160]

Just as Gerald's presence at a debate did not necessarily mean that he was interested in what was being discussed, so what he said when he did speak did not necessarily reflect what he thought. But even though it is impossible to know when he was arguing a case as an intellectual exercise and when he was presenting a point of view in which he believed, it is probably safe to assume that he had an interest in the subjects on which he chose to speak. He spoke on at least four occasions. He made one speech on the Anglo-American Alliance, one on whether duelling was justifiable, one on whether the liberty of the press was desirable and another on whether old-age pensions were necessary. Gerald argued that duelling was justifiable and that the introduction of pensions for the elderly was unnecessary.[161]

There is no doubt then that Gerald cut a substantial figure by the time he left Eton for Cambridge in the summer of 1899. 'In the Eleven' and 'In the Eton Society', there was not much more that a boy could achieve at the school.[162] The Rev. Donaldson's valedictory comments on Gerald's Eton career capture something both of the world in which he had been educated and of the young man that Eton (Temple Grove and his family) had produced. Donaldson was happy with what he saw. He was 'sorry' that Howard-Smith was 'leaving: a thoroly [sic] sound healthy minded good fellow: not a great scholar, but might get a 2nd. In the [?] Trip. Hv [sic] much affn [sic] for him + hope he is going to do his family + House credit.'

Childhood, adolescence and class

What then have we learned about the late Victorian and Edwardian middle- and upper middle-class family? This chapter appears, on the face of it, to confirm much of what is said about the way in which such families brought up their children – or rather their sons. Gerald's parents employed staff to look after him (and help run their home) when he was young; they sent him away to prep school at the age of nine, and then on to Eton when he was thirteen years old. Everything that we know about Gerald suggests that he, like his prep school and public school contemporaries, probably emerged at the age of nineteen, if not upright and manly, then 'pretty easily recognized by speech manner, dress and behaviour'.[163] His parents had got what they wanted. Gerald, it seems, had been socialised, at home and at school, into the rules, practices and behaviour of the upper middle-class world into which he was born, the upper middle-class world in which it was intended that he should make his way.

Yet it is easy to be misled. It is tempting to make big claims, to smooth over complications, to attribute a spurious uniformity to social groups with which, by virtue of chronology or class, we share little in common – with which perhaps we have little instinctive sympathy or understanding. In all events, Gerald Howard-Smith's childhood and adolescence should not be taken as an exemplar of the way in which the late nineteenth- and early twentieth-century upper middle class brought up its sons. The upper middle-class's socialisation of its children was no more uniform, no more uniformly successful, than that undertaken by any other class.

Gerald's parents sent him to not just any private school, but to Temple Grove, one of the best known and best regarded prep schools in the whole of southern England, and then on to Eton, the most famous and most highly regarded school in the country, if not the whole world. This, of course, was far from typical. Prep schools and public schools, it must be remembered, were strikingly heterogeneous, varying widely in resources, size, success, longevity and social standing. Some schools, it should not be forgotten, marketed themselves primarily, if not exclusively, on the basis that they were cheap.[164]

Neither should it be assumed that Gerald Howard-Smith's experience at Temple Grove and Eton was typical even of those who were at school with him. He was at once less gifted academically and more gifted athletically than many of his Eton contemporaries. A talented all-round sportsman, he struggled with his writing, excelled at the high jump and at cricket and received the school's ultimate accolade when he was elected a member of Pop. Indeed, his membership of Pop alone confirms, if confirmation were needed, that Gerald's experience cannot be taken as typical even of those who were at school with him. Seldon and Walsh put it like this:

> Even within a school the boys differed greatly. Raymond Asquith said of one Etonian officer he defended in a court martial in 1916 that he was 'a perfect man of his type – insolent, languid, fearless and of a virile elegance which is most engaging'. Yet Eton in the same era produced prize-winning physicist, Henry Moseley; a leading composer, George Butterworth; a committed social Reformer, Stephen Hobhouse; several distinguished headmasters; and many others for whom the terms 'insolent' and 'languid' could not be less apt.[165]

*Hetero*geneity then was as important as *homo*geneity. The way in which Philip and Mary Howard-Smith brought up Gerald is of interest, not for its typicality, but for the insights that it offers into the upper middle-class world, in all its gradations and variety, in which he grew up.

Notes

1. T. Travers, *The Killing Ground* (Barnsley: Pen & Sword, 1987), p. 5, cited in Anthony Seldon and David Walsh, *Public Schools and the Great War: The Generation Lost* (Barnsley: Pen & Sword, 2013), p. 39.
2. F.M.L. Thompson, *The Rise of Respectable Society: A Social History of Victorian Britain 1830–1900* (London: Fontana, 1988), p. 145. For prep schools, see Donald Leinster-Mackay, *The Rise of the English Prep School* (Lewes: Falmer Press, 1984) and Vvyen Brendon, *Prep School Children: A Class Apart over Two Centuries* (London: Continuum, 2009). For public schools, see T.J. Chandler, 'The Structuring of Manliness and the Development of Rugby Football at the Public Schools and Oxbridge, 1830–1880', in J. Nauright and T.J.L. Chandler (eds), *Making Men: Rugby and Masculine Identity* (London: Cass, 1999) and J.A. Mangan, 'Bullies, Beatings, Battles and Bruises: "Great Days and Jolly Days" at One Mid-Victorian Public School', in Mike Huggins and J.A. Mangan (eds), *Disreputable Pleasures: Less Virtuous Victorians at Play* (London: Frank Cass, 2004).
3. Eton College Archives, SCH/HOUSE/SAD, MEL 24, [now 01], Donaldson House Notes, Election 1899.
4. *Morning Post*, October 10, 1893.
5. Census of England and Wales, 1861, RG09/91/90/31.
6. Census of England and Wales, 1861, RG09/ 91/90/31; *Post Office London Directory*, 1881, p. 620; J. Foster, *Men-at-the-Bar: A Biographical Handlist* (London: Hazell, Watson and Viney, 1885), p. 434; *Who's Who*, 1913, p. 1,866. Philip received his MA in 1873: see *Daily News*, May 16, 1873.
7. Census of England and Wales, 1871, RG10/195/10/14; *Post Office London Directory*, 1881, p. 768.
8. For his work in the revision courts, see, for example, *Barrow's Worcester Journal*, September 12, 1885; *Derby Mercury*, September 30, 1885. Also P.W.J. Bartrip, 'The State and the Steam-Boiler in Nineteenth-Century Britain', *International Review of Social History*, 25, 1, 1980, esp. pp. 94–5.
9. *Midland Counties Express*, May 17, 1919.
10. www.plimsoll.org/resources/SCCLibraries/WreckReports/14394.asp [October 2013], Board of Trade Wreck Report 14394, 1880.
11. Board of Trade Wreck Report 15140, 1883. See also *London Gazette*, August 19, 1887.
12. www.livesonline.rcseng.ac.uk/biogs/E002867b.htm [October 2013].
13. Census of England and Wales, 1871, RG10/29/89/99.
14. Thompson, *Respectable Society*, p. 173.
15. A. Light, *Mrs Woolf and the Servants* (London: Penguin, 2007), p. 30. See, too, Elizabeth Buettner, *Empire Families: Britons and Late Imperial India* (Oxford: Oxford University Press, 2004).
16. Stephen Koss, *The Rise and Fall of the Political Press in Britain* (London: Fontana, 1990), p. 159. I owe this reference to Dilwyn Porter. Philip gave as his address not his home, Avenue Road, Hampstead, but his place of work, King's Bench-walk, Temple.
17. Light, *Mrs Woolf*, p. 30.
18. Hermione Hobhouse, *Survey of London: volume 42: Kensington Square to Earl's Court* (London: English Heritage, 1986), pp. 239–48.
19. Census of England and Wales, 1881, RG11/47/103/18.
20. Census of England and Wales, 1881, RG1147/103/18.
21. *Standard*, January 24, 1880.
22. Thompson, *Respectable Society*, p. 126.
23. Census of England and Wales, 1881, RG11/ 50/46/45. They may also have employed non-live-in staff such as laundresses and gardeners for whom no records survive.
24. Census of England and Wales, 1891, RG12/34/3/1.

Home, school and socialisation 27

25 John Benson, *Affluence and Authority: A Social History of Twentieth-Century Britain* (London: Arnold, 2005), p. 16.
26 J. Burnett, *Useful Toil: Autobiographies of Working People from the 1820s to the 1920s* (London: Routledge, 1994), pp. 137–8.
27 Burnett, *Useful Toil*, p. 137.
28 Perkin, *Professional Society*, pp. 28–9.
29 L. Davidoff, M. Little, J. Fink and K. Holden, *The Family Story: Blood, Contract and Intimacy 1830–1960* (London: Longman, 1999), pp. 158–9.
30 Burnett, *Useful Toil*, p. 142. Also, Census of England and Wales, 1881, RG19/54/45.
31 *Who was Who, 1916–1928*, p. 975.
32 Census of England and Wales, 1881, RG11/ 50/46/45.
33 www.cricketarchive.com/Archive/Players/864/864934.html [October 2013].
34 Henry and Emily's home, Buckhill House, was a large, late eighteenth-century building that had been improved during the course of the following century.
35 Census of England and Wales, 1891, RG12/1597/5; F.M.L. Thompson, *English Landed Society in the Nineteenth Century* (London: Routledge & Kegan Paul, 1963), p.10. For the role that Henry and the estate played locally, see, for instance, *North Wilts Herald*, April 3, 10, 17, 1891.
36 F.M.L. Thompson, 'Social Control in Victorian Britain', *Economic History Review*, xxxiv, 3, 1981.
37 Burnett, *Useful Toil*, pp. 146–8.
38 Thompson, *Respectable Society*, p. 145. Also Thompson, 'Social Control', p. 190.
39 M.D. Hill, *Eton and Elsewhere* (London: John Murray, 1928), pp. 28–9.
40 It took its name from the Rev. J.H. Edgar who was headmaster from 1880 until 1893. Information from Christine Vickers; S. Wright, *Waterfield's School: A Preparatory School in its Victorian Heyday* (Guildford: Heron Ghyll Press, 1994), pp. 186, 202.
41 M. Batchelor, *Cradle of Empire: A Preparatory School through Nine Reigns* (Chichester: Phillimore, 1981), p. 46; John Benson, *The Working Class in Britain, 1850–1939* (London: Longman, 1989), p. 41.
42 East Sussex Record Office, Temple Grove School, TGS, 2/2/2, Admissions Book.
43 Vvyen Brendon, *Prep School Children: A Class Apart over Two Centuries* (London: Continuum, 2009), p. 53.
44 TGS, 2/2/2, Admissions Book.
45 TGS, 2/2/2, Admissions Book.
46 Robert Graves, *Goodbye to All That* (London: Penguin, 2000), p. 24.
47 TGS, 14/1/1, *General Rules for the Conduct of Temple Grove School*, 1880.
48 Wright, *Waterfield's School*, p. 200. At least one early twentieth-century ghost story is based at Temple Grove: Dublin Core, 'A School Story', *More Ghost Stories of an Antiquary* (London: Arnold, 1911).
49 TGS/17/8/1, C.C. Barclay, 'Reminiscences of Temple Grove', p. 1.
50 Wright, *Waterfield's School*, p. 201.
51 TGS, 17/8/1, Notes by A.L. Keigwin.
52 D. Leinster-Mackay, 'The Origins of the Incorporated Association of Preparatory Schools (IAPS) and its Early Concerns: A Centennial Acknowledgement', *History of Education*, 22, 1993, p. 115.
53 L.S.R. Byrne and E.L. Churchill, *Changing Eton: A Survey of Conditions Based on the History of Eton since the Royal Commission of 1862–4* (London: Jonathan Cape, 1937), p. 8.
54 Byrne and Churchill, *Changing Eton*, p. 9.
55 TGS, 14/1/1, *General Rules*; Barclay, 'Reminiscences', p. 3.
56 Batchelor, *Cradle of Empire*, p. 50; R.D. Pearce, 'The Prep School and Imperialism: The Example of Orwell's St Cyprian's', *Journal of Educational Administration and History*, 23, 1, 1991, pp. 44–5.

28 *Privilege*

57 The two boarding houses, it was said, helped the 'small boys' to settle in. TGS, 14/6/1/1, *Temple Grove, East Sheen*, c. 1890.
58 Byrne and Churchill, *Changing Eton*, p. 3. Also *Temple Grove Magazine*, July 1916, pp. 1–2.
59 Batchelor, *Cradle of Empire*, p. 50; Leinster-Mackay, 'Origins', p. 114.
60 Leinster-Mackay, *English Prep School*, p. 194. See, more broadly, John Benson, '"Get a Blue and You Will See Your Money Back Again": Staffing and Marketing the English Prep School, 1890–1912', *History of Education*, 43, 3, 2014.
61 Leinster-Mackay, *English Prep School*, pp. 194–5.
62 Byrne and Churchill, *Changing Eton*, pp. 5–6.
63 Wright, *Waterfield's School*, p. 164. Also Byrne and Churchill, *Changing Eton*, p. 5.
64 Byrne and Churchill, *Changing Eton*, pp. 5–6.
65 *Temple Grove Magazine*, July 1916. Also Wright, *Waterfield's School*, pp. 195–6, 162.
66 *Temple Grove Magazine*, December 1916, p. 9. For more on the importance of prep school sport, see E.F. Benson (who attended Temple Grove), *David Blaize* (New York: George H. Doran, 1916), pp. 72–3.
67 Wright, *Waterfield's School*, p. 171. Also, p. 112.
68 Batchelor, *Cradle of Empire*, pp. 57–8.
69 Batchelor, *Cradle of Empire*, p. 60.
70 Thompson, 'Social Control', p. 192.
71 Byrne and Churchill, *Changing Eton*, p. 12.
72 Hill, *Eton*, pp. 29–30.
73 Peace, 'Prep School and Imperialism', p. 51.
74 He secured a place, but not a scholarship. TGS, 6/2/1; 17/1/1.
75 Wright, *Waterfield's School*, p. 72.
76 Batchelor, *Cradle of Empire*, p. 48.
77 Cited in Chandler, 'Manliness', p. 26. See Barbara English, 'The Education of the Landed Elite in England c. 1815–c.1870', *Journal of Educational Administration and History*, 23, 1, 1991.
78 John Tosh, *A Man's Place: Masculinity and the Middle-Class Home in Victorian England* (London: Yale University Press, 2007), p. 118.
79 Chandler, 'Manliness', p. 26.
80 Shane Leslie, *The End of a Chapter* (New York: Charles Scribner's Sons, 1916), p. 30.
81 L. Simpson, 'Imperialism, National Efficiency and Education, 1900–1905', *Journal of Educational Administration and History*, 16, 1, 1984.
82 Simpson, 'Imperialism', pp. 29, 32–33; Jennifer S. Kushnier, 'Educating Boys to be Queer: Braddon's *Lady Audley's Secret*', *Victorian Literature and Culture*, 2002, pp. 61–4.
83 Cited in Simpson, 'Imperialism', p. 29. See also Kushnier, 'Educating Boys to be Queer'; C. Dewey, '"Socratic Teachers": Part I – The Opposition to the Cult of Athletics at Eton, 1870–1914', *International Journal of the History of Sport*, 12, 1995.
84 *Eton College Chronicle*, November 10, 1898. See Seldon and Walsh, *Public Schools*.
85 Harold Perkin, *The Rise of Professional Society: England since 1880* (London: Routledge, 1989), p. 368.
86 Patrick Joyce, *The State of Freedom: A Social History of the British State since 1800* (Cambridge: Cambridge University Press, 2013), p. 283.
87 *Eton Calendar*, Lent 1894, p. 106.
88 For example, Hill, *Eton*, pp. 34–40; Clare Rose, *Making, Selling and Wearing Boys' Clothes in Late-Victorian England* (London: Ashgate, 2010).
89 See Joyce, *Freedom*, pp. 267–8; Jane Hamlett, *Material Relations: Domestic Interiors and Middle-Class Families in England, 1850–1910* (Manchester: Manchester University Press, 2010), pp. 148–9. Also Jane Hamlett's paper, 'Schools for Boys', which she kindly allowed me to see in advance of publication.

90　*Eton Calendar*, Michaelmas, 1893, p. 28.
91　Byrne and Churchill, *Changing Eton*, p. 131; Joyce, *Freedom*, pp. 267–8.
92　Eton College Archives, SCH/HOUS/SAD, MEL 24, Easter 1893.
93　MEL 24, Christmas 1894, Election 1895.
94　MEL 24, Easter 1895.
95　MEL 24, Christmas, 1896.
96　*Eton Calendar*, Michaelmas, 1893, p. 28; Lent, 1894, p. 41; Summer 1899, p. 17.
97　Eton College Archives, SCH/CCF/2/2, Eton College Officers Training Corps, Corps Records, 1895.
98　MEL 24, Easter 1894.
99　MEL 24, Christmas 1897.
100　MEL 24, Easter 1897.
101　MEL 24, Election 1896.
102　MEL 24, Christmas 1897.
103　MEL 24, Election 1896.
104　*Eton Calendar*, Summer 1899, p. 17.
105　Joyce, *Freedom*, ch. 7.
106　SCH/CCF/2/2, Corps Records, 1895.
107　*Eton College Chronicle*, January 30, 1896.
108　*Eton College Chronicle*, October 24, 1895.
109　Seldon and Walsh, *Public Schools*, pp. 24–7. According to Shane Leslie, 'military proficiency was rated low.' Leslie, *End of a Chapter*, p. 43.
110　*Play*, December 15, 1896; Joyce, *Freedom*, p. 280.
111　*Eton College Chronicle*, October 11, 1895; February 6, 1897.
112　'One Who Would Have Gone' to *Eton College Chronicle*, October 10, 1896.
113　Rev. S.A. Donaldson, 'Higher Religious Education', *The Parents' Review: A Monthly Magazine of Home-Training and Culture*, 3, 1892–3.
114　MEL 24, 1896. For the role of the chapel, see Hamlett, 'Schools for Boys', pp. 8–10.
115　Joyce, *Freedom*, pp. 278–9; Tony Mason and Eliza Riedi, *Sport and the Military: The British Armed Forces 1880–1960* (Cambridge: Cambridge University Press, 2010), ch. 2.
116　*Eton College Chronicle*, June 13, 1895. Also Leslie, *End of a Chapter*, p. 34.
117　*Eton College Chronicle*, March 14, 1896.
118　*Eton College Chronicle*, February 29, 1896.
119　*Eton College Chronicle*, March 11, 1899. He also came second in the hurdles: *Eton College Chronicle*, March 16, 1899.
120　Richard Holt, *Sport and the British: A Modern History* (Oxford: Oxford University Press, 1990), p. 77.
121　*Eton College Chronicle*, January 27, 1898.
122　*Eton College Chronicle*, October 16, 1896. Also November 6, 1896.
123　Eton College Archives, 'Mixed Wall Game', 1873–1905, October 20, 1898.
124　'Mixed Wall Game', 1873–1905, 1898.
125　*Eton College Chronicle*, November 30, 1898.
126　Hill, *Eton*, p. 97.
127　Holt, *Sport and the British*, p. 77.
128　J.W. Pawson, *The Field Game* (Eton: Spottiswoode, Ballantyne & Co., 1935), p. 3.
129　Eton College Archives, Field, 1893–1904, pp. 172–6, 209.
130　*Eton College Chronicle*, December 14, 1898. Also Field, 1893–1904, p. 206; Old Etonian Association, *The Eton Register* (Eton: Spottiswoode, 1901), p. xv.
131　He played as a forward. *Eton College Chronicle*, March 7, 1899.
132　Still valuable is T. Mason, *Association Football & English Society 1863–1915* (Brighton: Harvester, 1981).
133　*Eton College Chronicle*, February 6, 1896.

30 *Privilege*

134 *Eton College Chronicle*, November 6, 1897. See also 'Centre Forward' to *Eton College Chronicle*, February 13, 1896.
135 *Eton College Chronicle*, February 25, 1898.
136 Hill, *Eton*, p. 214.
137 *Eton College Chronicle*, March 18, 1897.
138 *Eton College Chronicle*, March 18, 1897, March 25, 1898, March 16, 1899.
139 Thompson, *Respectable Society*, p. 299.
140 D. Frith, *The Golden Age of Cricket 1890–1914* (Ware: Omega Books, 1983); Holt, *Sport*, section 2.
141 *Eton College Chronicle*, May 23, 1895.
142 Harris was the captain of the English cricket team 1879–84.
143 *Eton College Chronicle*, July 24, 1896. Also May 14, 1896.
144 *Eton College Chronicle*, May 13, 27, 29 1897; June 22, 1897.
145 *Eton College Chronicle*, October 1, 1897.
146 *Eton College Chronicle*, May 27, 1898; *Annual Register*, 1899, p. 460.
147 *Eton Register*, p. xiv.
148 Cited in Holt, *Sport*, p. 115. See George R. Sims, *Living London: Its Work and its Play its Humour and its Pathos its Sights and its Scenes* (London: Cassell, 1902), vol. 2, p. 149. Cf. P.S.H. Lawrence, *An Eton Camera 1920–1959* (Salisbury: Michael Russell, 1983), pp. 12–13.
149 F.S. Ashley-Cooper, *Eton v. Harrow At The Wicket: With Some Biographical Notes, Poems, and Genealogical Tables* (London: St James's Press, 1922), p. 98.
150 *Eton College Chronicle*, July 16, 1898. Also June 23, 1898.
151 *Daily Mail*, July 15, 1899.
152 *Eton College Chronicle*, June 22, 1899.
153 *Eton College Chronicle*, July 20, 1899.
154 MEL 24, Christmas 1896.
155 MEL 24, Easter 1898.
156 MEL 24, Christmas 1898. Also MEL 24, Election 1898.
157 *Eton College Chronicle*, September 22, 29, 1898.
158 Eton Archives, Eton Society, 1895–1908, 1895; 'S.F.P.' to *Eton College Chronicle*, January 26, 1899.
159 National Trust Image Collection No. 881823.
160 It is dangerous, of course, to argue from a negative, but Gerald was not recorded as absent from Pop's debates of September 23, October, 7, 14, 21, 28, 1898. Eton Archives, Eton Society, 1895–1908.
161 Eton Society, 1895–1908, 1898 *passim*.
162 *Eton College Chronicle*, September 29, 1899.
163 Thompson, *Respectable Society*, p. 145.
164 For example, *Standard*, August 31, 1892. See Benson, 'Get a Blue'; Hamlett, *Material Relations*, pp. 150–151; Seldon and Walsh, *Public Schools*, p. 21.
165 Seldon and Walsh, *Public Schools*, p. 21.

2 'AN UNASSAILABLE DISTINCTION THROUGH LIFE': UNIVERSITY, SPORT AND STATUS

Bloods and Blues

Just as we tend to have a picture in our mind of the late Victorian and Edwardian upper middle-class family, so too we have a sense of what it was like to be a university student in late nineteenth- and early twentieth-century Oxford and Cambridge. We envisage a world of wealth, power and privilege, of precious, young dilettantes or sporty, young 'bloods' living lives of idleness and indulgence, interspersed perhaps with the occasional visit to a library or lecture theatre. '"Oxbridge" between 1875 and 1914', confirms J.A. Mangan caustically, 'was more a place of privileged play than it was a centre of meritocratic cerebral effort'.[1] Contemporaries agreed: 'the visitor to Oxford and Cambridge is often impressed with the idea that recreation and amusement form the real work here, and that study is merely useful insofar as it goes to fill up some corner of the day's routine, which cannot be otherwise allocated.'[2]

Trinity College was even more powerful and privileged than the rest of the two universities. By far the largest college in Cambridge, it was known as a training ground 'for England's governing classes, in Parliament, the civil service, the Church, and in colonial government, and educated men who would become prime ministers, viceroys, governors general and members of Cabinets.'[3] When the historian G.M. Trevelyan went up to Trinity in 1893, notes his biographer, it served only to widen his already impressive range of contacts and connections: 'sixty-eight out of the 105 MPs from Cambridge were from Trinity, the highest number from any Oxbridge college, accounting for one MP in ten. At the same time, one-third of Gladstone's last cabinet was composed of Trinity men, including Sir William Harcourt, Earl Spencer, and Trevelyan's own father.'[4]

Trinity was also a keen sporting college.[5] When Cambridge won the university boat race against Oxford during the spring of Gerald's first year, the entire crew and cox, with only a single exception, came from Trinity.[6] Trinity's sporting focus was unusual, but not exceptionally so. By the turn of the century, the two ancient universities set enormous store by the physical, moral, military – and other – benefits that sport was believed to inculcate. There should be more military training at university, claimed the *Cambridge Chronicle* in

1900, but undergraduate sport made a valuable contribution to safeguarding the nation's defences. 'Men trained in the athletic field can be turned into first class soldiers in a much shorter time than those where nerves and sinews have not been hardened by constant and regulated practice.'[7] Indeed, sport, it was believed, paid social as well as military dividends. 'To win a dark or light Blue at Athletics', it was said, 'gives men an unassailable distinction through life'.[8]

But how accurate is such a picture? Once again, we have to ask ourselves how far our views of late Victorian and Edwardian upper middle-class life are clouded by nostalgia and/or by irritation. Did the young men of the two ancient universities devote themselves as single-mindedly as we are led to believe to the pleasures of the sports field? And if they did, and did so successfully, did it really open the doors and pay the dividends – social and otherwise – that many appeared to believe. One wonders again whether Gerald Howard-Smith and his young, upper middle-class contemporaries were quite so conformist, quite so homogeneous, quite so prepared to submit to the prevailing culture as the existing consensus is inclined to suggest.

Trinity

Gerald Howard-Smith went up to Trinity in the autumn of 1899. The move from school to university could be difficult, but Gerald was hardly stepping into the unknown. His father had been to Trinity before him. The way in which his parents had brought him up – at home in Kensington, at school at Temple Grove and then at Eton – had prepared him, as little else could, for what lay ahead. Ten years at boarding school meant, most obviously, that he was used both to living away from home and to living in a communal environment.[9]

Gerald, like Trevelyan six years before, came to Trinity with contacts and connections. Although Gerald's were less impressive than Trevelyan's, they did much, one imagines, both to secure his admission to Trinity and, once there, to smooth his passage into undergraduate life. Eton had close links with Trinity and every year a large number of Old Etonians ended up at Trinity (and, of course, at other Oxbridge colleges). Of the one hundred and eighty-three young men joining Trinity in 1899, twenty-three (13 per cent) had been to Eton, and three (Gerald, Edward Geoffrey St Aubyn and Charles Hotson Murray Ebden) had been members of Pop.[10] Indeed, the ties between Eton and Trinity were so close that the 'Trinity Etonians' had their own soccer team, which played matches against the 'Trinity Harrovians' as well as against teams described, in tellingly dismissive terms, as the 'Trinity Rest' and the 'Trinity Rest II'.[11]

How then did Gerald spend his time at Cambridge? We do not know a great deal, it must be said, about his academic career – a reflection, perhaps, of the interest that he, and others like him, took in what one might have thought would be at the core of university life. What we do know is that Gerald, like the majority of those who went up with him, did so without winning a scholarship. Tutored by the classicist James Duff, he studied classics, theology and mathematics, graduating with an ordinary degree in 1902.[12] 'The ordinary degree man', it was explained a few years later, 'leaves Cambridge with a certificate enabling him to step into the clerical, legal, or teaching professions'.[13]

However seriously Gerald took his studies, he certainly devoted much of his time to athletics and cricket. It seems likely, in fact, that his sporting interests and sporting prowess proved major factors in smoothing his progress from childhood to adolescence, from schoolboy to undergraduate. As Richard Holt explains: 'Going on to university, and that usually meant Oxford or Cambridge, was unlikely to be a difficult transition for the public school sportsman. The academic demands of the ancient universities were not particularly onerous and the college system fitted into the patterns of communal living and rivalries learned in school houses.'[14] The sporting relationship between school and university, it has been pointed out, was cyclical – not to say incestuous. 'Worshipped "bloods" at school became admired "blues" at university and were enthusiastically head-hunted by the schools as games masters, who in turn sent their "bloods" on to the universities.'[15]

Sport was everywhere. 'The ideology of athleticism was never as dominant in the universities as it was in the schools,' concedes J.A. Mangan, 'and it varied in intensity from college to college and from period to period, but it became woven tightly into the social and educational fabric of college life.'[16] There were sports clubs and societies to join, training sessions to attend, committee meetings to go to, balls and dances to dress up for. Gerald, for example, joined the Third Trinity Boat Club (one of the college's two rowing clubs) as soon as he arrived in Cambridge. Four years later, the club invited him (in his capacity as President of the Cambridge University Athletic Club) to the Trinity May Ball which it held at the Corn Exchange.[17] So it was that when the mathematician Walter William Rouse-Ball looked back at the part played by college athletic clubs during his years as a Fellow of Trinity between 1878 and 1905, he concluded that the 'growth of organised recreations of this kind will strike the future historian as one of the outstanding features of the last century'.[18]

Athletics

Gerald made his mark at Cambridge in both athletics and cricket. Athletics was taken much more seriously, and aroused much more interest, in Oxbridge circles than it did at Eton.[19] Cambridge University Athletic Club (CUAC) had been founded in 1857 (followed shortly afterwards by Oxford University Athletic Club). Competing against one another for the first time a few years later, their inter-Varsity matches, CUAC stresses to this day, predated the birth of the modern Olympics by more than three decades.[20] It was a rivalry which, as with the boat race, marked an important occasion in the national sporting calendar. In 1900, for example, 6–7,000 spectators turned up to watch Oxford take on Gerald and the rest of the Cambridge team at the Queen's Club (near to his home) in West Kensington.[21]

Gerald joined CUAC as soon as he could, and began competing straight away. At the Cambridge Freshmen's Sports, which the club organised at the start of the academic year to assess newcomers' potential, Gerald acquitted himself very creditably. But although he won the high jump, it was not enough to secure him a place in the Cambridge team that was selected the following spring to compete against Oxford in the annual inter-Varsity meeting.[22] Undeterred, he continued to compete, in both hurdles and high jump, at college meetings across the university (and occasionally in Oxford) during the remainder of the 1899–1900 season, and again throughout the winter of 1900–1901.[23]

His efforts paid off. In March 1901, eighteen months into his time at Cambridge, he won the high jump at the University sports.[24] Although conceding that the conditions were unfavourable, the sporting paper the *Field* was distinctly underwhelmed:

> For the high jump, owing to the prevalence of the strong wind, the posts and bar were shifted from the usual position, and the competitors, instead of alighting in the soft pit, had to land on grass. The change may have had some effect, but probably H-Smith is not equal to more than 5ft 7in [1.70 metres].[25]

Whatever the *Field*'s reservations, Gerald's victory was enough to secure him selection to the Cambridge team that faced Oxford four weeks later. Held at Queen's Club on the Friday afternoon before the boat race, the 'dull, cold, and windy' weather was again conducive neither to large attendances nor to outstanding performances. Nevertheless, there was 'a goodly crowd' of 6,000 or so on hand to see Gerald build on his promising early season form with a winning leap of five feet 10¼ inches [1.78 metres]. The *Field* was surprised but impressed: 'Bulkeley, on whom Oxford's hopes depended, failed to clear 5ft 6in [1.68 metres], while Howard Smith, who was reported to have done 4½in [11cm.] better than this in practice a few days back, quite surprisingly corroborated the rumour.'[26]

Gerald's good form continued into 1902.[27] He showed what he was capable of at a 'well patronised' meeting held at Fenner's early in March. On the first day of the two-day event, he won his heat of the one hundred and twenty yards hurdles by four yards [3.7 metres] in just over seventeen seconds, a victory which he repeated the following day in the final in a fractionally quicker time.[28] Despite a poor performance in the high jump at the University handicaps the previous November, he was back to winning ways with a leap of five feet nine inches [1.75 metres]. He won, claimed the *Field* enthusiastically, but as we shall see below perhaps not altogether metaphorically, 'without taking off his coat'.[29]

Results such as these qualified him, as they had the previous year, to represent Cambridge in the inter-Varsity match against Oxford. Once again,

'The weather was bad, the ground was sodden, but the company was large and the sport was excellent.'[30] With several thousand spectators in attendance, it was said that 'the grounds presented an animated appearance when the proceedings commenced at half-past two.'[31] Although Cambridge lost by five events to four, Gerald again performed very creditably, finishing third in the one hundred and twenty yards hurdles (despite falling at the second barrier). He was the clear favourite in the high jump, which he won with five feet 9¾ inches [1.78 metres], a height that left him 1½ inches [3.8 cm.] clear of his nearest challenger.[32] 'This event was always looked upon as a certainty for Howard-Smith', remarked the *Pall Mall Gazette*. 'Last year he won with a leap of 5 ft. 10¼ in. [1.78 metres]. In America last summer he cleared 6 ft. [1.83 metres].'[33] In fact, concluded the *Cambridge Chronicle* contentedly, the standard of Oxbridge high jumping was as high as it had been thirty and forty years before.[34]

Gerald's final year at Cambridge, 1903, saw his standing rise, both nationally and to some extent internationally, to new and impressive heights.[35] The *Field*, for instance, ran a series of stories on university athletics that, *inter alia*, extolled his exploits. 'The Light Blue president has for some time had an ankle under treatment', it reported in March, 'but it had sufficiently recovered to enable him to appear at the high jump, which he won from C.C. Doorly, the performances of both men being above the average.'[36] But it was Gerald's performance against London Athletic Club – for whom Doorly was competing – that had the *Field* reaching for its superlatives. In a passage that is worth quoting at some length, it lauds Gerald not just for the quality of his jumping but also for the upper middle-class insouciance with which he won the event:

> The third item was the high jump, and yet another sensation was in store for the spectators. All four competitors cleared 5 ft 4 ft [*sic*] [1.63 metres], but when it came to 5 ft 6 in [1.68 metres], three of them broke down, Doorly most unaccountably, because on the 9th inst he cleared 5 ft 9 in. [1.75 metres] However, the bar was raised to 5 ft 8 in [1.73 metres], and Howard-Smith treated it as a soft thing, not even removing his sweater. Then the Varsity president had the bar put up to 6 ft [1.83 metres], and amid deafening cheers he cleared it well at his first effort, which evidently satisfied him, for he gathered up his garments and returned to the pavilion, having gained another record for Fenner's.[37]

Success, sociability and distinction

Although athletics was an individual (and individualistic) sport, it provided numerous opportunities – at Oxford and Cambridge, in particular – for sporting sociability. The relationship between sporting success, sporting sociability and social distinction is inevitably difficult to disentangle with any certainty.[38] The problems are compounded in Gerald's case by having to decide whether, and to what extent, the economic, social, and cultural advantages with which he had been brought up meant that the doors that sport opened for him were already at least partly ajar.

Whatever the complications of attributing cause and effect in such matters, there is no doubting that Gerald benefited – and benefited substantially – from the social contacts arising from his sporting interests and accomplishments. College sports clubs developed, it has been seen, into a key component of late nineteenth- and early twentieth-century Oxbridge life.[39] Indeed, twenty-five years before Gerald went up to Cambridge, a *Punch* cartoon showed a university rowing club room overlooking the river: it was replete with undergraduates in rowing kit, alongside, one is not surprised to see, a wine bottle and wine glasses.[40] Ten years later, George Nugent, a student at King's College, joined the boat club, he recalled, not to row but to 'wear the blazer' and enjoy the privilege of 'occasionally going down to the river' to 'see our college boat practising, or of running and shouting advice to it, when it is in for a race'.[41]

For those, like Gerald, with the ability and application to participate at a high level, university-wide sports clubs such as the CUAC assumed more importance still. Gerald, for example, was elected secretary of CUAC for the 1902 season, and went on to serve as club president in 1903.[42] The sociability that such clubs encouraged – and the attribution and circulation of status that they fostered – were mutually reinforcing. When the Third Trinity Boat Club invited Gerald to the 1903 Trinity May Ball in his capacity as President of CUAC, it invited, too, the presidents of the Cambridge University Association Football Club, the Cambridge University Boat Club, the Cambridge University Cricket Club and the Cambridge University Rugby Union Football Club.[43]

Sporting sociability, whether elite, middle class or plebeian, was always likely to peak while teams were on tour. Whatever their scale and seriousness, sports tours provided teammates with opportunities not just to travel and compete but also, of course, to socialise, to reinforce existing friendships and to forge new, possibly rewarding relationships. It is no surprise then that Oxford and Cambridge undergraduates (and graduates) were to the fore in organising such tours. The Corinthians, a London soccer team confined to university men and ex-public schoolboys, were known, for example, both for their attacking style of play and for their Christmas and Easter tours of the midlands and north of England. 'Not only did everybody love a lord', concludes Tony Mason, 'but they loved an amateur too, especially when he was a gentleman who was quite capable of giving the professionals a good run for their money.'[44]

Gerald was good enough, lucky enough – and well off enough – to take part in the two-month trip that a combined Oxford-Cambridge athletics team made to Canada and the United States of America during the late summer and autumn of 1901.[45] Trips on such a scale, it goes without saying, could be contemplated only by those from wealthy families – or by those who somehow managed to acquire wealthy backers.[46] Thus when plans were announced twelve years later to send a team of six British athletes on a three-month tour of South Africa, it was explained that their fares and hotels would be paid for them. However, the fact that the tourists would be responsible for their other living costs, and would also have to forfeit three months' earnings, meant, pointed out the *Cricket and Football Field* with some understatement, that 'the working class athlete seems to be barred from the trip.'[47]

The Oxford-Cambridge tour of Canada and the United States was some time in the planning. It was early in April that Harvard and Yale invited the Oxford and Cambridge Athletics Clubs to visit America for what would be the fourth in a series of transatlantic meetings that had begun seven years before.[48] A month or so later, it was confirmed that a party of Oxford and Cambridge athletes would visit New York (and Montreal) in September, 'when they will test their strength against the pick of Yale and Harvard Colleges.'[49] Gerald, a winner at the recent inter-Varsity match, was selected for the high jump.[50]

The eighteen-man party that left Liverpool for Boston in the middle of August was, as might be expected, strikingly homogeneous in background, circumstances and advantages. Privately educated, athletically gifted (and no doubt socially confident), its members were at one, of course, in being able to spend two months away on tour. Gerald was among friends – or at least among young men whom he knew well (sometimes very well indeed). Of the eighteen athletes selected, ten were from Cambridge and two were with Gerald at Trinity: the hammer thrower/high jumper Walter Edward Bonhote Henderson, and the middle-distance runner H.W.P MacNaughton, who had been a member of Pop at Eton at the same time as Gerald – and was one of those photographed with him outside the College chapel two years before.[51]

The tour also brought Gerald and his teammates into contact with a succession of businessmen, politicians and others prominent in public life. James Lees (later Sir Lees) Knowles led the team on the trip. A fine athlete in his own right, Knowles straddled the worlds of business and politics. He was chairman of his family firm Andrew Knowles & Sons, the largest colliery company in south Lancashire, whose workforce at the time of the tour was getting on for 4,000.[52] Elected Conservative MP for West Salford in 1886, he went on to serve as parliamentary secretary to two Presidents of the Board of Trade, and as Second Church Estates Commissioner, a crown appointment who acted as the link between government, parliament and the Church of England.[53]

Once in North America, Gerald and the team continued to mix with the great and the good. They were met on their arrival by a group of Harvard and Yale athletes who afforded them 'a hearty welcome'.[54] The American party was led by John White Hallowell, the captain of the Harvard team, and Evert Jansen Wendell, a Harvard graduate of independent means with extensive interests in athletics and philanthropy.[55] This 'ever-caring millionaire', it has been said, 'directed his considerable skills to helping others and in the service of his country'.[56]

Gerald and the rest of the team were watched by, hosted by and, no doubt, introduced to a series of leading figures in Canadian and American society. Lord Strathcona, the Canadian High Commissioner in London, attended the team's meeting against McGill, Montreal and Toronto Universities in

Montreal in the middle of September: 'and there was not one on the grounds more cordial in his congratulations than Lord Strathcona.'[57] Theodore Roosevelt was unable to preside a week later at the dinner held on the evening of the meeting against Yale and Harvard – but only because he had been elevated to the presidency following the assassination of William McKinley three weeks previously.[58] The team also made trips to Ottawa and Buffalo, and took tours of the Yale campus (including lunch at the New Haven Country Club) and the Harvard campus (followed by dinner in Boston at the exclusive Algonquin Club).[59] The tycoon Thomas Lipton invited them to watch, as his guests, his British yacht challenge for the prestigious and hotly contested America's Cup.[60]

On the field, Gerald, like the rest of the team, enjoyed mixed success, winning handsomely in Canada but losing heavily in America. Gerald came in for particular praise for the part he played in the tourists' victory over McGill, Montreal and Toronto in Montreal. 'The high jump was a splendid example of good athletics', noted the Montreal *Gazette*. 'Smith went 5ft. 10in. [1.78 metres], and afterwards did an exhibition that landed six feet even [1.83 metres]. He failed, however, at 6ft. 2in. [1.88 metres].'[61] He also came in for a certain amount of criticism when the team moved south to the United States. After finishing third (out of four) against Harvard and Yale in New York, it was said that he was 'made obviously nervous by the proximity of the competition to a grand-stand, [and] was unable to equal his best performance – half an inch [1.3 cm.] better than the mark at which the event was won'.[62]

Whatever Gerald's successes and failures on the field, whatever the contacts he made off it (and whether or not they proved useful in the years ahead), the tour must have made an impact. A trip of this length, on this scale can only have heightened Gerald's – and his teammates' – awareness of the world around them. It raised questions, in particular, about English attitudes towards sport and, thus, more generally about English, upper middle-class way of doing things. The *New York Times*, for example, ran a substantial article comparing the ways in which university athletes prepared on the two sides of the Atlantic. 'To an Englishman the method of training in vogue at Yale Field and Cohasset would be almost impossible, and doubtless seem a mystery. On the other hand, a Yale athlete who might drop in at the Montreal quarters would be astonished to find the Englishmen going through a full afternoon's series of outdoor sports, each man doing what he feels like doing and enjoying himself as if it were recreation.'[63]

It was an issue that drew on – and possibly contributed to – a broader contemporary awareness of the changing international order. For as is well known, some were alarmed and some were delighted that Britain appeared to be in relative, if not absolute, decline, while the United States seemed set to embark on a period of economic, social and cultural ascendancy.[64] The criticism of the team's preparations might have dented the tourists' self-assurance, but it certainly did not destroy it. Gerald and his teammates were able to console themselves that although they had been beaten, they had taken their defeat with good grace, affording their opponents 'all the credit that is their due'.[65]

Walter Henderson, who competed alongside Gerald in the high jump, quoted with approval the comment in one American newspaper that, 'There has been the best of feeling between the visitors and the visited. The Oxonians and the Cantabs are good sportsmen and good fellows. They don't think the world is coming to an end when they are beaten.'[66]

The Oxford-Cambridge tour of Canada and the United States of America in 1901 is important then for what it tells us both about Gerald's athletic prowess and about the privileged world to which that prowess gave him access. It shows, indeed it epitomises, the centrality of sport in late nineteenth- and early twentieth-century English university life. It is not surprising, of course, that sporting success and sporting status were intimately related; what is more surprising, perhaps, is that sporting status could provide even upper middle-class sportsmen with opportunities that would not otherwise have been available to them.

Back in England, Gerald resumed his involvement in top-level sport. Now halfway through his university career, he became a leading – if not *the* leading – figure in turn-of-the-century Cambridge athletics. It was a small world, but an important one for all that. For as Paul R. Deslandes suggests, British upper middle-class manliness was personified, for many at Oxbridge and beyond, by 'the Cambridge University Athletic Club runner's muscular body, handsome face, and self-assured stance'.[67] Indeed, it is this 'paragon of undergraduate masculinity' that Deslandes chooses to adorn the front cover of his book *Oxbridge Men: British Masculinity and the Undergraduate Experience, 1850–1920*.[68]

What use did Gerald make of his sporting skills and sporting status? He did all he could, it seems, to promote athletics across the university. As an administrator, an official and a competitor, he was as active off the field as he was on it. He helped organise sport at Trinity, and served CUAC as a committee member, as Honorary Secretary (1901–2) and finally as President (1902–3).[69] He was also ready to officiate at everything from inter-college contests, to the University's Freshmen's Trials, the University Handicaps and the University sports themselves.[70] These were sought after positions: Lees Knowles, the leader of the tour to Canada and the United States, was one of those officiating at the (admittedly higher status) inter-Varsity meetings.[71]

Gerald proved a hard act to follow. In the spring of 1904, the year after Gerald left Cambridge, the *Field* reviewed the state of university athletics. It was reasonably satisfied with what it saw. 'There have been signs for some years past of a want of progress if not an actual decline, in the pursuit of athletics at the public schools and the Universities; but, though the cult may be confined to a somewhat small number of enthusiasts, a high standard of performance is fortunately maintained.'[72] However, Gerald's leaving, it concluded, was a significant blow:

> The Light Blues have lost an excellent performer at the high jump in their late president, G. Howard-Smith, whose achievements, both in England and America, have seldom been equalled by amateurs.[73]

Cricket

Cricket was much more popular and much more fashionable than athletics. In fact, cricket stood apart.[74] The game was played, watched and supported by all classes in late nineteenth- and early twentieth-century England. The county game was still popular, enthusiasts recall nostalgically, with middle- and upper middle-class support doing much to give matches their distinctive character:

> A modern county cricketer would hardly recognise the packed grounds on which his counterpart played a hundred years ago, seemingly as part of an extended Georgian garden party, with gaudily clad spectators, and often their servants and pets, too, camped out around the boundary.[75]

Crowds flocked, too, we have seen, to the Eton–Harrow game at Lords. And they were just as keen to attend games between the Gentlemen and Players, and between Oxford and Cambridge.[76] The standard of play at the universities was often very high. Every member of the Oxford XI of 1895, for instance, played first-class county cricket, with four of them going on to represent England.[77] One of the four, P.F. ('Plum') Warner (Rugby and Oriel College, Oxford) played fifteen times for his country, captaining the team on ten occasions – and taking his fiancée Agnes with him on the 1903–4 tour of Australia.[78]

The way in which Oxbridge Blues played was highly valued. Men like Prince Ranjitsinhji (Trinity College, Cambridge) and C.B. Fry (Repton and Wadham College, Oxford), another who had been in the Oxford XI of 1895, were major national figures, revered as 'public school, imperial sportsmen, espousing the values of fair play'. Fry, it has been said, 'was deified by the public. He played cricket for England, with a classically correct technique, scoring 3,147 runs in 1901 including six successive hundreds. He captained Oxford at cricket, soccer and athletics, then played as an international at both association and rugby football, while building a career as a journalist.'[79]

Gerald, therefore, had a lot to live up to – not to say a lot to aspire to. If ever there were a sport in late Victorian and Edwardian England that promised distinction and status, it was university cricket. Certainly, cricket at Cambridge enjoyed the highest possible standing. Its demands were considerable, its facilities exemplary. Founded in 1820, Cambridge University Cricket Club (CUCC) had established itself at Fenner's in 1848 and soon afterwards began playing its great rivals Oxford at Lords, the headquarters of world cricket.[80] Between 1871 and 1887, almost 380,000 people – an average of more than 22,000 spectators a year – made their way to northwest London to watch Oxford take on Cambridge in their much anticipated annual contests.[81]

Needless to say, membership of CUAC was expensive. There was an entrance fee of one guinea, together with an annual subscription of the same amount.[82] But this was far from the end of it. There was clothing and equipment to buy, travel to and from matches to see to, food and drink to pay for, not to mention all the other costs associated with the life of a university sportsman. It would be easy for even a modestly ambitious player to spend £1–10–0 (£1.50) and more on his bat, pads and gloves alone, a sum it would take a coalminer, for example, a full week of work to earn.[83] These were costs, it goes without saying, which confirmed, indeed reinforced, CUAC's social and economic exclusivity.

The young gentlemen able and willing to pay such fees received in return a range of benefits, some exclusively social and honorific. Members were entitled, for instance, to wear the club colours – a not insubstantial benefit, we have seen, in the eyes of some undergraduates. They were also entitled to free admission at Fenner's both to the ground and to the pavilion (where tea, wine and light refreshments were served, but only to members).[84] Members were also allowed to bring two lady guests free to most games (whereas gentlemen guests could be admitted only by the special invitation of the president). Once in the ground, there had long been strict rules as to who could go where. Members, and members only, were allowed to sit in the pavilion, on the roof and under the veranda; members and members only were allowed to take lady guests to the seats in front of the pavilion.[85] Members were given priority, too, when it came to admission to the most important games: in the summer of 1900, Gerald's first summer in Cambridge, the MCC committee placed one hundred and fifty ten shilling tickets to the Varsity match at the disposal of the CUCC committee.[86]

The club also provided its members with the facilities to help them improve their skills. Players had access to the club's nets, where they were able – in an intriguing insight into contemporary views of the relative importance of batting and bowling, of amateurs and professionals – to bat against professional bowlers whom the club brought in to bowl against them.[87] So when the ground opened for practice at the beginning of the 1900 season, the club announced that it would cost members two shillings an hour to hire the county bowlers whom the club had engaged to provide them with batting practice.[88]

Gerald, it must be said, found the transition from school cricket to university cricket less easy than that from school athletics to university athletics. He was less talented a cricketer than he was an athlete and there was more competition to represent the university at cricket than there was at the hurdles or the high jump. In all events, Gerald was not regarded as one of the more promising newcomers to Cambridge cricket during his first year at university.[89] This view of his potential seemed to be borne out when he played poorly in the two-day freshmen's trial which was held at the beginning of May. He was run out for just one run and took just one wicket for sixty-one runs (conceding a wide and a number of no balls).[90]

Gerald, however, was good enough – and well enough connected – to turn out for a team such as the Eton Ramblers. This was a club, it goes without saying, which boasted both impeccable credentials and impressive connections. He played for them twice in the summer of 1900, once against Malvern College and once against the Free Foresters, both matches taking place in

Malvern on the ground belonging to the town's College.[91] The match against the Free Foresters, which took place at the beginning of August, exemplified not just the level of cricket at which Gerald was playing but also the level of society in which he was making his way.

The Eton Ramblers, as their name suggests, recruited Old Etonians, gifted players from privileged backgrounds. Their opening batsman against the Free Foresters, Robert Cunliffe Gosling, had been educated, like Gerald, at Eton and Trinity, before going on to captain England at soccer – and in 1902 becoming High Sheriff of Essex. Batting at number three was Charles Hotson Murray Ebden, who had been with Gerald at Eton and was now his contemporary at Cambridge. Both young men, it might be remembered, had been elected to Pop and both had been photographed the year before – posing languidly – outside the Chapel.[92] Coming in after Ebden at number four for the Ramblers was Henry John (later Sir Henry John) Mourdant. He, too, had been educated at Eton (and King's College) Cambridge, he, too, played first-class cricket (for Middlesex) – and in due course, on the death of his cousin Sir Osbert Mordaunt in 1934, became the 12th Baronet of the Mordaunt Baronets.[93]

The Ramblers' opponents, the Free Foresters, were also socially exclusive.[94] It was a club that, like the Ramblers, took account of social standing as well as cricketing prowess in everything that it did. Founded in 1856, the club took its name from the fact that members were 'free' to play against (as well as for) the club and because they were drawn originally from the Forest of Needwood in Staffordshire and the Forest of Arden in Warwickshire. However, by the time Gerald came up against them, they recruited from across the Midlands (as well as from officers in the armed forces), and played their matches against 'County, University, College Schools, Regimental XI's and … recognised clubs in desirable localities'. In spite of – or more likely because of – such connections, the Foresters were, for many years, the only amateur club to feature in the first-class fixture list.[95]

Gerald was also good enough – and well connected enough – to be selected for teams associated with that bastion of the game, the Marylebone Cricket Club: the MCC itself, the 'MCC and Ground' and the 'Gentlemen of Marylebone Cricket Club'. So between the end of May and the middle of July 1900, he played, at Lords, against the club side Hampstead, against Haverford College, against the Minor Counties and against the Cambridge team that he was not yet able to get into. The MCC sides in which Gerald played, it must be said, were not always very well regarded. 'The team representing the M.C.C at Cambridge yesterday', the *Morning Post* observed sourly towards the end of May, 'was only a moderate one'.[96]

Whether or not such criticisms were justified, playing for the MCC brought Gerald into contact with some of the leading cricketers of the day. His most memorable game, in this respect at least, was probably that against the London County Cricket Club, because it meant facing the redoubtable W.G. Grace. Coming towards the end of his career, Grace had been enticed by the offer of running the club from its base at Crystal Palace.[97] Although it did not become the serious cricketing project that its supporters envisaged, it recruited good players and enjoyed a respectable and attractive fixture list.[98] In all events, the London team proved far too good for Gerald, who did not bowl and was dismissed for a duck.[99]

But Gerald was nothing if not a trier and he was determined to do better the following summer. He began well. Playing in the opening game of Cambridge's 1901 season, the Seniors' Match, he scored ten (out of one hundred and eighty-four runs), and took two (out of four) wickets.[100] Ten days later, he had an exceptional game. Playing for the university against 'Mr A.J. Webbe's Eleven' in Cambridge's first trial match, he performed better (in the first innings at least) than he, his teammates, his captain or anybody else can ever have anticipated. 'The visitors were dismissed for 164 runs', reported the *Cambridge Chronicle*, 'G. Howard-Smith, the fifth bowler tried, taking six wickets inside eleven overs at a cost of only 23 runs.'[101] The *Daily Mail* was impressed.

> The most promising feature of the cricket was the success in bowling met with by G. Howard Smith, the high jumper, whose fast and medium paced deliveries proved very difficult to play. Taking two wickets in his first over, he altogether dismissed six batsmen for 23 runs, and in the present dearth of good bowlers appears to be a distinct find.[102]

Such early season form earned Gerald a place in the team the university chose to play against Yorkshire at the end of May. Not surprisingly, perhaps, he found the transition from university cricket to county cricket difficult to negotiate. Selected as an all-rounder, he scored just nine runs in his two innings, and took two just wickets for one hundred and three runs in the first innings, and one for twenty-nine in the second.[103] Nevertheless, he was selected a week later to play against another county side, Worcestershire. He had a marginally better game as Cambridge won by eight wickets. Although he scored only two runs (in his one appearance at the crease) and had match figures of no wickets for thirty-eight runs, he did take three catches in Worcestershire's first innings.[104]

Gerald was selected again when the university took on the touring South Africans. Such tours aroused great interest. 'I do not doubt', it was observed a few months later, 'that these friendly contests in our national games tend to foster the good feeling which, happily, exists between all parts of the Empire'.[105] Moreover, as Geoffery Levett has pointed out in a recent study of colonial tours to early twentieth-century London, it can be 'hard to believe that there was ever an element of self-doubt about the fitness of the Edwardian sportsman. The popular image of the era continues to be that of a sporting Golden Age, "a time of complacency, security and opulent pride for Britain and her splendid Empire".'[106]

But what happened when such certainties were challenged? We have seen already that Oxford and Cambridge's defeat later in the year by Harvard and Yale in America led to a degree of reflection and reappraisal. How much greater the impact was likely to be when the defeat was at home rather than abroad, when it involved the national game rather than a minority sport such as athletics. 'Victorious cricketers from the colonies could claim', it has been pointed out, 'a share of self-discipline, doggedness, detachment, and team spirit that was so often proclaimed by the British as intrinsic to the game. Beating the imperial ruler on the field therefore buttressed claims to equal worth off it'.[107]

Cambridge lost to the touring South Africans, a defeat that probably had more impact than one might now imagine. It is true, of course, that the losing team comprised the best players in Cambridge, not the best players in the country. But it was a comprehensive defeat, the South Africans, winning the match by an innings and two hundred and fifteen runs.[108] Moreover, the Cambridge team represented, it was commonly believed, the cream of upper- and upper middle-class masculinity. Levett makes the point: 'Poor performances against colonial teams provoked a fear that the products of the public school system were failing to demonstrate the skills that were supposed to justify their leadership role in the political and social life of the nation and empire, as well as on the sports field.'[109]

Gerald himself had a mixed game against the South Africans. He did moderately well with the bat, scoring four not out in the first innings and twenty-one not out in the second; but performed less well with the ball, bowling twenty-two overs, with a return of just one wicket for one hundred and nineteen runs. It was not enough to earn him his Blue. But it was a close run thing, with Gerald in contention for a place in the team to face Oxford until the very last moment. The Cambridge captain 'has now virtually completed his side to oppose Oxford at Lord's next Thursday', reported the *Daily Mail* at the end of June, 'the only question being as to whether the eleventh place will be filled by L.T. Driffield or G. Howard-Smith, a choice which may not be made till the morning of the match'.[110] It was Gerald who lost out.

It was a blow, but assuaged perhaps by the fact that he had been selected to join the combined Oxford and Cambridge athletics team on its forthcoming tour of Canada and the United States of America. Although the trip raised questions, it has been seen, about the English team's preparations, it did little, it seemed, to dent the tourists' belief in either themselves or the English way of doing things. The scale of the tour, the coverage it received and the confirmation it provided of Gerald's standing in the sport all did a good deal, presumably, to take his mind off being overlooked for the game against Oxford.

However disappointed he was, Gerald was back on the cricket field as soon as he could at the beginning of the 1902 season. The first game of the summer in Cambridge was traditionally between two teams of 'Seniors', and Gerald had the honour of captaining one of them.[111] The captain of the opposing team, Noel Oneley Tagart had been brought up, like Gerald, in the Kensington district of the capital. Living just a couple or so miles away from one another, both had enjoyed comfortable upper middle-class childhoods, both had been educated at public school (Gerald at Eton, Noel at Clifton) and both had gone on to become contemporaries at Cambridge.[112]

University, sport and status 45

Yet again, Gerald did not do enough to do to get his Blue. Unfortunately for him, the competition for places was almost certainly stiffer than in previous years, the captains of the Oxford and Cambridge teams having agreed that undergraduates returning from a year or more of military service in the Boer War should be eligible for selection for twelve months longer than usual.[113] Whatever the reason, Gerald missed out. He did not play against Surrey, Sussex or Yorkshire, he was chosen neither for the Varsity match nor for the other 'great match of the season', the game against the touring Australians.[114] And when he did play for the university – against London County, for example – it did not go well. He was out for a duck in his one innings and did not manage to take any wickets.[115]

Gerald pressed on, playing at all the levels available to him. The omens were certainly better than in previous years. He began representing the university more regularly, playing in matches, for example, against Surrey, Sussex, Warwickshire and Yorkshire.[116] Not that he was always successful. Sometimes it went very badly indeed: he had to face the ignominy, for instance, of having his fast bowling no-balled eleven times in the match against Yorkshire.[117] Nevertheless, at the beginning of July, he was selected, at long last, to play for Cambridge against Oxford in the Varsity match at Lord's.

Figure 2.1 Gerald Howard-Smith (back row, second from left) and a Trinity College Cricket XI, 1903.
(Reproduced by permission of the Master and Fellows of Trinity College, Cambridge)

46 *Privilege*

As in previous years, even the choosing of the two teams made the pages of the national press. The *Daily Mail* ran its story under the heading, 'The Rival Blues 'Varsity Elevens for Next Week's Great Match'. It explained that, 'The Light Blue eleven having been completed with the bestowal yesterday of caps on Messrs. Godsell and Howard-Smith, and seven of the Oxford team having been definitely selected, it is now possible to set out the two sides as in all probability they will face each other for the inter-'varsity match at Lord's next Thursday.'[118]

When the match got underway, neither Gerald nor Cambridge excelled. It was a strikingly – almost a hopelessly – one-sided game, which Oxford won by getting on for three hundred runs. Gerald batted twice, scoring eleven runs in his first innings and nought not out in his second; the one wicket he managed to take came at a cost of eighty-six runs. He was not alone in his failure to perform. The team as a whole never got into the game: 'The margin of 268 runs was, in the run of the play, fully deserved, for a sedate comparison between the two sides by anybody who watched the play closely could only result in one conclusion – that the Oxonians were, all round, the better team.'[119]

Fortunately for Gerald and his teammates, the Oxford-Cambridge match was not just about cricket, not just about who won and who lost. A major event in the social calendar, it was of interest to those from all classes who followed the national game. For the privileged few who watched the game at Lord's, there was the opportunity to relive their youth, to renew old contacts and perhaps to meet friends of friends. For the twenty-two players as well as for the thousands of spectators – it was an occasion at which to see and to be seen. Cricket, points out Mike Huggins, was a sport which, like horse racing and yachting, 'allowed the elite to indulge their passion for pleasure and pageantry alongside high spending'.[120]

The 1903 match at Lord's between Oxford and Cambridge marked the high point – indeed the end point – of Gerald's three-year, first-class cricket career. Between 1901 and 1903, he played three times for the Marylebone Cricket Club and seventeen times for Cambridge University. His was not a distinguished record. In the twenty games he played, he scored one hundred and eighty-nine runs at an average of just over eleven (with a best score of twenty-three); he took twenty-nine wickets at an average of forty-four (albeit with impressive best figures of six for twenty-three).[121] But cricket was Gerald's second sport and he left Cambridge a double Blue

Publicity, plaudits and prospects

Gerald's undergraduate career seems, on the face of it, to confirm Mangan's view that late nineteenth- and early twentieth-century Oxbridge 'was more a place of privileged play than it was a centre of meritocratic cerebral effort'.[122] Even though training regimes were lax by modern standards, university-level sport was demanding and time consuming. Gerald must have spent a large proportion of his time at Cambridge practising and competing in – not to mention discussing, organising and travelling to and from – athletic events, cricket matches and the other sports in which he was interested. No sooner was athletics over in the spring than he began playing cricket. The latter, of course, was notoriously time consuming: each summer while he was at Cambridge, Gerald played in a succession of one-, two- and three-day games: some were at Fenner's, but others were at Lord's, at grounds in London and at venues across the south (and occasionally the north) of England.[123]

Gerald's sporting performances brought him considerable publicity. The Oxford-Cambridge athletics meeting at Queen's Club, the Oxford-Cambridge cricket match at Lord's, along with the Oxford-Cambridge boat race on the Thames, were all regarded as occasions of national – not to say international – significance.[124] His athletics exploits, particularly his involvement in the tour of Canada and the United States, meant, we have seen, that he was singled out for individual attention and congratulation. His cricketing exploits were much less newsworthy with the result, as might be expected, that they were reported in much less detail and only once, so far as is known, with any particular enthusiasm. But Gerald left Cambridge a double Blue – and this at a time when these things mattered, and mattered a great deal.[125]

But this is by no means the end of the matter. It is one thing to show that Gerald – or anybody else – excelled at university sport, gleaning publicity and plaudits, locally, nationally and internationally, as he did so. It is quite another to assume that sporting prowess brought 'unassailable distinction', let alone paid material dividends, enabling graduates to translate their youthful achievements on the sports field into significant, long-term advantages. Whether or not Gerald was able to do so we will see in the following chapter.

Notes

1 J.A. Mangan, 'Lamentable Barbarians and Pitiful Sheep: Rhetoric of Protest and Pleasure in Late Victorian and Edwardian "Oxbridge"', *Victorian Studies*, summer 1991, p. 476. See, too, Nick Mansfield, 'Grads and Snobs: John Brown, Town and Gown in Early Twentieth-Century Cambridge', *History Workshop Journal*, 35, 1993.
2 Cited in Mangan, 'Lamentable Barbarians', p. 476.
3 Barbara English, 'The Education of the Landed Elite in England c.1815–c.1870', *Journal of Educational Administration and History*, 23, 1, 1991, p. 24. See also Paul R. Deslandes, 'Competitive Examinations and the Culture of Masculinity in Oxbridge Undergraduate Life, 1850–1920', *History of Education Quarterly*, 42, 4, 2002, p. 544.
4 David Cannadine, *G.M. Trevelyan: A Life in History* (London: Fontana, 1993), p. 20.
5 T.J.L. Chandler, 'The Structuring of Manliness and the Development of Rugby Football at the Public Schools and Oxbridge, 1830–1880', in J. Nauright and T.J.L. Chandler (eds), *Making Men: Rugby and Masculine Identity* (London: Cass, 1999), p. 20.
6 *Sporting Chronicle*, April 2, 1900. Also March 19, 1900.
7 *Cambridge Chronicle*, April 6, 1900. See, for example, Mike Huggins, *The Victorians and Sport* (London: Hambledon, 2004), p. 32; Tony Mason and Eliza Riedi, *Sport*

48 *Privilege*

and the Military: The British Armed Forces 1880–1960 (Cambridge: Cambridge University Press, 2010), pp. 3–4.
8 Shane Leslie, *The End of a Chapter* (New York: Charles Scribner's Sons, 1916), p. 90. Also Eric Parker, 'Private Schools: Ancient and Modern', *Longman's Magazine*, November 1896/April 1897, cited in Donald Leinster-Mackay, *The Rise of the English Prep School* (Lewes: Falmer Press, 1984), p. 196. See, too, Eric Parker in *The Preparatory Schools Review*, 11, 1898.
9 Patrick Joyce, *The State of Freedom: A Social History of the British State since 1800* (Cambridge: Cambridge University Press, 2013), ch.7.
10 Trinity College Library, *Admissions Trinity College Cambridge. 1851–1900*, pp. 1, 120–21,146.
11 *Cambridge Chronicle*, March 21, 1902. Also *Morning Post*, December 1, 1900.
12 J.A. Venn, *Alumni Cantabrigiensis*, part 2, vol. 5 (Cambridge: Cambridge University Press, 1953), p. 552; www.trinithcollegechapel.com/about/memorials/brasses/duff-jd [May 2015]; information from Adam Green and Jonathan Smith.
13 Leslie, *End of a Chapter*, p. 90.
14 Richard Holt, *Sport and the British: A Modern History* (Oxford: Oxford University Press, 1989), p. 83.
15 J.A. Mangan, 'Bloods, Blues and Barbarians: Some Aspects of Late Victorian Oxbridge', in M. Huggins and J.A. Mangan (eds), *Disreputable Pleasures: Less Virtuous Victorians at Play* (London: Cass, 2004), p. 40. See, too, John Benson, '"Get a Blue and You Will See Your Money Back Again": Staffing and Marketing the English Prep School, 1890–1912', *History of Education*, 43, 3, 2014.
16 Mangan, 'Lamentable Barbarians', p. 477.
17 Trinity College Library, 28/2/f.14.
18 Cited in Mangan, 'Lamentable Barbarians', p. 474. See W.W. Rouse-Ball, *A History of the First Trinity Boat Club* (Cambridge: Bowes & Bowes, 1908).
19 *Field*, March 31, 1900.
20 www.cuac.org.uk/the-early-days [February 2014].
21 *Sporting Chronicle*, March 31, 1900; *Cambridge Chronicle*, April 6, 1900. See Paul R. Deslandes, *Oxbridge Men: British Masculinity and the Undergraduate Experience, 1850–1920* (Bloomington: Indiana University Press, 2005), dust cover and p. 44, which take a Cambridge University Athletic Club runner as a 'paragon of undergraduate masculinity'.
22 *Daily Mail*, October 28, 1899; *Field*, October 28, November 4, 1899; *Sporting Chronicle*, March 31, 1900.
23 *Field*, November 25, 1899; February 24, March 3, November 17, 1900; *Sporting Chronicle*, March 31, 1900; *Pall Mall Gazette*, November 15, 1900.
24 *Daily Mail*, March 4, 1901.
25 *Field*, March 9, 1901.
26 *Field*, March 30, 1901. See, too, *Cambridge Chronicle*, April 5, 1901. Gerald also finished third (out of four) in the hurdles.
27 *Field*, November 30, 1901; February 8, March 1, 1902.
28 *Cambridge Chronicle*, March 14, 1902.
29 *Field*, March 15, 1902.
30 *Illustrated London News*, March 29, 1902.
31 *Pall Mall Gazette*, March 22, 1902.
32 *Cambridge Chronicle*, March 28, 1902.
33 *Pall Mall Gazette*, March 22, 1902. See, also, *Penny Illustrated Paper*, March 22, 1902.
34 *Cambridge Chronicle*, March 28, 1902.
35 See, for instance, *New York Times*, March 29, 1903; *Otago Witness*, May 20, 1903.
36 *Field*, March 14, 1903. Also *Field*, April 4, 1902; *Daily Mail*, March 28, 1903.

37 *Field*, March 21, 1903. See, more broadly, D.J. Taylor, *On the Corinthian Spirit: The Decline of Amateurism in Sport* (London: Yellow Jersey Press, 2006).
38 Holt, *Sport*, pp. 113–117. See also Hamish Telfer, 'Ludism, Laughter and Liquor: Homosocial Behaviour in Late Victorian Scottish Harrier Clubs', in Huggins and Mangan (eds), *Disreputable Pleasures*.
39 Mangan, 'Lamentable Barbarians', p. 474.
40 Mike Huggins, 'Cartoons and Comic Periodicals, 1841–1901: A Satirical Sociology of Victorian Sporting Life', in Huggins and Mangan (eds), *Disreputable Pleasures*, pp. 141–2.
41 Deslandes, *Oxbridge Men*, p. 163.
42 *Cambridge Chronicle*, May 31, 1903.
43 Trinity College Library, 28/2/f.14.
44 Mason, *Association Football*, p. 216. The Corinthians also toured Europe and the Empire. See Dilwyn Porter, 'Amateur Football in England, 1948–63: The Pegasus Phenomenon', *Contemporary British History*, 14, 2000, pp. 1–2
45 This section draws heavily on John Benson, 'Athletics, Class and Nation: The Oxford- Cambridge University Tour of Canada and the United States of America, 1901', *Sport in History*, 33, 1, 2013.
46 *Cambridge Chronicle*, May 24, 1901.
47 *Cricket and Football Field*, July 12, 1913.
48 *Cambridge Chronicle*, April 5, 1901.
49 *Cambridge Chronicle*, May 10, 1901. Also May 24, 1901.
50 *Cambridge Chronicle*, July 19, 1901.
51 National Trust, Inventory 881823, Lanhydrock, Cornwall, Portrait of Eton Society, 1899; *Daily Mail*, August 24, 1901; *New York Times*, September 24, 1901.
52 Raymond Challinor, *The Lancashire and Cheshire Miners* (Newcastle: Frank Graham, 1972), p. 261.
53 See Frank Cranmer, 'Church-State Relations in the United Kingdom: A Westminster View', *Ecclesiastical Law Journal*, 6, 2001.
54 *Daily Mail*, August 24, 1901.
55 *New York Times*, August 29, 1917. See J.A. Lucas, 'Four "Mysterious" Citizens of the United States that Served on the International Olympic Committee during the Period 1900–1917: Theodore Stanton; James Hazen Hyde; Allison Vincent Armour and Evert Jansen Wendell', *Fifth International Symposium for Olympic Research*, 2000.
56 Lucas, 'Four "Mysterious" Citizens', p. 200.
57 *Montreal Gazette*, September 16, 1901. Also *New York Times*, September 15, 1901.
58 *New York Times*, September 20, 1901.
59 *New York Times*, September 20, 1901; *Harvard Crimson*, September 30, October 1, 2, 1901; *Yale Daily News*, October 5, 1901.
60 *Cambridge Chronicle*, August 16, 1901.
61 *Gazette*, September 16, 1901. Also *Cambridge Chronicle*, September 13, 1901.
62 Caspar Whitney, 'The Sportsman's View-Point', *Outing*, xxxix, 2, November 1901, p. 235. Also p. 236. Diwyn Porter suggests that this might have been because spectators in America were more vociferous than in England.
63 *New York Times*, September 15, 1901. Also *Tatler*, September 11, 1901. For a fuller discussion, see Benson, 'Athletics, Class and Nation', pp. 10–13.
64 See, for example, Ernest Edwin Williams, *Made in Germany* (London: Heinemann, 1896); Frederick Arthur MacKenzie, *The American Invaders: Their Plans, Tactics and Progress* (London: Street & Smith, 1901).
65 *Penny Illustrated*, October 19, 1901.
66 Cambridge University Library, *Centenary 28th June 1995: Transatlantic Series History and Match Programme* (N.P., 1995), p. 15.

50 *Privilege*

67 Deslandes, *Oxbridge Men*, p. 44.
68 Deslandes, *Oxbridge Men*, front cover.
69 *Field*, November 2, 1901, March 15, 1902; February 14, 1903; Paul Willcox, *Oxford v. Cambridge Athletics Sports 125th Anniversary* (N.P., 1989), p. 58; information from Jonathan Smith.
70 *Field*, November 30, 1901; February 22, March 15, November 1, 1902; March 14, 1903.
71 *Field*, March 22, 1902; April 4, 1903; Willcox, *Oxford v. Cambridge*, p. 32.
72 *Field*, April 2, 1904.
73 *Field*, March 12, 1904.
74 F.M.L. Thompson, *The Rise of Respectable Society: A Social History of Victorian Britain, 1830–1900* (London: Fontana, 1988), p. 299.
75 Christopher Sandford, *The Final Over: The Cricketers of Summer 1914* (Stroud: History Press, 2014), p. 18. Also David Frith, *The Golden Age of Cricket 1890–1914* (Ware: Omega Books, 1978), p. 17.
76 Frith, *Golden Age*, p. 17.
77 Frith, *Golden Age*, p. 142.
78 Frith, *Golden Age*, p. 158.
79 Huggins, *Victorians and Sport*, pp. 179–80. See, also, Frith, *Golden Age*, ch. 6; Holt, *Sport*, p. 99.
80 See W.J. Ford, *The Cambridge University Cricket Club* (Edinburgh: Blackwood, 1902).
81 Holt, *Sport*, p. 115.
82 Cambridge University Archives, CUCCII, 8, Membership Book.
83 www.ogimages.bl.uk/images/014/014EVA000000000U8040A000 [August 2015]; *John Wisden's Cricketers' Almanack for 1906*, frontpiece; John Benson, *The Working Class in Britain, 1850–1939* (London, Longman, 1989), p. 41.
84 CUCCII, 9, *Membership of the C.U. Cricket Club*, April 1902.
85 CUCCII, 9, President's Book, pp. 44, c. 1875.
86 CUCCII, 9, Committee Minutes, May 28, 1900.
87 *Membership of the C.U. Cricket Club*, April 1902. See Lincoln Allison, 'Batsman and Bowler: The Key Relation of Victorian England', *Journal of Sport History*, 7, 2, 1980.
88 CUCCII, 9, *Arrangements and Matches for 1900*.
89 *Sporting Chronicle*, April 12, 1900.
90 *Cambridge Chronicle*, May 4, 11, 1900.
91 For example, *Birmingham Daily Post*, July 31, 1900.
92 National Trust, Inventory 881823.
93 http://cricketarchive.com/Archive/Players/4/4882/4882.html [April 2014].
94 See P. Whitcombe and M. Parsons, *The Free Foresters 1856–2006* (NP., ND.).
95 www.ukcricket.org/freeforesters [December 2011].
96 *Morning Post*, May 22, 1900. See, also, *Cambridge Chronicle*, May 25, 1900; *Standard*, June 20, 1900; *Huddersfield Examiner*, July 14, 1900.
97 R. Low, *W G Grace: An Intimate Biography* (London: Metro Publishing, 2010), p. 168; Richard Tomlinson, *Amazing Grace: The Man who was W.G.* (London: Little Brown, 2015), ch. 30.
98 Low, *W G Grace*, pp. 279–84.
99 *Standard*, June 27, 1900; *Morning Post*, June 28, 1900.
100 *Sporting Chronicle*, April 30, 1901.
101 *Cambridge Chronicle*, May 10, 1901. Also *Sporting Chronicle*, May 13, 1901. In the second innings of the match, he took one for 61. *Cambridge Chronicle*, May 17, 1901. For other games in which he played during May, see *Cambridge Chronicle*, May 24, 1901; *Sporting Chronicle*, May 20, 1901.
102 *Daily Mail*, May 10, 1901.

University, sport and status 51

103 *Sporting Chronicle*, May 27, 1901; *Cambridge Chronicle*, May 31, 1901.
104 *Daily Mail*, June 3, 1901.
105 *Pall Mall Gazette*, September 17, 1901.
106 Geoffrey Levett, 'Sport and the Imperial City: Colonial Tours in Edwardian London', *London Journal*, 35, 1, 2010, p. 39.
107 Sean Scalmer, 'Cricket, Imperialism and Class Domination', *Journal of Labor and Society*, 10, 2007, p. 437.
108 *Sporting Chronicle*, June 12, 1901; *Cambridge Chronicle*, June 14, 1901.
109 Levett, 'Sport and the Imperial City', p. 55.
110 *Daily Mail*, June 29, 1901.
111 *Daily Mail*, April 29, 1902; *Cambridge Chronicle*, May 2, 1902.
112 Census of England and Wales, 1881, RG11/21/49/29.
113 CUCCII, 9, Minutes of Committee, October 28, 1901.
114 *Cambridge Chronicle*, June 13, 1902. Also May 16; June 6, 27, 30; July 4, 1902.
115 *Cambridge Chronicle*, June 20 1902.
116 http://cricketarchive.com/Archive/Players/30/30415/First-Class_Matches.html [July 2009]. He played too against the touring Philadelphians. *New York Times*, June 11, 28, 1903.
117 *Daily Mail*, May 30, 1903.
118 *Daily Mail*, June 27, 1903. Richard Godsell also played for Gloucestershire.
119 Reference not retrievable.
120 Huggins, *Victorians and Sport*, p. 28.
121 www.cricketarchive.com/Archive/Player/30/30415/30415.html [December 2011].
122 Mangan, 'Lamentable Barbarians', p. 476.
123 www.cricketarchive.com/Archive/Players/30/30415/First-Class_Matches.html [July 2009].
124 Leslie, *End of a Chapter*, p. 90; Benson, 'Get a Blue', p. 1.
125 Deslandes, *Oxbridge Men*.

Part II
CAREER

3 'GENTLEMANLY MANNERS AND REFINED HABITS': LONDON, THE HOME COUNTIES AND TEACHING

Blues and benefits

It is easy to assume that Oxbridge Blues – particularly double Blues – segued effortlessly from the world of academia to the world of work, from the sports field to posts in the law, the church, the army or the higher reaches of the British and Imperial civil service. Whether or not they excelled at sport, Oxford and Cambridge graduates dominated the upper echelons of both the ancient professions and the burgeoning government service. All senior judges, of course, were university graduates (usually from Oxford or Cambridge) – and more than three-quarters of them had been to a public or other private school (usually Eton or Harrow).[1] It was much the same in all professions. The great majority of civil service heads of departments, confirms Harold Perkin, 'had been to public or other private schools ..., a large if declining proportion of these to Eton or Harrow ... and the share of Oxbridge graduates was increasing'.[2]

The transition from university to work was smoother still, one feels sure, for those graduates who brought with them not just the patina of an Oxbridge education but the added sheen of sporting success. Some contemporaries believed, we have seen, that winning a Blue conferred 'an unassailable distinction through life'[3] – or, more prosaically, that if you could 'get a blue ... you will see your money back again'.[4] The few historians who have looked at the matter tend to agree. 'Jobs for the Blues' were commonplace, believes Tony Mason.[5] Some prep schools, claims Donald Leinster-Mackay, were packed with Blues and other sporting celebrities: '[A]t Dunchurch Hall Preparatory School the headmaster was a former Oxford cricket Blue, and of six assistant masters, two had played Rugby for England, one had captained Kent at cricket, one was a famous Corinthian and soccer international, and one had played hockey for England.'[6]

The view that sporting success shaped the career choices – and enhanced the career prospects – of Oxbridge graduates is supported by a good deal of the available biographical and autobiographical evidence. Field Marshall Sir Douglas Haig, for instance, is probably the most contentious general in British history, but he did not decide on a career in the army until he was an undergraduate at Brasenose College, Oxford, during the early 1880s. It may be, suggests his biographer Gary Sheffield, that Haig's choice 'was connected with his love of horses, and his discovery that he was a talented polo player'.[7] Lieutenant-Colonel Cyril Pelham Foley is remembered, in some circles at least, for his 'very special distinction of being in the Eton elevens of 1886–7 when both matches with Winchester and Harrow were won, and then helping Cambridge beat Oxford three times – 1889 to 1891'.[8] His transition from university to the upper reaches of government was, by his own account, virtually seamless:

> I left Cambridge in 1891, and in the following year was taken on the Irish Staff of Lord Houghton, now Lord Crewe. During that and the ensuing winter I shared a small house at Leighton Buzzard with the Hon. Charles Hanbury-Tracey, and hunted principally with the Whaddon Chase, then under the mastership of Mr. Selby Lowndes, and with Lord Rothschild's staghounds.[9]

The suggestion that Haig, Foley and others like them benefited, and benefited greatly, from their social background, university education and sporting accomplishment seems little more than a statement of the obvious. But questions remain. How typical were men like Haig and Foley of Gerald Howard-Smith and other young undergraduates at late nineteenth- and early twentieth-century Oxford and Cambridge? And if they were typical of their Oxbridge contemporaries, is it possible to distinguish between social background, a public school education, three or four years at Oxford or Cambridge, family contacts, sporting interests and sporting success in determining the career choices and subsequent career paths of young men such as Gerald Howard-Smith?

Direction and redirection

One wonders, then, how Gerald coped with leaving Cambridge. The university was a world – a world within a world – in which he had excelled. A double Blue, he had been president of the university athletics club, he had proved himself a world-class high jumper, he had played first-class cricket, he may well have become, like other sportsmen, a role model, a 'paragon of undergraduate masculinity'.[10] His sporting interests had not only taken up much of his time while at university but meant that he was well known in Oxbridge circles, that he even had a certain standing in the wider worlds of athletics and cricket.

It could not, it did not, last. When they left university, Blues like Gerald generally had no choice, one would think, but to curtail their involvement in top-level sport. Gerald certainly cut back: he went on no more high-profile athletics tours, he played no more first-class cricket, he disappeared more or less completely from the pages of the national sporting press. What then should he do with the rest of his life? What direction should he take? How was he to replace the structure, the satisfaction, the kudos that athletics and cricket had provided?

It is a widely held view, after all, that retirement, whether voluntary or involuntary, from top-level sport, tended – and tends – to be stressful, debilitating and, in all too many cases, catastrophic. Even the most privileged were susceptible. To take just one early twentieth-century example, a recent biography of F.R. (Frank) Foster (1889–1958), who captained Warwickshire to cricket's county championship in 1911, played for the amateur 'Gentlemen' against the professional 'Players', and toured Australia with England, explains how 'his life fell apart' after he gave up playing. He was badly injured in a road accident; '[H]e was a failure in the family menswear business; he separated from his wife and children; took to hanging around Soho; went bankrupt and committed fraud. Despite his playing achievements he was banned from Warwickshire's Edgbaston ground, and died in a psychiatric hospital.'[11]

This emphasis on the disruptive effects of retirement from first-class cricket has been reinforced in recent years by a growing concern with what seems to be the disproportionate number of ex-players who have gone on to take their own lives. Whatever the statistical and other limitations of David Frith's pioneering studies of cricket and suicide, they have drawn attention to the issue. It is clear that over the years, many players, whether amateur or professional, celebrities or journeymen, have faced extreme difficulties in coming to terms with the realities of retirement.[12] It is an anxiety that was brought to a head towards the end of 2011 when Peter Roebuck, who twenty years before had contributed the foreword to David Frith's first book on cricketing suicide, himself jumped to his death from the sixth floor of a South African hotel.[13] Cricket, concludes, Frith, 'is stuck with its dreadful burden'.[14]

Accordingly, it is the aim of this, the first part of the chapter to consider how Gerald Howard-Smith coped with leaving Cambridge, with abandoning, abruptly perhaps, life as a full-time or nearly full-time, top-level sportsman. It will be suggested that he found it much less traumatic than the existing literature would lead one to expect. A career in university sport was inherently finite, of course. But there were other reasons, it seems, for his successful adjustment: his domestic circumstances and the fact that he managed to retain more elements than one might imagine of his previous existence.

Gerald had a secure, and seemingly supportive, home life on which to fall back. Although he had been away at boarding school since the age of nine and had spent his late teens and early twenties at university, he never really left home. Terms were short and he returned to his parents' home in Kensington during his vacations from Cambridge.[15] After graduating, Gerald moved back, it seems almost certain, to the family home in Kensington, and then lived with his parents, more or less continuously, for the rest of his life. Indeed, he continued to do so even when this meant uprooting himself from London and the Home Counties, the world in which he had been brought up and spent the first twenty or so years of his life. When Philip and Mary lived in London, he lived in London. When Philip and Mary moved from London to the West Midlands, he followed, dividing his time initially between the two, before finally settling down with them on the outskirts of Wolverhampton.

The family's move from the capital was occasioned by Philip's burgeoning career: his appointment as Recorder of Bridgnorth in 1900 and then, five years later, as Judge of the County Court Circuit 5, an area of the West Midlands covering Atherstone, Lichfield, Rugeley, Tamworth, West Bromwich and Wolverhampton.[16] So it was that early in the new century, Gerald's parents made their home at 'the Ford House', in Bushbury, an area described as 'a delightful rural suburb of Wolverhampton'.[17] With its library, drawing room, dining room and five bedrooms, its servants' rooms and domestic offices, its cottage and outbuildings, its stabling, paddock and orchard, not to mention its miniature lake and pleasure gardens set in more than ten acres of land, the Ford House was a home fit for a judge – and for his family.[18]

Living with one's parents when an adult was not necessarily the recipe, of course, for domestic harmony. And Gerald, it must be remembered, lived with Philip and Mary, not just for a few months after leaving university, but for ten years and more. With no personal or family papers to consult, there is no way of knowing for sure how well Gerald and his parents got on. However, some conjecture is possible – and probably plausible and persuasive.

Gerald and his parents did, indeed, seem to get on. They had the advantage, of course, of living in large houses and being able to pay others to take on the day-to-day drudgery that such accommodation inevitably entailed. They also had the advantage – and advantage it was in this context, at least – of spending time away from one another. Whatever one thinks of applying the concept of 'separate spheres' to late nineteenth- and early twentieth-century middle-class families, there is no denying that the Howard-Smiths spent a good deal of time apart.[19] Gerald's father had his office, belonged to clubs in London and Lichfield and travelled, as we have seen, to courts and inquiries across the country.[20] Although terms were short, Gerald and his brother spent a good part of their formative years away being educated. By the time Gerald returned from Cambridge in 1902, Charles was at Winchester, before going on five years later to Oxford.[21]

It was normal, of course, for parents like Philip and Mary to send their sons away to school – and less likely therefore to generate the resentment and ill-feeling that those of us from other eras and other social backgrounds might imagine. Certainly, by the time he graduated, Gerald and his father had interests in common. Not only did Gerald eventually follow Philip into the law and practise near him, but their shared love of cricket meant that in the summer at least they spent substantial, and probably increasing, periods of their leisure time together. Ten years after coming back home to live, Gerald was made captain of Wolverhampton Cricket Club; Philip, a keen supporter, began umpiring at home games.[22]

There are other reasons, too, for supposing that Gerald might have got along with his parents without too much friction. Nineteenth- and early twentieth-century autobiographers can be understandably reticent about family disagreements.[23] However, it has been suggested that while young middle- and upper middle-class men like Gerald might chafe at their parents' – particularly their fathers' – financial control over their lives, overt rebellion was rare.[24] 'Fathers controlled the purse strings', concludes John Tosh, 'and hence were able to determine their sons' disposable income, their access to education and training, and their place of residence. In an economically unstable world, middle-class youths did not lightly cast aside their financial cushion and peer into the abyss.'[25]

In fact, Gerald was able to live more independently than such parental control might suggest. Even after the family's move to Wolverhampton (and before he began earning), Gerald kept/acquired a base in London. When he sat his intermediate law examination in 1907, he gave his address as 24 Darlington Street, Wolverhampton, the offices, we shall see later, of the firm to which he was articled.[26] When he sat his final examination two years later, the address he gave was in London, not in Wolverhampton. But it was not 31 Bedford Row, where he was articled, but a flat at 16 Upper Montagu Street in the desirable, central London district of Marylebone.[27]

It seems then that by providing him with a home in which to live – a base from which to operate – Gerald's parents helped him to adapt more readily than might otherwise have been the case to life after Cambridge. But Gerald still had choices to make. He needed to decide, in particular whether, and with what seriousness, to maintain the sporting interests that had taken up so much of his time and done so much to provide him, one must assume, with a sense of who he was. It was – and is – notoriously difficult, of course, for sportsmen to know when to retire, to decide whether it would be best to drop down a level, to play on a part-time or occasional basis, or to quit their chosen sport/s altogether. Still only in his early to mid-twenties, Gerald pressed on: he began to play football again, he continued with his athletics and he remained an active, and successful, cricketer, albeit on the club and minor county circuit, rather than at the first-class level.

He revived his football career. Gerald, we saw earlier, had played while at Eton. The game, which had only been recently introduced to the school, proved surprisingly popular for what is commonly thought of as a working-class sport. Gerald was good enough to represent the school, but not good enough to escape the censure of the *Eton College Chronicle*. 'H.-Smith got away several times', it reported in 1898, 'but failed to pass soon enough, but eventually scored from a good pass'.[28] He did not play football, so far as is known, while he was at Cambridge, athletics presumably taking up his time during the winter months.

But once he left university, Gerald made the time to resume his football career. During his first two to three years in Wolverhampton, he travelled down to London on Saturday mornings during the winter in order to play for the Old Etonians. This was a club which, like its cricketing namesake, was based in the south of England and recruited from among the most privileged young men in the country. When the Old Etonians lost to Blackburn Olympic in the cup final of 1883, for example, the *Athletic News* made much of the contrast between the two teams: the Old Boys 'were all educated gentlemen, and undoubted "swells" when compared with their rough and ready opponents, every man of whom has inherited the primeval curse, and has to earn his bread by the sweat of his brow'.[29] Thereafter, the Old Etonians, like other gentlemanly clubs, played mostly against old boys' teams from soccer-playing public schools.[30] This suited Gerald, who retained his links with the Old Etonians for a number of years after leaving Cambridge. Staying overnight with a friend in the capital, he gave up these sporting – and no doubt social – weekends only, it was said, when his 'professional success attracted too much work'.[31]

Not that playing football meant abandoning athletics. Training regimes in both sports were lax, of course, by later standards. Corinthian attitudes retained their potency, particularly in the circles that Gerald frequented. William John Oakley a former president of Oxford University Athletic Club, who represented England at both soccer and athletics, knew what was required. It did not sound too demanding: 'As for training in the strict sense for football that is not necessary. Beyond knocking off a little smoking and going early to bed just before a big match, I do not find training at all necessary. Personally I keep fit by playing fives.'[32]

We do not know whether Gerald played fives or trained hard for football and athletics, let alone whether he intensified or cut back on his workload after leaving Cambridge. But he continued to compete, and compete very successfully, in the high jump. He did not do so, it seems, anywhere in the Midlands, but remained in/returned to the south of England, turning out several times for the London Athletic Club (LAC). Founded in 1863 by 'gentlemen who are engaged for the most part in Mercantile Houses', the club retained its air of exclusivity.[33] The LAC was 'by far the most important of all the clubs with similar objects in London', reported Charles Dickens Jnr in 1882. Charging new members an entrance fee of one guinea, together with an annual subscription of the same amount, the club boasted an 'excellent' ground in Chelsea. The cab fare from Charing Cross, Dickens added helpfully, was two shillings – from the Bank of England three shillings.[34]

The LAC's social superiority was exemplified, and no doubt confirmed, by the annual meetings it organised against Oxford and Cambridge universities. Those held in March each year provided 'a fairly accurate forecast', it was said, of what was likely to happen in the Varsity match a few weeks later at nearby Queen's Club.[35] Gerald jumped for London in several of these competitions. He did particularly well in 1904. Back in a sporting – and social – milieu with which he was so familiar, he found himself up against Edward (E.E.) Leader (Charterhouse and Trinity) who went on to compete in the London Olympics of 1908. 'The high jump found ex-president Howard-Smith quite in his old form', enthused the *Field*. But he did not have it all his own way: 'Leader showing most marked improvement, the old Blue had to do his very best to secure the event, and the performances of both men were exceptionally good.'[36]

Gerald was back the following year, this time competing for the LAC in away fixtures against Oxford and Cambridge. Jumping alongside him in March against Cambridge was Walter (W.E.B.) Henderson who had both been with him at Trinity and gone on tour with him to Canada and the United States of America.[37] His teammate in November against Oxford was Edward Leader, his Trinity contemporary who had pushed him so hard the previous year when competing for Cambridge. As the *Daily Mail* observed drily, Oxford versus London was something of a misnomer: it was 'to some extent a case of Oxford v. Cambridge, as the L.A.C. numbers many Light and Dark Blues among its members'.[38] Gerald was not only victorious for London against both Oxford and Cambridge, but jumped, against Oxford at least, with what seems to have become his stereotypical Corinthian insouciance. 'Howard Smith, as usual', reported the *Mail*, 'came to the rescue of the L.A.C. in the high jump – doing his preliminary leaps, as is his custom, in his jacket, and after disrobing clearing 5ft. 10in'.[39]

Cricket, of course, was Gerald's other major sport. The decision whether or not to retire was at once less difficult and more difficult for cricketers than it was for many other sportsmen. It was less difficult insofar as cricket was less demanding physically than sports such as football and athletics: batsmen, in particular, were able to continue playing to a good standard even as they grew older and became less fit and agile. It was a more difficult decision insofar as cricket was particularly time consuming: as they grew older, even well off amateurs like Howard-Smith found it difficult to combine the demands of the first-class game with the exigencies of earning a living. 'After leaving Cambridge he became quite a first-class bowler and a formidable batsman as well', claimed one of his friends, 'but he never had time for first-class cricket'.[40] The *Cricket and Football Field* recognised the problem. 'Year by year there is a marked diminution in the number of amateurs who find it possible to give up four solid months of the year to a game which, however enjoyable it may be, is hardly calculated to assist them in the more serious side of life.'[41]

Gerald continued to play cricket on an occasional/part-time basis – and always with those from the same, or similar, privileged circles with which he was accustomed. During the three to four years after leaving Cambridge, he turned out, as he had while an undergraduate, for prestigious teams like Windsor Home Park, the Free Foresters and the Marylebone Cricket Club (MCC).[42] He found it difficult, as before, when playing at first-class, or nearly first-class, level. So although he was a member of the MCC team that beat Wiltshire by an innings and ninety runs in August 1904, he did not cover himself with glory: he contributed just one run to the MCC's total of four hundred and forty-five for nine, he did not bowl in Wiltshire's first innings, and in the second he took three wickets but at a cost of seventy runs.[43]

Gerald did much better, as might be expected, when playing at a slightly lower level. He turned out, as we have seen, for Windsor Home Park, a prestigious club on the outskirts of London. Replete with royal connections, the club's ground had Windsor castle as a backdrop and its teams had been captained, on a number of occasions, by Prince Christian Victor of Schleswig-Holstein, one of Queen Victoria's grandsons and the only member of the royal family ever to play first-class cricket.[44] This, then, was the sort of club for which Gerald was invited to play – the sort of club at which he was able to excel. 'G. Howard-Smith, the old Oxford [sic] Blue', had an outstanding game against Slough, reported the *Slough, Eton and Windsor Observer* in the summer of 1906. Taking four wickets for fifteen runs, and scoring eighty-five runs, he 'played most attractive and correct cricket, and hit twelve 4's, three 3's, and seven 2's'.[45]

What was important was not just that Gerald knew how to play, but that he knew how to behave. All the clubs he played for after leaving Cambridge – Windsor Home Park, the Free Foresters, the MCC and the Eton Ramblers – were based in and around London and recruited with an eye on social acceptability as well as on playing ability.[46] The gentleman amateur was supposed to play, of course, with a certain flair, a certain nonchalance. Richard Holt cites the case of Gerald's namesake, G.O. Smith (Charterhouse and Keble College, Oxford). A slightly built figure, he 'would casually saunter on to the pitch for a cup final just as he strolled to the wicket to score the odd century for Oxford'. Hard training was bad form. 'The Corinthian of my day never trained', remarked Smith, 'and I can safely say the need of it was never felt'.[47]

Cricket, choices and careers

But did this mean, as the *Cricket and Football Field* suggested a few years after Gerald left university, that playing cricket and forging a career were mutually exclusive, that however enjoyable cricket might be, it was 'hardly calculated to assist … in the more serious side of life'.[48] Other observers, we saw at the beginning of the chapter, took a markedly different view. 'To win a dark or light Blue at athletics', claimed one, 'gives men an unassailable distinction through life'.[49] Get a Blue, believed another, and 'you will see your money back again'.[50]

It is the aim of this, the second part of the chapter to examine the decisions that Gerald Howard-Smith took with regard to his future career. It will consider in particular whether he benefited or suffered from – or perhaps was unaffected by – focusing so single-mindedly on sport, notably athletics and cricket, while in his late teens and early twenties. The suggestion will be that he did benefit, at least in the short term. It will be shown that while Gerald's sporting accomplishments almost certainly helped him to gain a foothold in the world of prep school teaching, they did not prevent him abandoning it with apparent alacrity when confronted with the realities of life in this sector of early twentieth-century private education.[51]

Prep school teaching had obvious attractions. It provided a haven, it has been said, for the second rate, those with literary aspirations and/or those without the connections needed to secure higher paid, higher status employment elsewhere.[52] It was suggested at the turn of the century, for example, that, 'a young man entering upon the scholastic profession with no special aptitudes or distinctions can hardly do better than by associating himself with the headmaster of a well-known preparatory school, gaining his confidence and marrying his daughter.'[53] Misogynous cynicism aside, prep school teaching held obvious attractions for Blues – or double Blues like Gerald – with a raft of sporting accomplishments to their name. One can see that working in a well-run school, in a pleasant part of the country might appear a tempting option. 'The young man fresh from the University usually finds everything delightful. The boys are jolly, especially out of school. He has plenty of outdoor exercise and rejoices in the games, as he did at College, and he finds his long holidays, with a sufficiency of money in his pocket, delightful also.'[54]

It is easy then to see why young Blues might wish to work at prep schools and easy to see why prep schools might wish to employ them.[55] It was a system, J.A. Mangan believes, that became self-sustaining. 'Worshipped "bloods" at [public] school became admired "blues" at university and were enthusiastically head-hunted by the schools as games masters, who in turn sent their "bloods" on to the universities.'[56] The Blues' combination of youthful enthusiasm, sporting standing and social acceptability made them an attractive proposition, concluded the second master of Hurstpierpoint College in 1897: 'A large percentage of famous "blues", and of athletic celebrities are to be found occupying at least temporarily, masterships in schools, in which position they are of the highest value to the athletics. A man fresh from the University ... knows what to wear and how to wear it; he knows, e.g., that belts are plebeian, and that caps should be worn so as not to show a fringe.'[57]

Gerald, it must be said, took his time to turn to prep school teaching. He spent several years, as we have seen, continuing with his sporting interests, enjoying the life, one imagines, of a young man about town. It was not until 1906, several years after leaving Cambridge, that he finally entered the labour market. Perhaps his parents decided it was time for him to get a job, perhaps he was chafing at his lack of financial autonomy, perhaps he was beginning to tire of his lack of long-term prospects. Whatever the catalyst, Gerald decided to return to the prep school world in which he himself had received his early education. The two schools at which he taught – or perhaps coached – were both on the outskirts of London: Northaw Place, near Potters Bar; and Stoke House, not far from Slough.

Northaw Place Preparatory School had been founded in 1881 by the Reverend Frederick John Hall and occupied a late seventeenth-century mansion, surrounded by a large park and well- laid-out gardens, near Potters Bar, fifteen miles or so to the north of the capital. Yet despite the grandeur of its setting, the school was smaller, less exclusive and less highly regarded than Temple Grove where Gerald had received his early education.[58] Indeed, when the census was taken in the spring of 1901, five years before Gerald joined the school, it employed only two assistant masters and educated fewer than forty boys, most of whom were drawn, as one might expect, from London and the Home Counties.[59]

The two clergymen who ran Northaw Place in the years before the First World War, the Reverend Hall and the Reverend W.F. Money, took a resolutely narrow view of the prep school curriculum. They were interested, it has been said, 'in cricket and in the bible, in that order, and in very little else'.[60] The teaching, it seems, was dull and unimaginative, with enormous emphasis placed on the inculcation of scriptural knowledge. Clement Atlee, the future prime minister, was a pupil at the school for four years, leaving at exactly the time that Gerald began teaching there in the spring/early summer of 1906. 'Had Christianity not been so firmly entrenched', observes Atlee's biographer acidly, 'cricket would assuredly have replaced it'.[61]

There is no doubting Northaw Park's cultivation of 'cricket worship'.[62] However, this did not mean that it sought out Blues like Gerald to teach and/or coach its forty or so boys. Perhaps the school was too small or too poor to pursue such a policy; perhaps Hall and Money felt that what was most important was getting their pupils into the public schools that their families wished. In all events, there is no indication of any Blues other than Gerald working at the school. In 1914, eight years after he left, Northaw Place employed just five members of staff – none of whom, so far as one can judge, displayed any particular aptitude for sport.[63]

The other school at which Gerald worked in the summer of 1906, Stoke House Preparatory School, was also physically impressive, sited as it was in its own grounds of twenty acres or so at Stoke Poges, a mile or so to the north of Slough.[64] It was much the same size as Northaw Place, but probably slightly better staffed and almost certainly more successful academically.[65] Proud of its record in securing scholarships to major public schools, it claimed in 1913, for instance, to have educated some eight hundred boys since its opening in 1867. Of these, seventy-four, it announced with considerable satisfaction, had gone on to Winchester, one hundred and fifty to Charterhouse and one hundred and eighty to Eton.[66] Such advantages did not come cheap: its fees in 1909 were one hundred and twenty-five guineas a year – with an additional charge of a guinea a term to meet the costs of laundry.[67]

Stoke House, like most prep schools, set great store on the inculcation of patriotic attitudes. The boys raised money for the *Daily Mail*'s fund for the Union Jack Club, and listened to lectures on Britain's place in the world. 'We had a most awfully patriotic chap yesterday who gave us a ripping lecture on dreadnoughts', recalled one young pupil, 'it was so interesting, and we had magic lantern slides.'[68] Stoke House, like most prep schools, also set great store on sport. Edward Hagarty Parry, who took over the school from his father in 1892, had been an outstanding footballer, captaining both Charterhouse School and Oxford University, winning the FA cup with the Old Carthusians in 1881 and playing three times for England (once against Scotland and twice against Wales).[69] It is not surprising therefore that sport – athletics, cricket, fives and particularly football – played a major part in the day-to-day life of the school.[70] It boasted cricket and football fields, a gymnasium, a swimming pool and a fives court.[71]

When twelve-year old Jim Neville joined Stoke House in 1909 (just after Gerald was there), his letters home to his parents were full of the teams he hoped to play for, the teams he was chosen to play for, the matches they won, the matches they lost. There was a lot to tell: 'We have a red and blue shirt as well as a cap when we get our colours', he explained to his mother.[72] 'Well to begin with', he went on proudly, 'I think that I must tell you that in the match yesterday I got my "Colours".'[73] It was not just a matter of winning and losing, he made clear to his father: 'We played St. Georges yesterday [and lost], but Mr Parry was not angry, as he said we played up alright.'[74]

Stoke House seemed made then for a Blue like Gerald. Although he only worked at the school during the summer of 1906, he kept in contact after he left. Returning three years later to play cricket in a match against the school staff, he performed well, scoring thirty-eight out of a total of two hundred and fifty-four, and taking four (and possibly five) wickets.[75] Even ten years after his brief period of teaching/coaching at Stoke House, he was remembered, it seems, with both respect and affection. When he was killed in action in 1916, the school magazine marked his death with more than conventional pieties. His obituary refers explicitly to his sporting prowess. Gerald Howard-Smith, 'a very well-known cricketer and athlete at Eton and Cambridge, was with us at Stoke Poges for the summer term of 1906, leaving us to take up legal work. He was immensely popular with everybody and as a soldier was brave beyond comparison.'[76]

Again however, Gerald was seemingly the exception that proves the rule. For all his popularity, for all his sporting prowess and for all the emphasis that Stoke House placed on sport, its staffroom was no more packed with Blues than those at Temple Grove or Northaw Place. Neither, so far as is known, did the school make any effort to publicise the presence of the one Blue it did employ. The boys (and their families) knew, no doubt, whether their masters had any claim to sporting – or other – fame. Twelve-year old Jim Neville was present at the match in which Gerald played so well against the Stoke House staff in 1909. However, he was struck by the performance, not of the ex-master Howard-Smith, but of one of the current masters, N.D.C. Ross, who scored eighty-four runs. Mr Ross, an impressed Jim Neville told his mother, had been not a Blue like Howard-Smith but captain of his college at Cambridge.[77]

Gerald Howard-Smith's teaching career had not amounted to much: a maximum perhaps of three months teaching/coaching, during the spring and early summer of 1906, at two small prep schools on the outskirts of London. But although his career was so brief, it offers a revealing insight into early twentieth-century private school education. It suggests most obviously – and not very surprisingly – that you did not need teaching experience, let alone a teaching qualification, in order to secure a post in a prep school. It is telling, for example, that when a four-week teaching Diploma for prep school assistants was started at Oxford in 1897, it attracted just seven teachers – not all of them from prep schools. 'Some headmasters', explained Leinster-Mackay, 'opposed the course, fearing that trained assistant masters would entertain ideas, contrary to their own, on how *their* schools should be run'.[78]

It helped, of course, to have the right contacts when applying for a job in a prep school (or anywhere else). But what was needed too was social standing, self-confidence – and no doubt the sense of entitlement that so often went along with them. So it was that late nineteenth- and early twentieth-century prep schools recruited men like Gerald Howard-Smith on the basis of their social background as well as – or as much as – on the basis of their educational attainment and pedagogical potential.

Even those with a stake in the system, could see its drawbacks. 'Year by year', claimed one London prep school headmaster, 'the universities turn out a certain proportion of men who having done nothing particular at their Public Schools have at 19 gone to the university with no clear idea, except that they would like a continuance of the pleasant time they had enjoyed at school.' Three years later, he complained, they left university and thought they might try prep school teaching. He cited the letter he received from one such applicant – which ended by referring to what the young man presumably thought to be some of his most important qualifications for the post:

> I am fond of sports, being experienced in football association, fives, swimming, sculling, punting, canoeing, boat sailing, rowing, photography, etc. I am fond of music, and sing and play the violin also. Enclosed you will find three copies of testimonials which please return.
>
> I am very fond of boys, and am said to be of gentlemanly manners and refined habits, etc., etc.[79]

The headmaster was – or affected to be – horrified: 'It is dreadful to think what harm might be done in a school by a person sufficiently fatuous to urge his fondness for punting, canoeing, boat sailing, etc. – the pet forms of slacking at Oxford, as constituting serious qualifications for a mastership.' Nevertheless, he offered the writer of the letter an interview.[80]

Gerald Howard-Smith was at one, then, with many prep school masters (and coaches) in not having a teaching qualification. But, in other respects, his fledgling teaching career challenges the little that is known – or thought to be known – about early twentieth-century prep school education. Whatever Gerald's inadequacies, it seems unlikely that he conformed to the stereotype of the listless idler that the London headmaster criticised so trenchantly. Indeed, Gerald's career raises a number of other intriguing issues. Is it true that late nineteenth- and early twentieth-century prep schools were packed with Oxbridge Blues like Gerald? If it is true that the schools recruited Gerald and his like with such enthusiasm, what use did they make of them in their marketing? And was Gerald usual or unusual in showing so little staying power when it came to building a career in the teaching profession?

Such questions, although obvious and important, are a good deal easier to ask than they are to answer satisfactorily. It is difficult to judge the typicality of Gerald Howard-Smith because so little is known about other prep school teachers. And it is not easy to assess the representativeness of Northaw Place and Stoke House because we know so little about other prep schools – and what little we do know suggests that they were strikingly heterogeneous, varying widely in the resources at their disposal, as well as in their size, success, longevity and social standing.[81]

However, help is at hand. Schools' advertising in newspapers and trade directories can be – and has been – used in order to understand better the still little known world of 'teaching in the market-place'.[82] Also useful – and much more manageable – is *Paton's List of Schools and Tutors*. Published annually, it was designed, it explained, 'with a view to assisting Parents in their choice of Schools by placing before them in a concise and practical form particulars of *many* of the best English Schools for Boys and Girls'.[83] However, it can be used, too, by historians wishing to analyse the ways in which late nineteenth- and early twentieth-century private schools marketed themselves to parents, guardians and other interested parties.

Paton's List confirms that the schools at which Gerald taught, Northaw Place and Stoke House, were at one with their peers in the emphasis that they placed on sport (along with drill, gymnastics and other forms of physical activity). More than 90 per cent of the one hundred and forty-two English boys' prep schools advertising in *Paton's* in 1911–12 stressed their sporting ethos, the place of sport in their curricula, the care with which they taught and supervised it and the superiority of their sporting (and other) facilities.[84] Stoke House's listing emphasised, for instance, that it offered its pupils 'cricket and football fields, a good playground, a fives court ... a gymnasium ... and a swimming bath, 60 ft. by 25 ft'.[85]

Indeed, by the time Gerald worked at Northaw Place and Stoke House, some commentators were becoming concerned by the proliferation of prep school facilities, by what they saw as the softening of prep school education. The *Spectator* explained in 1910, for instance, that it thought that provision had become almost too impressive: 'the playing-fields must be large and the cricket-pitch perfect; there must be a fully equipped gymnasium, a playroom for wet afternoons, an outdoor and an indoor miniature rifle range, and a swimming-bath with water which can be nicely warmed; there must be riding-classes and dancing-classes; the assistant-masters must teach the boys football and cricket, if not get them every one into the eleven.'[86]

But all was not quite as it seemed. Despite the *Spectator*'s concerns, Gerald and his fellow Blues employed in the sector were valued less highly than they probably hoped – and less highly certainly than the school's emphasis on sport would lead one to suppose. The prep schools advertising in *Paton's* in 1911–12 – during what is generally regarded as the apogee of athleticism's hold over private education – made virtually no reference to the employment of specialist sports coaches and teachers: there was no trumpeting of the 'internationals, Blues, or at least county players as staff members', whom Leinster-Mackay believed to be so important.[87]

68 *Career*

Stoke House again was at one with its competitors. Just two of the one hundred and forty-two entries in *Paton*'s mentioned the provision of such high-level, specialised coaching. Even the two establishments that did so, Beechmont School in Sevenoaks and Tredennyke School in Worcester, made it clear that their provision was available only on a seasonal – and in all probability a part-time – basis. At Beechmont, the boys' games, it noted, were 'organised, and always superintended by the Masters, assisted in the summer by a cricket professional.'[88] At Tredennyke, both cricket and football, it was emphasised, were 'carefully supervised, and a professional cricket instructor attends during the summer months.'[89]

What is striking is that not one of the one hundred and forty-two schools advertising in Paton's in 1911–12 made any reference at all to employing an Oxford or Cambridge Blue. This does not mean, of course, that they did not do so. But it is instructive for all that. For while it would obviously be wrong to suggest that Gerald Howard-Smith was the only Oxbridge Blue to secure a prep school post in the years before the First World War, the schools' failure to publicise the existence of such staff provides an indication of the weight that they accorded – or rather did not accord – to the employment of these talented and privileged young men.

Blues, benefits and options

Gerald Howard-Smith knew, like others from his privileged background, that prep school teaching might be socially acceptable, tolerably well paid and reassuringly agreeable – but only in the short term. The trouble was that there was little in the way of a career structure: there were few housemaster or head of year posts to be had in schools employing just a handful of teachers. Headmasters, it was true, could earn a very good living. 'They charge handsome fees', claimed the *Daily Mail*, 'they take large numbers of little boys; and in the administration of their schools they are not put to heavy expenses. Many a preparatory schoolmaster must enjoy an income of £1,000 per annum; not a few enjoy incomes reaching to £2,000 and £3,000, and two or three at least even more.'[90] Those working under the head did much less well. The young man employed in a prep school must not, he was warned, 'look forward to remaining an assistant-master in such a school, or he will always be a poor man. In such a position he cannot hope to start with a salary of more than £100 a year, besides board and lodging, which is worth to him another £50 or £70, though advertisements may be seen offering as little as £50. He cannot hope to end **With More than £200**.'[91]

So although it may be tempting to view prep schools as an integral part of England's late Victorian and Edwardian heyday, it is easy to see why Gerald-Howard-Smith – and those like him – might not wish to commit themselves to teaching for more than a short period of time. They simply did not regard it as a long-term option. Indeed, insofar as one can judge, Gerald never intended to make teaching his career. It was an interlude, no doubt a pleasant enough interlude, between school, university and work, between youth and manhood, between dependence and independence. Gerald, it must not be forgotten, had options. He came from a good family and his father was building a successful career in the law; he had not just been to public school and university, he had been to Eton and Trinity College, Cambridge; he had not only shown an interest in sport, he had excelled at athletics and cricket, acquiring, for a few years at least, a national and even international profile.

But when Gerald turned his attention finally to finding other, more permanent and more lucrative ways of earning a living, what influenced him most, it seems, was his family background and, in particular, his father's legal experience and professional connections. Although Gerald was in his mid-twenties and well used to living away from home, he turned – both professionally and geographically – to his family, to what they knew and did best. He followed his father's (and grandfather's) example by embarking on a career in the law; he followed his father's (and mother's) example by leaving the London and the Home Counties in which he had spent the first twenty-five years of his life in order to live with his parents on the outskirts of Wolverhampton, an unlikely destination one might think for a London-born, Eton- and Cambridge-educated double Blue.

Notes

1 Harold Perkin, *The Rise of Professional Society: England since 1880* (London: Routledge, 1989), pp. 88–9.
2 Perkin, *Professional Society*, p. 90.
3 Shane Leslie, *The End of a Chapter* (New York: Charles Scribner's Sons, 1916), p. 90.
4 Eric Parker, 'Private Schools: Ancient and Modern', *Longman's Magazine*, November 1896/April 1897, cited in Donald Leinster-Mackay, *The Rise of the English Prep School* (Lewes: Falmer Press, 1984), p. 196. Also Eric Parker in *The Preparatory Schools Review*, 11, 1898.
5 Tony Mason, *Sport in Britain* (London: Faber & Faber, 1988), p. 36.
6 Leinster-Mackay, *English Prep School*, pp. 193–4. Also Leslie, *End of a Chapter*, p. 28.
7 Gary Sheffield, *The Chief: Douglas Haig and the British Army* (London: Aurum, 2011), p. 15.
8 www.espncricinfo.com/england/content/player/13105.html [May 2014]. See, also, David Frith, *The Golden Age of Cricket 1890–1914* (Ware: Omega Books, 1983), pp. 110, 144.
9 Lieut.-Col. Cyril P. Foley, *Autumn Foliage* (London: Methuen, 1935), pp. 27–8.
10 Paul R. Deslandes, *Oxbridge Men: British Masculinity and the Undergraduate Experience, 1850–1920* (Bloomington: Indiana University Press, 2005), p. 44.
11 R. Brooke, *F.R. Foster, The Fields were Sudden Bare* (Cardiff: ACS Publications, 2011), back cover. Also Keith Booth, *Tom Richardson: A Bowler Pure and Simple* (Cardiff: ACS Publications, 2012).
12 D. Frith, *By his own Hand: A Study of Cricket's Suicides* (London: Hutchinson, 1991); D. Frith, *Silence of the Heart: Cricket Suicides* (Edinburgh: Mainstream Publishing, 2001). See, too, studies such as J. Hundertmark, 'Cricketers and Mental Health Concerns', *Australian Psychiatry: Bulletin of Royal Australian and New Zealand College of Psychiatrists*, 15, 6, 2007.
13 *Daily Mail*, November 13, 2011.

70 Career

14 Frith, *By his own Hand*, 14. See, too, D. Lavallee, S. Gordon and J.R. Grove, 'Retirement from Sport and the Loss of Athletic Identity', *Journal of Personal and Interpersonal Loss*, 2, 2, 1997; J.R. Grove, D. Lavallee and S. Gordon, 'Coping with Retirement from Sport: The Influence of Athletic Identity', *Journal of Applied Sport Psychology*, 9, 2, 1997.
15 Census of England and Wales, 1901, RG13/38/74/56.
16 *London Gazette*, August 29, 1900; *Kelly's Directory of Herefordshire and Shropshire*, 1900, p. 39; *Leicester Chronicle and Leicestershire Mercury*, September 1, 1900; *Tom's Official Directory*, 1909, p. 198.
17 J.P. Jones, *The Heart of the Midlands: The Official Guide to Wolverhampton and its Surroundings 'The Green Borderland of the Black Country'* (Wolverhampton, NP., 1906), p. 132.
18 Wolverhampton Archives, D-NAJ/F19, Nock and Joseland, Sales Material, 1919.
19 For three recent, very different takes on 'separate spheres', see John Tosh, *A Man's Place: Masculinity and the Middle-Class Home in Victorian England* (London: Yale University Press, 2007); Eleanor Gordon and Gwyneth Nair, *Murder and Morality in Victorian Britain: The Story of Madeleine Smith* (Manchester: Manchester University Press, 2009); Jane Hamlett, *Material Relations: Domestic Interiors and Middle-Class Families in England, 1850–1910* (Manchester: Manchester University Press, 2010).
20 Information from Joanne Peck; *Who Was Who 1916–1928* (London: Adam & Charles Black, 1947), p. 975.
21 *Daily Mail*, November 8, 1907; *London Gazette*, January 1, 1932.
22 *Express and Star*, July 13, 1912; *Midland Counties Express*, May 17, 1919.
23 Information from Laura Ugolini.
24 Deslandes, *Oxbridge Men*, p. 68. See, for instance, Mark Tellar, *A Young Man's Passage* (London: Home and Van Thal, 1952), p. 196.
25 Tosh, *Man's Place*, p. 121.
26 University of London, Institute of Advanced Legal Studies (IALS), Law Society, Examination Records, LSOC09/30, Intermediate Examination Results, 1907.
27 IALS, LSOC10/32, Final Examination Results, 1909.
28 *Eton College Chronicle*, February 25, 1908.
29 Cited in Tony Mason, *Association Football & English Society 1863–1915* (Brighton: Harvester, 1981), p. 54.
30 I am grateful to Dilwyn Porter on this point.
31 *Eton College Chronicle*, May 11, 1916.
32 *Pall Mall Gazette*, October 3, 1901. See, too, Sir Oliver Lodge in *Sporting Star*, September 20, 1904; Holt, *Sport and the British*, pp. 99–100; John Benson, 'Athletics, Class and Nation: The Oxford- Cambridge University Tour of Canada and the United States of America, 1901', *Sport in History*, 31, 1, 2013, pp. 10–13.
33 www.londonac.org.uk/history [May 2014].
34 Charles Dickens Jnr, *Dickens's Dictionary of London, 1882. (Fourth Year) An Unconventional Handbook* (London: Macmillan, 1882), p. 27.
35 M.Z. Kuttner, 'A Start for a Challenge Cup', in George R. Sims (ed.), *Living London: Its Work and Its Play, Its Humour and Its Pathos, Its Sights and Its Scenes* (London: Cassell, 1902), vol. I, p. 176.
36 *Field*, March 19, 1904. There are echoes here, Dilwyn Porter points out, of C.B. Fry breaking the world long jump record while at Oxford in 1892. But see Iain Wilton, *C.B. Fry: King of Sport* (London: Metro, 2002), p. 50.
37 *Field*, March 25, 1904; *Daily Mail*, March 14, 1905.
38 *Daily Mail*, November 23, 1905. Also November 24, 1905.
39 *Daily Mail*, November 24, 1905.
40 *Eton College Chronicle*, May 11, 1916. I am grateful to Anthony Whitaker for this reference (and for much other assistance).

London, the Home Counties and teaching 71

41 *Cricket and Football Field*, August 16, 1913. See P. Cain, 'Education, Income and Status: Amateur Cricketers in England and Wales c.1840–c.1930', *Sport in History*, 30, 3, 2010, pp. 369–70.
42 *Slough, Eton and Windsor Observer*, September 8, 1904;
43 www.cricketarchive.com/Archive/Scorecards/129/129170.html [May 2014].
44 *St James Gazette*, October 30, 1900.
45 *Slough, Eton and Windsor Observer*, July 7, 1906. See, also, June 30, 1906.
46 Gerald played for the Eton Ramblers. See *Slough, Eton and Windsor Observer*, June 30, 1906.
47 Holt, *Sport and the British*, p. 100.
48 *Cricket and Football Field*, August 16, 1913.
49 Leslie, *End of a Chapter*, p. 90.
50 Parker, 'Private Schools'.
51 The following section draws heavily on John Benson, '"Get a Blue and You Will See Your Money Back Again": Staffing and Marketing the English Prep School, 1890–1912', *History of Education*, 43, 3, 2014.
52 Leinster-Mackay, *English Prep School*, p. 215.
53 *Daily Mail*, April 4, 1903.
54 C.C. Cotterrill, 'The Masters of a Preparatory School', in Board of Education, *Special Reports on Educational Subjects, Volume 6. Preparatory Schools for Boys: Their Place in English Secondary Education* (HMSO, 1900), p. 22.
55 T. Mason, *Sport in Britain* (London: Faber & Faber, 1988), p. 36.
56 Mangan, 'Bloods', p. 40. See 'Cross-Fertilization in Schools', *Educational Times and Journal of the College of Preceptors*, lxiii, 1910, p. 110.
57 *Play*, January 15, 1897.
58 *Paton's List of Schools and Tutors (An Aid to Parents in the Selection of Schools.): Fourteenth Annual Edition, 1911–1912* (London: J. and J. Paton, 1912), p. 125; Roy Jenkins, *Mr. Atlee: An Interim Biography* (London: Heinemann, 1948), p. 9.
59 Information from Anthony Whitaker.
60 F. Beckett, 'Clement Atlee', www.labourhistory.org.uk [May 2011].
61 Jenkins, *Mr. Atlee*, p. 10.
62 Jenkins, *Mr. Atlee*, p. 10.
63 Information from Anthony Whitaker.
64 *Paton's List*, 209; *The Schoolmaster's Yearbook and Directory: A Reference Book of Secondary Education in England and Wales* (London: Sonnenschein, 1906), p. 521. Stoke House moved to Seaford in 1913.
65 Census of England and Wales, 1901, RG19/1344/133/62; Norfolk Record Office, NEV11/23/2, Stoke House School, 'Jim's Letters', E.H. Parry to Mr Neville, January 26, 1909; *Stoke House, Stoke Poges, Bucks. School List*.
66 *Stoke House Annals*, August 1913. Also NEV11/23/2, *School List. May*, 1909; *Daily Mail*, August 10, 1900.
67 *School List*.
68 NEV11/23/2, Jim Neville to his mother, December 5, 1909. Also *Daily Mail*, July 8, 1907.
69 *Paton's List*, p. 125; www.englandfootballersonline.com/TeamPlyrsBiosP [March 2013].
70 NEV11/23/2, *School List, 1909; Slough Observer*, August 22, 1903; May 4, 1907.
71 *Paton's List*, p. 209.
72 NEV11/23/2, Jim Neville to his mother, December 12, 1909.
73 NEV11/23/2, Jim Neville to his mother, December 5, 1909.
74 NEV11/23/2, Jim Neville to his father, November 14, 1909.
75 *Stoke House Annals*, July 1909.
76 *Stoke House Annals*, August 1916, p. 10.
77 NEV/11/23/1, Jim Neville to his mother, June 27, 1909.

78 Leinster-Mackay, *English Prep School*, p. 208.
79 H. Frampton Stallard, 'The Troubles of a Schoolmaster', *Preparatory Schools Review*, March 1904, p. 129.
80 Frampton Stallard, 'Troubles', p. 129.
81 *Daily Mail*, February 14, 1911; Leinster-Mackay, *English Prep School*. Some schools, as we saw earlier, marketed themselves exclusively, so far as one can judge, on the basis that they were cheap. See *Standard*, August 31, 1892.
82 See, for example, John Money, 'Teaching in the Market-Place, or "Caesar Adsum Jam Forte: Pompey Aderat": The Retailing of Knowledge in Provincial England during the Eighteenth Century', in John Brewer and Roy Porter (eds), *Consumption and the World of Goods* (London: Routledge, 1993), pp. 343–6; C.Y. Ferdinand, 'Selling it to the Provinces: News and Commerce round Eighteenth-Century Salisbury', in Brewer and Porters (eds), *Consumption*, pp. 400–401.
83 *Paton's List*, Introduction.
84 *Paton's List*, pp. 58–234. A.J.C. Dowding, Games in Preparatory Schools', in *Special Reports*, p. 349. One of the schools advertising, Park House, was not, in fact, a prep school.
85 *Paton's List*, p. 209. Northaw Place did not have an entry, but see, for example, pp. 85, 88, 99, 105, 106, 148, 157, 162, 192. Also *Preparatory Schools Review*, March 1904, pp. 122–3, 125–6.
86 *Spectator*, September 10, 1910.
87 Leinster-Mackay, *English Prep School*, pp. 193–4.
88 *Paton's List*, 201.
89 *Paton's List*, p. 232. Also *Daily Mail*, September 23, 1905; Dowding, 'Games in Preparatory Schools', 352.
90 *Daily Mail*, April 4, 1903.
91 *Daily Mail*, April 4, 1903. Bold in original.

4 'A GENTLEMAN OF EXPERIENCE': WOLVERHAMPTON, THE LAW AND SPORT

Class and place

Gerald Howard-Smith, one imagines, would find life difficult – would be a fish out of water – in a place like Wolverhampton. The town, after all, was about as far socially, culturally and economically – if not geographically – from London and the Home Counties as it was possible to get. Wolverhampton, like the Black Country to its south and east, had a long-standing reputation for dullness, backwardness and provincialism. *Punch*, it has been said, reacted with 'abusive astonishment' when it learned that Queen Victoria had decided to visit the town on one of her first public appearances following the death of her beloved husband, Prince Albert in 1861.[1]

Surprising or not, Gerald's decision to move to Wolverhampton from the south of England enables us to explore further certain key aspects of late nineteenth- and early twentieth-century England. Class, class identity and class relationships remain, of course, among the most complex and contentious issues with which historians and social scientists ever have to deal.[2] Yet for all the attention that has been lavished on the working class, there has been much less interest in the middle class. It is only recently, one is tempted to say, that there has been any serious investigation of the ways in which the various groups comprising the late Victorian and Edwardian middle class interacted with one another.[3] Some believe however that, 'The distinctions of status and wealth to be found within the middle class were greater than in either the working class or the upper class.'[4]

How then does Gerald Howard-Smith's move to Wolverhampton help us to understand class, class identity and class relations in late nineteenth- and early twentieth-century England? It raises a series of questions – most obviously about the ways in which, and the extent to which, upper middle-class Gerald adapted to what seems, on the face of it, to have been the totally alien environment of working-class Wolverhampton? His move north also alerts us to the scale and significance of the economic, social, cultural and other differences that distinguished London and the Home Counties from Wolverhampton and what is now known as the West Midlands (and, indeed, probably most of the rest of the country). Then too Gerald's move to Wolverhampton makes us

74 *Career*

think about the relationship between class and place, to wonder whether the gap between London's upper middle class and the West Midlands middle class – let alone working class – could ever be bridged.

Gerald Howard-Smith, it will be suggested, coped much better than one might imagine. This finding, if true, is of some significance, revealing a good deal about not only Gerald, but also about metropolitan-provincial relations and about the relationships that existed – or could exist – between the different groups comprising the late Victorian and Edwardian middle class. The suggestion, more specifically, is that it was Gerald's family contacts, his sporting interests and, to a lesser extent, his legal career that enabled him both to isolate himself from working-class Wolverhampton and to integrate himself into the middle-class networks that existed in the area in which he was now living and working.[5]

Wolverhampton

Wolverhampton, it bears repeating, was not an obvious destination for a young man like Gerald Howard-Smith. A quintessentially working-class town to the northwest of Birmingham, it was worlds away from the upper middle-class world of Kensington, Temple Grove, Eton, Cambridge, the MCC, the London Athletics Club, prep school teaching and tours of North America. Although Wolverhampton, like the Black Country, had an active local aristocracy and a substantial middle class, it was dominated and defined by its large working-class population, many of whom continued to live in truly wretched conditions.[6] The town's medical officers pressed constantly for improvements to be made, complaining even at the turn of the century that: 'Improper feeding, lack of care, neglect of cleanliness and ventilation, insufficient food, clothing and shelter account probably for the greatest part of our fatalities.' It was a damning indictment, and one that local Marxist historian George Barnsby chose as 'a fitting comment on 150 years of industrialisation in the Black Country and the worsening situation in the 1890s in particular'.[7]

Even those more inclined to accept the long-term benefits of industrialisation recognised the extent of Wolverhampton's economic and social problems, conceding that the town's reputation remained both damaged and damaging. So although the town's 1902 *Red Book* was resolutely positive, the best it could find to say was that Wolverhampton had 'acquired, very unfairly, a name for smoke and dirt'. However, it insisted that there were grounds for optimism:

> Thanks to the vigilance of the Corporation, the Tettenhall, Compton, Merridale, Lea and Penn Roads ... are rapidly assuming an appearance which, in a very short space of time, will vie even with such resorts as Leamington and Cheltenham. Modern improvements, comprising widened streets, complete sewerage systems, good water supply, abolition of insanitary houses and dens of iniquity which existed years ago, have

tended to promote the general healthfulness of the town which is evidenced by the low position in the mortality returns.[8]

Wolverhampton, it hardly needs saying, never did vie with resorts such as Leamington and Cheltenham. So why then did Gerald Howard-Smith leave the capital with all its delights for a West Midlands town with seemingly so little to commend it? The reason he did so, it was suggested in the previous chapter, was in order to follow his father, Philip Howard-Smith. Called to the Bar in 1870, Philip went on, as we saw earlier, to become a member of the Oxford Circuit and a Revising Barrister, a role that brought him to various hearings, some of which were held in the West Midlands.[9] 'I attended many of his courts in South Staffordshire', recalled a Wolverhampton journalist, 'and was always struck with his judicious mixture of commonsense law as applied to Parliamentary and local government voting lists'.[10] Nevertheless, Philip was probably best known, in the West Midlands and elsewhere, for representing the Board of Trade in cases that, locally at least, attracted considerable attention in the press.[11] Indeed, it was said after his death that it was as a Board of Trade Commissioner for Inquiring into the Causes of Boiler Explosions that he 'was at his best'.[12]

It was presumably Philip's experience as a Revising Barrister and Board of Trade representative – and perhaps some familiarity with the West Midlands – that led to his appointment in 1900 as Recorder of Bridgnorth.[13] Although it was only fifteen miles or so from Wolverhampton, the two places were very different: the former, a market town serving a rural hinterland in Shropshire; the latter, we have seen, an industrial town on the edge of the (tellingly named) Black Country.[14] The Recordership was a largely honorific position and Philip was able to combine his duties in Shropshire with living in London, with the work he had been undertaking for the Board of Trade – and with assisting the International Commission of Inquiry which sat in Paris to investigate the Dogger Bank Incident of 1904 in which the Russian navy killed three fishermen when it fired on trawlers from the Hull fleet.[15]

Philip had to give up such activities five years later when he was appointed Judge of the County Court Circuit 5, an area of the West Midlands covering Atherstone, Lichfield, Rugeley, Tamworth, West Bromwich and Wolverhampton.[16] Despite their name, county courts were organised, not on a county basis, but by dividing the country into sixty circuits, a process that established courts in more than five hundred towns. Each of the courts had an average 'range of jurisdiction' of seven miles, a reasonable distance it was felt for plaintiffs and defendants to walk in order to attend hearings in which they were involved. Whether or not plaintiffs and defendants walked to court, by the time Philip took up his post, the county court system had been in place for more than half a century and was dealing with getting on for 1.5 million small claims a year.[17]

His Honour Judge Philip Howard-Smith, as he now was, began sitting as a County Court Judge in 1905 and continued to do so until his death in 1919.

Deliberating on a wide range of issues, some trivial and some important, mostly routine but occasionally controversial, he acquired a reputation for introducing 'an element of humour into the cases that came before him'.[18] It was an approach that sometimes led him into trouble. 'The publicity given to the casual observations of Judge H. Smith in Wolverhampton County Court seems likely to have a repressive effect on his Honour's occasional displays of his sense of humour', observed the *Midland Counties Express* in 1912. Philip was scared to say anything, he complained, 'for what I say appears in the London newspapers'.[19]

When they moved up from London, Philip and Mary could have chosen to live, if not in the Bridgnorth area, then virtually anywhere in, or within striking distance of, the large swathe of the West Midlands covered by County Court Circuit 5. However, the couple decided to move, not to Atherstone, Lichfield (another market town), Rugeley, Tamworth or West Bromwich, but to Wolverhampton.[20] They made their home, it must be said, not in Wolverhampton itself, but at the impressive Ford House, Bushbury, on the Staffordshire–Shropshire border. It was here, in what was described as 'a delightfully rural suburb of Wolverhampton', that Gerald was to be based for the remaining ten years or so of his life.[21]

Adolescence, manhood and middle age

Gerald was in a curiously anomalous position. By the time he moved to Wolverhampton, he was in his mid-twenties: no longer a child and no longer a youth. But was he a man? It remains unclear what Gerald, his parents, his family and others made of the position in which he found himself. Some presumably saw him as fully adult; some probably viewed him as insufficiently independent to be fully mature; while there were some, strange though it may seem, who possibly considered him old enough to be approaching middle age. Age and ageing were – and remain – more complicated, more cut across by class, gender and generation than is often realised.

'The progress of the middle-class boy from infancy to manhood', claims John Tosh, 'was marked by a sequence of well-defined stages'.[22] It was widely accepted, it seems, that there were significant turning points in male lives and that these were marked, *inter alia*, by new patterns of acquisition and consumption. The 'great symbols of initiation into the brotherhood of men', Laura Ugolini reminds us, 'are the first watch, the first pair of long trousers and the first cigarette'.[23] So although boys did not experience a uniform *rite de passage*, the journey to manhood, Tosh concludes, 'began in domestic dependence and ended in domestic authority. In between these two versions of domesticity a young man needed to demonstrate to himself, his father and his peers that he could live without the comforts of home and the ministrations of its female inmates, so that when he came to form a household of his own he would do so on the right terms.'[24]

If age and independence were important, so, too, was generation. Boys' progress from infancy to manhood tended to begin later, and to take longer, the later they were born. There were significant differences, one will not be surprised to learn, between the classes. Paul Deslandes explains the crucial changes affecting privileged young men like Gerald who grew up during the late nineteenth and early twentieth centuries. 'For men from the upper middle classes ... rising rates of attendance at public schools and universities, longer periods of financial dependence, and ample time for leisure and entertainment extended the experience of youth in the latter half of the nineteenth century.'[25] However, the final transition to manhood, concludes Tosh, always depended on marriage.[26]

To what extent then did Gerald's progress from infancy, through youth to manhood follow the sequence of well-defined stages suggested by Tosh; to what extent was his progress, or lack of it, delayed by the educational, financial and other changes delineated by Deslandes? Does the fact that Gerald did not marry mean that he was never able to make the final transition to full manhood? These are difficult questions, compounded, of course, by the fact that Gerald and his family left no personal papers or other records of the sort that one would like to be able to use when undertaking an autobiographical study such as this.

What can be said is that by the time Gerald moved to Wolverhampton, he had proved himself able to 'live without the comforts of home and the ministrations of its female inmates'. He had been educated at boarding school and although terms were short he had spent a good part of his formative years separated from his parents. Then after Temple Grove and Eton, he went on to Cambridge, spending still more of his young life away from home studying and playing sport, most notably, we have seen, in Canada and the United States of America.

What can be said, too, is that by the time Gerald arrived in Wolverhampton, he had forged an identity that was his and his alone. He was known, nationally and to some extent internationally, not – or not primarily – for his family background, but as a young man with considerable sporting accomplishments to his name. When newspapers and magazines reported his cricketing and athletic exploits, they made no mention of his parents, his brother or his extended family. What they considered newsworthy were his Eton background, his university credentials, his Corinthian swagger. 'G. Howard-Smith, the old Oxford [sic] Blue played most attractive and correct cricket, and hit twelve 4's, three 3's, and seven 2's.'[27] 'Howard Smith, as usual, came to the rescue of the L.A.C. in the high jump – doing his preliminary leaps, as is his custom, in his jacket, and after disrobing clearing 5ft. 10in.'[28]

But there were complications. Despite his years of boarding and his significant sporting profile, Gerald, like a number of his upper middle-class contemporaries, remained financially dependent on his parents. Although he was now in his mid-twenties, he had worked, so far as we know, for no more than a few months during the spring and early summer of 1906. However, the most powerful barrier to Gerald being recognised as fully mature was almost certainly the fact that he was still single. The two were related. Getting married and settling down were hugely important. Marriage, it was widely believed, was a vital marker, a fundamental staging post in the transition from dependent adolescence to independent adulthood. 'Before marriage', points out Jane Hamlett, 'middle-class men usually lived either at home or in bachelor establishments, and women at home. Marriage thus marked a crucial point in the life cycle when a new home was established and was also seen as synonymous with financial independence.'[29]

Gerald's transition from adolescence to adulthood, from youth to manhood was complicated still further by the view, held in some quarters, that one's mid-twenties marked not the arrival of adulthood, but the onset virtually of early middle age.[30] This is not as unlikely as it may seem. The years selected to define middle age (and other stages of the life course) changed, as one might expect, according to changing economic, social, cultural and demographic circumstances. So although the middle and upper middle classes aged later (and, indeed, aged better) than those from the working class, Gerald was approaching what a number of contemporaries were accustomed to regarding as the unwanted descent into middle age. Others felt, it must be said, that middle age brought professional benefits. 'It is, no doubt, very much to the advantage of a young practitioner to exhibit a modern antique appearance', suggested the *Family Doctor* in 1890, 'and nothing contributes so greatly to this end as a head which is innocent of hair'.[31]

Whatever the outcome of such demographic cost-benefit analysis, the chronology of middle age was changing. When Gerald was growing up during the second half of the nineteenth century, those responsible for the compilation of the census were confident that middle age could be defined as the period of life which began around the age of thirty.[32] By the time Gerald himself was approaching thirty, during the late 1900s, life expectancy was on the rise and many commentators were coming round to the view that middle age began, not at thirty, but at thirty-five. Middle age, a correspondent to the *Lancet* explained confidently in 1914, was 'the period ... that lies between 35 and 50 years'.[33]

Whatever the precise chronology of middle age – and whatever the professional benefits of baldness – there is no doubt that most people associated the middle years of life with decline, decay and regret.[34] In 1909, for example, just as Gerald was settling into Wolverhampton, a contributor to *Punch* put his 'reflections on middle-age' into verse. They might have been addressed to Gerald personally:

Ah! How often you and I, my Gerald

Taking count of Time's appalling pace

Watching those insidious signs that herald

Chronic apathy of form and face

Noting how our legs are not so lissom

Nor our waists so waspish as of old

And the joys of youth how much we miss 'em

Vanished like the Age of Gold.[35]

The law

Even if some of Gerald's contemporaries in Wolverhampton regarded him initially as an overgrown – and perhaps overindulged – adolescent, his choice of career probably helped to set minds at rest. The law, after all, was one of the oldest of all professions; and provincial solicitors, whose ranks Gerald was about to join, were regarded, and certainly regarded themselves, as stalwart pillars of their local communities. Contemporary commentators recognised – and sometimes regretted – the power exercised by medicine, the church and the law. A profession, claimed Anthony Trollope in 1867, was 'a calling by which a gentleman, not born to the inheritance of a gentleman's allowance of good things, might ingeniously obtain the same by some exercise of his abilities'.[36] Others were a good deal more cynical. It was in 1906, the very year that Gerald was beginning his legal training, that George Bernard Shaw delivered his celebrated aphorism that all professions were 'conspiracies against the laity'.[37]

Gerald, of course, came from a family of lawyers. It may seem odd therefore that he chose to become a solicitor rather than a barrister like his father. The Bar, as is well known, traditionally enjoyed the higher standing of the two branches of the profession. But attitudes, it seems, were changing. According to the vice-chancellor of Gerald's (and Philip's) alma mater, Cambridge University, it had been unusual in the mid-nineteenth century, when Philip was setting out, for undergraduates like him to go on to become solicitors. However, fifty years later, it was common for them to do so – 'a fact', he explained with steely self-assurance, 'showing an improvement in the status of solicitors'.[38]

Whatever Gerald's reasons for eschewing the Bar, his father's contacts in Shropshire and South Staffordshire presumably provided him with significant advantages as he sought to make his way in the profession. It was Philip Howard-Smith's connections, one assumes, that helped his son to join one of the best known practices in Wolverhampton. Underhill and Thorneycroft (later Underhill, Thorneycroft and Smith) was an important local business with offices in a well-thought of area close to the centre of the town. His new colleagues, as might be expected, participated in a range of activities, professional, personal and sporting, which embedded them in the local community – and probably helped to ease a newcomer's move into the area.[39]

By the time Gerald began his articles, probably in the summer or autumn of 1906, his principal in the firm, James E. Underhill, held a number of official appointments in and around Wolverhampton: he was Clerk to the Tipton Justices, he was Commissioner for Oaths and Perpetual Commissioner and he was Law Clerk to the South Staffordshire Mines Drainage Commissioners.[40]

80 *Career*

In fact, Gerald had two principals, rather than one, to advise and assist him. He was articled not just to James E. Underhill in Wolverhampton but also to William Hamilton Underhill, a partner in the London firm of Greene and Underhill. With four other solicitors and an architect in residence, and offices in prestigious Bedford Row, Greene and Underhill was a substantial undertaking at the very heart of London's legal district.[41]

The vice-chancellor of Cambridge was right in assuming the potency of the link between the law, status and the two ancient universities.[42] As a Cambridge graduate, Gerald did not have to sit the Law Society's preliminary examination, a hurdle that those who were not exempted had to surmount 'before entering into articles of clerkship to solicitors'.[43] Held both in London and major provincial cities, these preliminary examinations were sat mainly, as might be expected, by those younger than Gerald and/or those who had not enjoyed the educational and other advantages from which he had benefited. Thus those taking the preliminary examination were tested on topics such as elementary Latin and 'writing for dictation', on the history of England and the geography of Europe, subjects that Oxbridge graduates such as Gerald were assumed, no doubt correctly, to have mastered long before.[44]

The first professional hurdle that Howard-Smith had to face, therefore, was the Law Society's intermediate examination, which he sat in October 1907. Despite his supposed academic limitations in his early years at Eton, he performed very well. Of thirteen Oxbridge graduates (and one Dublin graduate) among the one hundred and ninety-five candidates sitting the examination, he was one of only twenty-three to be awarded a first-class pass.[45] He was equally successful in his final examination which he sat a little under two years later. Of the two hundred and seventy-eight candidates taking the examination alongside him in July 1909, he was one of two hundred and fourteen to pass, and one of just forty-three to be awarded an 'honorary distinction'.[46] It was a promising start to his fledgling career.

It did not take Gerald long to establish himself in Wolverhampton. Indeed, Underhill and Thorneycroft thought so well of their former pupil that they invited him – within a year of qualifying – to join them as a partner in the firm at which he had undertaken his training.[47] Although few details of his legal career are now available, it seems that he became increasingly busy and increasingly successful.[48] There is some indication perhaps of the way his career developed in the fact that when he died in 1916, at the age of thirty-six, he left an estate valued at just over £3,000 – and this at a time when most shopkeepers, schoolteachers, clerks and other white-collar workers earned considerably less than £160 a year.[49]

What little we know of Gerald's career tends to support David Sugarman's contention that it is misleading to draw too firm a distinction between lawyers as 'professionals, constrained by public-service limitations on their work' and lawyers as 'free-wheeling business people'.[50] It seems that Gerald, like many provincial solicitors took work when and where he could. So as Sugarman points out: 'In those areas of the country dominated by local trades and industry, notably the Midlands and north-west, solicitors' clients included the owners and managers of local coal mines, iron works, canal and railway companies, utilities, banks, and building societies.'[51] It proved a mutually beneficial relationship. When the Sunbeam Motor Company appointed the partner in another local firm to join its board of directors a couple of years after Gerald's death, it was explained that this greatly strengthened it 'on the legal side, a matter of no mean importance in these days when industry is compassed about with legal restrictions at every stage and turn'.[52]

Whatever preconceptions about trade and business Gerald may have brought with him from Eton and Cambridge, from London and the Home Counties, he took on clients in Wolverhampton from both manufacturing and transport. Underhill and Thorneycroft had a longstanding relationship, for example, with local pump and turbine maker, the Thomas Parker Company (and its successor the Rees Roturbo Manufacturing Company). James Underhill had attended the official opening of Thomas Parker's new factory in 1894; he was present the following year at the annual meeting of its directors and shareholders; and he was one of the original investors in the Rees Roturbo Company when it was established in 1909.[53] So it was probably in the natural order of things that three years later, Gerald was one of two witnesses when Edmund Scott Gustave Rees (who gave his name to the company) applied for a patent in the United States of America for the new and improved rotary condenser and self-condensing turbine that he had developed.[54]

Gerald also acted at least twice for the Great Western Railway Company, one of the two lines that ran through Wolverhampton. His involvement, it must be said, was not of the sort, or at the level, that made the legal profession wealthy.[55] These were mundane, run-of-the-mill cases that were dealt with, as befitted their lowly status, in the town's police court. On the first occasion, Gerald prosecuted a youth charged with stealing £1–5–8 (£1.30) from the company: the young man pleaded guilty and was put on probation for twelve months.[56] In the second more serious case, he prosecuted two men who were charged with stealing four cases of whisky and other property worth £40 that belonged to the Great Western: the defendants were committed for trial at the borough quarter sessions.[57]

Whether his work was in court or behind the scenes, for the public good or for local business, Gerald became recognised both for his legal connections and for his legal achievements. When he was appointed captain of Wolverhampton Cricket Club in the spring of 1912, it made the pages of the national, as well as the local, press. Family background, professional standing, sporting values, athletic achievement and social acceptability were all brought into the equation: 'Mr. G. Howard Smith', reported the *Daily Mail*, was 'the son of the local county court judge, who seldom misses one of the club's matches. The new captain, who is well known locally as one of the partners in a very old-established firm of solicitors, is just the man for the post. A sportsman in the best sense of the term, he is a capital bat and a deadly bowler, while no one will dispute his popularity.'[58]

It seems certain therefore that by 1912 – and probably when he arrived in Wolverhampton – Gerald was regarded neither as a late developer nor as an ageing has-been on the cusp of middle age, but as a young man embarking on what promised to be a lucrative and satisfying career. Some may still have harboured their doubts: it was perhaps not just those suspicious of the law and lawyers who wondered what had brought a Londoner, an Old Etonian and Cambridge Blue to the town. But whatever they made of Gerald initially, Wulfrunians would soon see a good deal more about him in the local press on which to base their opinions.

Sport

It was sport, as well as – in fact more than – the law, which enabled Gerald both to settle in Wolverhampton and to continue to mix in the sort of circles and live the sort of life with which he was familiar. It may be, of course, that he naturally gravitated, at play as well as at work, towards those of a similar background to himself. It may be that he felt the need, at some level, to isolate himself from the working-class character of the area to which he had moved. Whatever his reasons, the sports clubs he joined, and the teams he played for, were upper middle class (and aristocratic) in their leadership and management, if not always in their wider membership.

Gerald's time in Wolverhampton exemplifies the role that sport could – and quite often did – play in the lives of late Victorian and Edwardian middle-class men (and, to a much lesser extent, women). Sport, his years in the West Midlands confirm, was a social and economic lubricant of some importance, reflecting and reinforcing the differences and distinctions that underpinned late nineteenth- and early twentieth-century British society. As Richard Holt explains: 'The shared experience of public school [and university] offered a splendid excuse for a new kind of exclusive sociability later on.'[59] This was a world that Gerald knew well, the world of the gentleman amateur. Amateurism, Holt goes on, 'was an important and distinctive element in the ideology of the British elite through which divisions between land and money were effectively bridged whilst manual workers and the lower middle class were informally excluded'.[60]

Few teams epitomised amateurism as powerfully as the Old Etonians, the team of 'educated gentlemen' that Gerald played for when he resumed his football career after leaving Cambridge. It may have been a natural choice while he was living in London, but as we have seen he maintained his contact with the club even after moving a hundred and thirty miles or so north to Wolverhampton. 'The freemasonry of the public school was strong', Mike Huggins reminds us, 'the more so since numbers were extremely limited, making the old school tie a powerful symbol of comradeship'.[61] So it was that for some years in the mid- to late 1900s, Gerald travelled down to London on Saturday mornings, turning out for the team and staying overnight with a friend in the capital. Playing for the Old Etonians did little, of course, to integrate him into his new West Midlands surroundings, but he gave up his weekends in London only, it was said, when his 'professional success attracted too much work'.[62]

Gerald's other sporting interests did help him to assimilate. He joined South Staffordshire Golf Club, for instance, soon after his arrival in the West Midlands.[63] Opened towards the end of the previous century in an attractive setting on the rural fringe of Wolverhampton, it was regarded as by far the best in the area. 'The founders and early members of the South Staffordshire Golf Club', explains its historian, 'were from the middle class, professional and business community, though shortly after the turn of the century they were joined by some members of the local aristocracy'.[64] It continued to be socially exclusive, charging its playing members three guineas a year (five guineas a year from 1910) – sums equivalent to what the best paid working-class men might hope to earn in a fortnight (or in about a month from 1910).[65] Aware all the time of the need to counter any threats to their social exclusivity, those running the club agreed – at the same time as they increased the subscription – to cap the number of playing members at two hundred 'gentlemen' and eighty-five 'ladies'.[66]

Gerald played an increasingly active, albeit selective, part in the direction of club policy. He attended, for example, one of the three annual general meetings and two of the four special general meetings which were held between the beginning of 1910 and the end of 1912.[67] These included the meeting in the autumn of 1910 at which it was decided to increase subscriptions and limit the number of playing members.[68] It was on this occasion that he made his most telling intervention in the way that the South Staffordshire club was run. What happened is of particular interest because it provides one of the few occasions on which it is possible to discern something of Gerald's view of the world.

Challenging many contemporaries' – and no doubt many club members' – strongly held views, Gerald seconded a motion proposing a relaxation of the rules regulating the playing of golf on Sundays. The proposal was: 'That during the months October to April inclusive each year the restriction upon Sunday play, which provides that it may not commence before 1p.m. be removed.' After a lengthy discussion, it was agreed finally to accept an amendment put forward by Sir Charles Shaw (the Liberal MP for Stafford). The compromise he suggested stipulated that while the club house and professional's shop should remain closed until one o'clock on Sundays, members would be able to 'obtain access to the dressing room by special keys with numbered tallies to be provided by the Committee at a charge of 2/6 per annum each'.[69]

Gerald's support for a relaxation of the rules restricting Sunday access was perhaps less radical than it seems. By the end of the nineteenth century, notes Huggins, 'Sunday play was infiltrating the new suburban sports such as golf, croquet or lawn tennis, which could be played on private club premises, or in the gardens of the wealthy, despite church pressures for self-regulation.'[70] Nevertheless, Gerald's intervention should not be underestimated. Sunday observance continued to divide opinion and Sabbatarianism retained considerable influence. Sport, explains John Lowerson, 'was identified by many contemporaries as both a symptom and a cause of progressive religious decay in English society at the turn of the century'.[71] It must therefore have taken both conviction and self-confidence for Gerald to speak – and to speak in public – on what remained one of the most contentious issues of the day.

Despite his involvement in the affairs of the South Staffordshire Golf Club, Gerald's sporting interests in Wolverhampton centred, not on golf (or football or athletics), but on cricket. Cricket, like all sports, was played in many ways at many levels, and the step down from the first-class game that Gerald now took had its attractions as well as its drawbacks. Playing at a lower level gave him more chance to shine. Never fully convincing with either bat or ball while at university, he was able to perform exceptionally well, we saw above, when turning out for lesser teams such as Windsor Home Park and Hugh-Onslowe's XI. Playing at a lower level was also more compatible with earning a living. Matches were shorter, less frequent and less likely to take place on weekdays than those he had been involved in while a student. Self-employed and single with no wife or family to consider, Gerald was better placed than most to take up whatever invitations he found attractive and, as we shall see, combined his commitments to his colleagues at Underhill and Thorneycroft with playing for Wolverhampton, Staffordshire and other teams.

It was Gerald's combination of upper middle-class background, elite connections and cricketing skills that earned him his invitation in 1913 to play for the most privileged of these teams, the Free Foresters.[72] The 'gentlemen' of such clubs, it has been noted rather wistfully, 'played their cricket, exercised impeccable table manners (if they desired a return invitation), and danced the evening away'.[73] Whatever Gerald's table manners and dancing skills, he had played for the Eton Ramblers against the Foresters while a student at Cambridge, he had played previously with members of the current Foresters team and since his move to the Midlands, he had performed with some distinction for Wolverhampton and his adopted county of Staffordshire. He did not live too far away from the county ground, Stoke-on-Trent, where the game against Staffordshire was to be played – and he was available on the first Wednesday and Thursday in August when other potential members of the team would presumably be at work or away on holiday.[74]

The Foresters' two opening batsmen against Staffordshire were the epitome of early twentieth-century amateurism. Bernard Meakin was a member of the well-known pottery manufacturing family that bore his name. Born at Darlaston Hall, near Stone, he played cricket for Cambridge University and Gloucestershire, had captained Staffordshire County Cricket Club in 1911–12 and went on to become club president from 1946 to 1956.[75] His partner, Bernard Middleditch had attended Jesus College, Cambridge and played football for the Corinthians (and, on one occasion, for England).[76]

Neither were there any signs of the Foresters adjusting the class basis of their recruitment policy when it came to manning their bowling attack.[77] The team's two most successful bowlers against Staffordshire both had unimpeachably elitist credentials. Leg-break bowler Gordon Armytage Fairburn had been educated at Geelong College in Australia, before moving, like Middleditch, to Jesus College, Cambridge, where he gained his cricket Blue in 1913, 1914 and again in 1919.[78] His teammate, slow-medium bowler Francis Hugh Mugliston, a trainee with the Sudan civil service, was yet another who had been educated at Cambridge, where he gained his Blue a few years ahead of Fairburn.[79] The Foresters' two least successful bowlers against Staffordshire were just as well connected. There was Howard-Smith himself; and there was H.W. Etheliston, whose cricketing pedigree included being a member of the Household Brigade team which, in July 1902, had played against the Gentlemen of Marylebone Cricket Club at Lords, the home of world cricket.[80]

The Free Foresters, one can be sure, did not judge success solely by results on the field. This was just as well since neither the team nor Gerald acquitted themselves terribly well in the match against Staffordshire. The Foresters lost by an innings, Gerald taking just one catch, managing to secure just one wicket with his bowling and losing his own wicket twice without, as they say, troubling the scorers. Whether or not his poor performance was the reason, this was the first, last and only occasion that he ever played for the Free Foresters.

One of the reasons presumably that the Foresters called on Gerald was that since moving to the Midlands he had been selected twice (in 1908 and 1910) to play for – rather than against – his adopted county, Staffordshire. This was quite an accolade. The Staffordshire team competed and did well in the Minor Counties Championship, the tier below the County Championship. '[W]hen at anything like full strength', observed the *Cricket and Football Field* in 1913, 'they have proved themselves for some years the strongest county outside the first-class game.'[81] Indeed, when they *were* at full strength, they were able to include in their team the legendary Sydney Barnes. However condescending attitudes may have been towards professional players, Barnes was recognised as the outstanding bowler of his time: he played twenty-seven times for England, turned out for the MCC on twenty-three occasions – and was named Wisden cricketer of the year in 1910, the year in which Gerald played alongside him for Staffordshire.[82]

Gerald was a good cricketer, a very good cricketer. But his selection for Staffordshire, like his invitation to play for the Free Foresters, depended too, one suspects, on his social acceptability – not to mention his ability to take time off during the working week (The two matches that Gerald played in for Staffordshire both took place on a Monday and Tuesday). Certainly, the aristocratic leadership of Staffordshire County Cricket Club was becoming increasingly concerned about the declining interest in, and the increasing costs of, putting out a team. However, as Lord Lichfield suggested in 1913, there was a way out of the dilemma: 'They hoped to find more amateurs and so lessen the great expense of having so many professionals in each match, as in the past.'[83]

Whatever the reasons for Gerald's selection, whatever the balance between skill, status and availability in the minds of the selectors, he had a miserable first game. As an all-rounder, he hoped no doubt to be heavily involved every time he played. But this was a match in which he made no discernible contribution at all: although Staffordshire defeated Hertfordshire by two hundred and twenty-nine runs, Gerald took no catches, was not called on to bowl and was out twice without scoring.[84] He performed a great deal better in his second match, against Cheshire, which was played in 1910 at the ground belonging to Wolverhampton Cricket Club. On the first day of the game, he bowled 'very well', according to the local paper the *Express and Star*, 'and was treated with considerable respect by the batsman'. Then batting after lunch on the second day, he was involved in a partnership that, it was said, saw him 'keeping up his end well, and making some very nice strokes'.[85]

Wolverhampton's well-connected amateur contingent was well to the fore in the Staffordshire side. No doubt, the selectors, along with Lord Lichfield, had cost and convenience in mind when choosing their eleven, recognising the difficulties in particular of raising a team to play on a Monday and Tuesday. In all events, Wolverhampton Cricket Club was extremely well represented. There were five Wulfrunians (at least) in the team. Henry Duncan Stratton, who scored thirty-seven in the first innings of the match (and played for the MCC on four occasions), was a solicitor in Wolverhampton.[86] Raymond Charles Page was another Wolverhampton solicitor. Educated at Bradfield College in Berkshire (where he played against other public schools), he opened the batting against Cheshire, making the third highest score of thirty-five.[87] Raymond's younger brother, Edgar Wells Page, scored only eight, but was another who worked in Wolverhampton, although in his case as a chartered accountant rather than as a solicitor.[88] This was not the end of the Wolverhampton connection. The teammate with whom Gerald shared his batting partnership on the second day of the match, William John Beddows, was yet another Wulfrunian. Born in Tettenhall, near the Wolverhampton club's ground, Beddows was a grammar school boy who represented the county at both golf and cricket, played cricket for the 'Gentlemen of Staffordshire', went on to win the military cross, was promoted to colonel, served as a JP, and in 1939 become head of Wolverhampton's Local Defence Volunteer Force.[89]

It was playing for Wolverhampton, rather than Staffordshire or the Free Foresters, that Gerald was able to perform to his best. It was at Wolverhampton Cricket Club, it seems clear, that his sporting interests, social background and professional contacts coalesced to ease the potentially difficult transition from young, metropolitan sportsman to aspiring, provincial solicitor. It was here, on the fringes of working-class Wolverhampton, that upper middle-class Gerald was able to forge a new life for himself.[90]

Wolverhampton Cricket Club, like its near neighbour South Staffordshire Golf Club, was based, not in Wolverhampton itself, but in the village of Tettenhall, three miles or so to the west of the town centre. It was an attractive venue, in a desirable rural/semi-rural residential location.[91] Wulfrunians should go and watch a game there, urged the *Express and Star*'s cricket correspondent, and enjoy 'the pleasure that is to be derived from spending a few hours on the delightfully situated cricket field at Tettenhall'.[92] It would not be a difficult journey. The tram network had recently been electrified and, because of the area it served, the 'prestigious route' running from Wolverhampton railway station to Tettenhall village always benefited, it was said, from 'the best horses and the newest vehicles'.[93]

Cricket, unlike golf, was popular with all classes in society. But this did not mean that members of a club like Wolverhampton joined or competed, let alone socialised, on equal terms.[94] Founded in the early 1880s, by the time Gerald moved to the town it boasted 'an influential list of non-playing members' and an array of influential, local patrons such as 'the Earl of Dartmouth, Sir C.T. Mander, Bart, Colonel T.E. Hickman, M.P., Mr. Alfred Bird, M.P.'[95] Those responsible for running the club, which – like the golf club – was considered to be the best of its kind in the area, believed not surprisingly that it was crucial to maintain the social distances and distinctions that propriety demanded.[96]

They therefore established five classes of membership: life members, playing members, honorary members, junior playing members and temporary playing members – with even junior playing members (or their families) having to find a subscription of half a guinea a year.[97] Those running the club took considerable care, too, in deciding which teams might provide suitable opposition. The first team did not play in the Birmingham League – and certainly did not have anything to do with the Wolverhampton and District Works League which completed its first season in 1912.[98] The club chose instead to compete against teams such as Bournville, Harborne, Leamington, the Forest of Arden, Lichfield Garrison, Malvern College, Knowle and Dorridge, Market Drayton ('who as a rule have the assistance of some 'Varsity players'), Sutton Coldfield and the 'Old Hall Masters' from Wellington in Shropshire. They even had a fixture against the Free Foresters.[99] 'Any lessons on how to play the game', it has been claimed, 'would be dealt out in friendly matches, the *locus classicus* of the amateur ethic'.[100]

Even so, some considered the club's members to be insufficiently deferential. It was an issue that, as one might expect, was discussed – and regretted – by those in positions of local authority. The 'Committee of Officers' compiling the official history of the Sixth Battalion of the South Staffordshire Regiment (in which Gerald Howard-Smith was to serve as a second lieutenant and temporary lieutenant during the First World War) were only too aware of the difficulties that could arise. Although discipline in territorial force units such as the Sixth Battalion was supposedly more relaxed than in their regular army counterparts, they too had their difficulties:

> there was a large contingent of volunteers from the Wolverhampton Cricket Club, a magnificent contribution to the ranks, but the devil for officers, some of short experience, to rule! Frankly, the officers amused them: the officers had no alternative but to be amused themselves.[101]

Whatever the discipline or indiscipline of its members, Wolverhampton Cricket Club provided an environment in which Gerald was able to excel. It was reported within a month of his joining the club at the beginning of the 1907 season that he was 'again proving destructive' in a first-team match against nearby Stafford.[102] Five years later, he was appointed captain.[103] Succeeding the long-serving Henry Duncan Stratton (with whom he had played for Staffordshire two years before), he was welcomed in the local press as 'a gentleman of experience and one capable of imparting ripe judgement into his work'. It was a wise appointment, concluded the *Express and Star*: 'Mr. Howard Smith well deserved the distinction which the club has conferred upon him.'[104] It was an appointment, as we saw earlier, which made the pages not just of the local but of the national press.

Captaincy seemed to galvanise him. Although – or because – he was now in his early thirties, his performances with both bat and ball were reaching a peak. In the course of a single week during the early summer of 1914, for example, he scored a century against Harborne, and bowled uninterrupted throughout an entire innings against Sutton Coldfield.[105] His bowling continued to be singled out for particular praise: 'G.H. Smith bowled well';[106] 'Bayliss and Howard Smith did the damage among the Walsall batsmen.'[107] Gerald had become integral, it is clear, to Wolverhampton's success. The team was 'seriously handicapped', concluded the *Express and Star*, when their captain was unable to play.[108]

He was part of a tightly circumscribed group. Gerald, many of his teammates, and some at least of the club's officials were drawn from a narrow circle that was bound together by a mixture of personal, professional and sporting relationships. Living, working and socialising in this way can only have confirmed and reinforced Gerald's and his teammates' distance, physically, socially and culturally, from the majority of those living in the town in which, or near to which, they made their homes, made their living and spent their free time.

Whatever the discipline or indiscipline of the club's members, those playing for the first team were accustomed to, and seemingly accepted, contemporary notions of status and sportsmanship. There was no arguing, one assumes, with those officiating in matches. Gerald Howard-Smith's father, his Honour Judge Philip Howard-Smith, was a keen supporter of the club, often umpiring at home games.[109] When he did so first in the summer of 1912, his participation produced predictable attempts at humour. '"We shall be having some legal decisions", one gentleman remarked.' In the event, all passed off smoothly: '[I]t happened that during the time that his Honour was wearing the white coat in the field everything was clean, and the occasion for a verdict from him did not arise.'[110] Indeed, the attribution and circulation of status between Gerald, his father, Wolverhampton Cricket Club and other local clubs was mutually reinforcing. When Gerald was made first team captain at Wolverhampton, the *Express and Star* commented, it will be recalled, that 'Mr. Howard Smith, the new skipper, well deserved the distinction which the club has conferred upon him.'[111] When his father began umpiring for the club, the paper remarked that Sutton Coldfield 'were honoured in having his Honour Judge Howard Smith to officiate temporarily for them in the capacity of umpire'.[112]

Neither was there any doubting the social acceptability of those selected for the first team. Although Wolverhampton's players were scarcely of the same social standing as those from clubs like the Eton Ramblers or the Free Foresters, they comprised a secure and solid cross-section of Wolverhampton (and Black Country) middle-class and upper middle-class society. The teams that Gerald captained included clergymen, businessmen, solicitors and other professionals – their participation facilitated, no doubt, by the fact that those in business and the professions were often either self-employed or worked in family concerns. Many of them went on, if they had not already done so, to make a name for themselves in the life of Wolverhampton and its surrounding areas.[113]

This homogeneity can be seen by considering, to take but one example, the composition of the team which travelled to Malvern to play in a one-day, single-innings match against Malvern College on 23 May 1914.[114] Wolverhampton's two opening batsmen, Raymond Charles Page and his younger brother Edgar Wells Page, had played with Howard-Smith in Staffordshire's match against Cheshire four years earlier.[115] Raymond and Edgar were joined in the team chosen to play against Malvern by two more of their brothers: John Kenneth Samuel Page who had been to school at Repton, and Harold Aston Page, yet another solicitor in a family – and a team – that was packed with them. Harold went on to enjoy a successful local career, becoming, for instance, president of Wolverhampton Law Society, and a director of the Wolverhampton and District Permanent Building Society.[116] The third man to bat for Wolverhampton, Arthur Cecil Finnis, knew the Page family well. By the time of the match, he was the assistant secretary of a brewery company. But ten years or so earlier, he had been working as a bank clerk in London, where he and his family found space for three lodgers, one of whom was Wolverhampton-born, opening batsman Raymond Page, who at the turn of the century had been working in the capital as a solicitor's clerk.[117]

Arthur Finnis was followed, after Gerald Howard-Smith and John and Harold Page, by two players from business, rather than professional, backgrounds. George Frederick Beddows was the brother of William John Beddows who, it will be recalled, had partnered Gerald on the second day of Staffordshire's match against Cheshire in 1910. Both men worked in the family timber business, while a third brother was, or had finished, training to be a doctor.[118] The next man to bat, Percival Samuel Bayliss was a member of a highly successful local business family. Brought up in a large household (where he was looked after by six members of staff), Percival married in 1911 and set up home in Tettenhall with his wife (a friend and two servants).[119] Ten years later, he joined the board of Bayliss Jones and Bayliss, becoming joint managing director in 1928, by which time the firm had been taken over by GKN (Guest, Keen and Nettlefolds).[120]

The final member of the team for whom it has been possible to obtain information was Clifford Howl. Living in the Black Country, rather than

Wolverhampton, he had been educated at Eastbourne New College and the University of Birmingham and played not just for Wolverhampton but for the 'Gentlemen of Staffordshire'. Howl worked in the family firm (of sanitary and hydraulic engineers), joined the Territorial Army, played golf and cricket for Staffordshire and became a JP and president of Tipton Conservative Association.[121] He also went on, many years later, to chair the Tibbington (1916) Company, the successor to the Tibbington Collieries and Brickworks Ltd, which went into liquidation in 1916. The liquidator appointed to manage the winding up, it comes as no surprise to learn, was Samuel Wells Page, the father of the four brothers playing for Wolverhampton in the match against Malvern College.[122]

Class, place and sport

It is well known, of course, that golf clubs and cricket clubs served as fulcrums of middle- and upper middle-class sociability. It is less widely recognised that they functioned in this way even in the most working-class of towns. Wolverhampton, it goes without saying, never did vie 'with resorts such as Leamington and Cheltenham.'[123] But even – perhaps especially – in a town like Wolverhampton, a privileged background, parental support, professional standing and sporting prowess went a very long way. Even in a town like Wolverhampton, it was possible, and probably relatively easy, for a young man like Gerald Howard-Smith to isolate himself both at work and at play from most traces of the working-class town in which he worked, near to which he lived, and on the fringes of which he spent so much of his leisure time.

Notes

1. R.H. Trainor, *Black Country Elites: The Exercise of Authority in an Industrialized Area, 1830–1900* (Oxford: Clarendon Press, 1993), p. 23.
2. For introductions to the postmodernist attack on class-based analysis such as that in this book, see Keith Jenkins, *Rethinking History* (London: Routledge, 1991) and Alan Munslow, *Deconstructing History* (London: Routledge, 1997). Richard Evans and George Bernard, like many others, have mounted spirited defences: R.J. Evans, *In Defence of History* (London: Granta, 1997) and G.W. Bernard, 'History and Postmodernism', in G.W. Bernard (ed.), *Power and Politics in Tudor England* (Aldershot: Ashgate, 2000).
3. See, for example, Simon Gunn and Rachel Bell, *Middle Classes: Their Rise and Sprawl* (London: Cassell, 2002); John Tosh, *A Man's Place: Masculinity and the Middle-Class Home in Victorian England* (London: Yale University Press, 2007); Jane Hamlett, *Material Relations: Domestic Interiors and Middle-Class Families in England, 1850–1910* (Manchester: Manchester University Press, 2010).
4. Tosh, *Man's Place*, p. 13.
5. This discussion draws heavily on John Benson, 'Sport, Class and Place: Gerald Howard-Smith and Early Twentieth-Century Wolverhampton', *Midland History*, 37, 2, 2012.
6. Trainor, *Black Country Elites*, p. 7; John Benson, 'Black Country History and Labour History', *Midland History*, xv, 1990; Jon Lawrence, 'Class and Gender in

the Making of Urban Toryism, 1880–1914', *English Historical Review*, 108, 428, 1993. Also Jeremy Walters, *My Father's Wolverhampton 1905–1931* (Wolverhampton: Jeremy Walters, 2015).
7 G.J. Barnsby, *Social Conditions in the Black Country 1800–1900* (Wolverhampton: Integrated Publishing Services, 1980), p. 78. Also G. Barnsby, *A History of Housing in Wolverhampton 1750–1975* (Wolverhampton: Integrated Publishing Services, N.D.).
8 Cited in J. Hunter, *The First £100 Million: A History of the Staffordshire Building Society* (Wolverhampton: The Society, N.D.), p. 1. See, too, J.P. Jones, *The Heart of the Midlands: The Official Guide to Wolverhampton and its Surroundings, The Green Borderland of the Black Country* (Wolverhampton, N.P., 1906), p. iv.
9 For example, *Birmingham Daily Post*, September 21, 1900.
10 *Midland Counties Express*, May 17, 1919.
11 For example, *Daily News*, August 17, 1900; *Engineer*, January 18, 1901.
12 *Midland Counties Express*, May 17, 1919.
13 *London Gazette*, August 29, 1900.
14 See, for example, Trevor Rowley, *The Shropshire Landscape* (London: Hodder & Stoughton, 1972), pp. 187–93.
15 *Morning Post*, November 30, 1900; *Scarborough Evening News*, October 24, 1904; Karen K. Jackson, 'The Dogger Bank Incident and the Development of International Arbitration' (MA thesis, Texas Tech University, 1974); information from Malcolm Wanklyn.
16 *Leicester Chronicle and Leicestershire Mercury*, September 1, 1900; *Tom's Official Directory*, 1909, p. 198; *Who Was Who, 1916–1928*, p. 975.
17 Paul Johnson, 'Creditors, Debtors and the Law in Victorian and Edwardian England' (Economic History Department, London School of Economics, Working Paper No. 31, 1996), pp. 6–7. Also Paul Johnson, 'Class Law in Victorian England', *Past and Present*, 141, 1993; Paul Johnson, 'Small Debts and Economic Distress in England and Wales, 1857–1913', *Economic History Review*, xlvi, i, 1993.
18 *Midland Counties Express*, May 17, 1919. See, for example, *Midland Counties Express*, February 17, 1912.
19 *Midland Counties Express*, March 16, 1912.
20 See Marie B. Rowlands, *The West Midlands from AD 1000* (London: Longman, 1987).
21 Jones, *Heart of the Midlands*, p. 132.
22 Tosh, *Man's Place*, p. 103.
23 E.E. Wood, *Is This Theosophy?* (London: Rider, 1936), cited in Laura Ugolini, *Men and Menswear: Sartorial Consumption in Britain 1880–1939* (Aldershot: Ashgate, 2007), p. 32.
24 Tosh, *Man's Place*, p. 122.
25 Paul R. Deslandes, *Oxbridge Men: British Masculinity and the Undergraduate Experience, 1850–1920* (Bloomington: Indiana University Press, 2005), p. 48. See, too, Hamlett, *Material Relations*, p. 145.
26 Tosh, *Man's Place*, p. 108.
27 *Slough, Eton and Windsor Observer*, July 7, 1906.
28 *Daily Mail*, November 4, 1905.
29 Hamlett, *Material Relations*, p. 74.
30 For an overview, see John Benson, *Prime Time: A History of the Middle Aged in Twentieth-Century Britain* (London: Longman, 1997), ch. 2.
31 *Family Doctor*, January 25, 1900.
32 Census of England and Wales, 1871, *General Report*, p. xii.
33 'Active 54' to *Lancet*, September 5, 1914.
34 Benson, *Prime Time*.

35 *Punch*, January 27, 1909.
36 Cited in Harold Perkin, *The Rise of Professional Society: England since 1880* (London: Routledge, 1989), p. 84.
37 See J.R. Ashton, 'All Professions are Conspiracies against the Laity', *Journal of Epidemiology and Community Health*, 57, 2003.
38 *Pall Mall Gazette*, October 9, 1901.
39 For the partners' attendance at a funeral of one of the firm's members, see *Express and Star*, June 26, 1914.
40 *Kelly's Directory of Staffordshire*, 1904, pp. 554, 868.
41 *Post Office London Directory*, 1907, p. 22.
42 See, more broadly, Perkin, *Professional Society*.
43 University of London, Institute of Advanced Legal Studies (IALS), Law Society, Examination Records, LSOC/2/32, List of Candidates for Preliminary Examination, 1905.
44 IALS, LSOC/2/32. 1904.
45 IALS, LSOCO9/30, Intermediate Examination Results, 1907; *Weekly Notes*, November 23, 1907.
46 *Weekly Notes*, July 31, 1909.
47 Information from Richard Alderson.
48 *Eton College Chronicle*, May 11, 1916.
49 *Wills and Administrations*, 1916, p. 260; Perkin, *Professional Society*, p. 78.
50 David Sugarman, 'Simple Images and Complex Realities: English Lawyers and their Relationship to Business and Politics, 1750–1950', *Law and History Review*, 11, 2, 1993, p. 257.
51 Sugarman, 'Simple Images', pp. 278–9.
52 *Flight*, May 16, 1918.
53 *London Gazette*, July 28, 1908; www.historywebsite.co.uk/genealogy/Parker/TPLimited.htm [September 2014]; www.gracesguide.co.uk/Rees_Roturbo_Manufacturing_Co [September 2014].
54 United States Patent Office, Serial No. 673, 560, September 21, 1915.
55 Sugarman, 'Simple Images', p. 273.
56 *Midland Counties Express*, April 13, 1912.
57 *Midland Counties Express*, May 4, July 11, 1912.
58 *Daily Mail,* April 1, 1912.
59 Holt, *Sport and the British*, p. 114.
60 Holt, *Sport and the British*, p. 116.
61 Mike Huggins, *The Victorians and Sport* (London: Hambledon, 2004), pp. 193–4.
62 *Eton College Chronicle*, May 11, 1916.
63 South Staffordshire Golf Club (SSGC), 'Members' Subscriptions', 1908–17.
64 T. Boliver, *South Staffordshire Golf Club 1892–1992* (Wolverhampton: The Club, 1992), p. 8. See, also, D. Mellin, *Oxley Park Golf Club Diamond Jubilee 1913–1988 Celebration Handbook* (N.P., N.D.).
65 SSGC, 'Members' Subscriptions'; W. Vamplew, 'Sharing Space: Inclusion, Exclusion and Accommodation at the British Golf Club before 1914', *Journal of Sport and Social Issues*, 34, 3, 2010, 361; John Benson, *The Working Class in Britain, 1850–1939* (London, 1989), ch. 2.
66 SSGC, Minutes of Special General Meeting, November 26, 1910. The population of Wolverhampton in 1901 was getting on for 100,000: Barnsby, *Social Conditions*, p. 2. See Vamplew, 'Sharing Space'.
67 SSGC, Company Minute Book, 1908–1958.
68 SSGC, Minutes of Special General Meeting, November 26, 1910.
69 SSGC, Minutes of Special Meeting, November 26, 1910.
70 Huggins, *Victorians*, p. 73.

Wolverhampton, the law and sport 93

71 John Lowerson, 'Sport and the Victorian Sunday: The Beginnings of Middle-Class Apostasy', *International Journal of the History of Sport*, 1, 2, 1984, p. 202.
72 See P. Whitcombe and M. Parsons, *The Free Foresters 1856–2006* (NP., ND.).
73 D. Frith, *The Golden Age of Cricket 1890–1914* (London: Omega Books, 1983), p. 20.
74 www.cricketarchiv.com/Archive/Scorecards/286/2864.html [September 2012]; www.cricketarchiv.com/Archive/Scorecards/286/2864.html [September 2012].
75 www.cricketarchive.com/Archive/Players/31/31395/31395.html [March 2012]; Staffordshire County Record Office, D4245/5/1, img: 424.
76 T. Mason, *Association Football & English Society 1863–1915* (Brighton: Harvester, 1980), p. 216. Also D. Porter, 'Amateur Football in England, 1948–63: The Pegasus Phenomenon', *Contemporary British History*, 14, 2000, pp. 1–2.
77 It is commonly claimed that when teams recruited from across the social spectrum, the upper and middle class batted, while their working-class teammates bowled. L.M. Randall, 'Was the Professional Sportsman in Britain between 1870 and 1914 less a Labour Aristocrat and more a Wage Slave?', *Australian Society for Sports History Bulletin*, 7, 1988, p. 16; S. Wagg, '"Time Gentlemen Please": The Decline of Amateur Captaincy in English County Cricket', *Contemporary British History*, 14, 2000, p. 2.
78 www.cricketarchive.com/Archive/Players/29/29333.html [March 2012].
79 Census of England and Wales, 1911, RG14/PN/25391. Mugliston also played for the MCC: www.cricketarchive.com/Archive/Players/31/31610 [March 2012].
80 www.cricketarchive.com/Archive/Scorecards/302/302688.html [March 2012].
81 *Cricket and Football Field*, August 30, 1913.
82 J. Hill, *Sport, Leisure and Culture in Twentieth-Century Britain* (Basingstoke: Palgrave, 2002), pp. 31–2; P. Dixon and N. Garnham, 'Cricket Club Professionals in Victorian and Edwardian County Durham', *Sport in History*, 23, 2003; D. Frith, *Golden Age*, p. 162; Holt, *Sport and the British*, p. 176.
83 *Cricket and Football Field*, June 7, 1913.
84 *Express and Star*, August 24, 25, 1908; www.stats.cricketworld.com/Scorecards/87/87484.html [February 2013].
85 *Express and Star*, July, 18, 19, 1910.
86 www.cricketarchive.com/Scorecards/Archives/Players/33/33075/33075.html [March 2012]; *London Gazette*, December 2, 1898, November 15, 1907, May 11, 1909.
87 www.cricketarchive.com/Scorecards/216/216644.html [March 2012].
88 *London Gazette*, October 3, 1919; *Express and Star*, May 12, 1956.
89 *London Gazette*, March 14, 1939; www.cricketarchive.com [March 2012].
90 David Barnes tells me that the club's records have been mislaid, probably during the recent move to a new pavilion.
91 Jones, *Heart of the Midlands*, p. 83.
92 *Express and Star*, June 20, 1914. Also April 25, 1914.
93 Mills, *Tettenhall*, p. 6. Also Brew, *Tettenhall*, pp. 7, 9; S. Webb and P. Addenbrooke, *A History of Wolverhampton Transport, Volume One 1833–1930* (Birmingham and Wolverhampton: Birmingham Transport History Group, 1987), pp. 38–42.
94 Holt, *Sport and the British*, p. 175.
95 Wolverhampton Archives, L796358(P), *Wolverhampton Cricket Club*, 1882; *Express and Star*, April 26, 1913.
96 The third member of west Wolverhampton's sporting establishment was Newbridge Lawn Tennis Club. *Express and Star*, August 3, 1912. See also R.T. Everitt, *One Hundred Sporting Summers: A Celebration of Bilston Lawn Tennis Club's Centenary and the Town's Sporting Heritage* (Bilston: N.P., 1995).
97 *Express and Star*, April 25, 1914.
98 *Express and Star*, July 20, August 17, 1912.

94 *Career*

99 See, for instance, *Express and Star*, April 30, 1910; April 26, 1913; May 30, June 1, 8, 13, 15, 27, August 1, 1914.
100 D.J. Taylor, *On the Corinthian Spirit: The Decline of the Amateurism in Sport* (London: Yellow Jersey, 2006), pp. 50–51. I am grateful to Dilwyn Porter for this reference.
101 A Committee of Officers who Served with the Battalion, *The War History of the Sixth Battalion the South Staffordshire Regiment (T.F.)* (London: Heinemann, 1924), p. 7. See also A. Thornton, 'The Territorial Force in Staffordshire 1908–1915' (MPhil thesis, University of Birmingham, 2004), p. 138; and, more broadly, C. Veitch, '"Play up! Play up! And Win the War!" Football, the Nation and the First World War 1914–15', *Journal of Contemporary History*, 20, 1985; G.D. Sheffield, *Leadership in the Trenches: Officer-Man Relations, Morale and Discipline in the British Army in the Era of the First World War* (London: Palgrave, 2000); T. Collins, 'English Rugby Union and the First World War', *Historical Journal*, 45, 2002.
102 *Express and Star*, May 18, 1907. Also April 27, 1907; May 21, 1910; July 12, 1913.
103 *Daily Mail*, April 1, 1912. For public school leadership, see Cain, 'Education, Income and Status'.
104 *Express and Star*, April 27, 1912.
105 *Express and Star*, July 1, 8 1914.
106 *Express and Star*, July 4, 1914.
107 *Express and Star*, July 18, 1914.
108 *Express and Star*, June 27, 1914.
109 *Midland Counties Express*, May 17, 1919.
110 *Express and Star*, July 13, 1912.
111 *Express and Star*, April 27, 1912.
112 *Express and Star*, July 13, 1912.
113 The team the club put out to play against Stafford in the spring of 1911 contained two clergymen. *Express and Star*, May 8, 1911.
114 For the game, see *Express and Star*, May 22, 1914.
115 *Express and Star*, May 15, 1956. Also May 12, 1956.
116 Census of England and Wales, 1911, RG14/PN/16767; RG14/PN/17007. The three brothers, their sister and parents were looked after by a lady help, a cook, a housemaid and a parlour maid. For Harold Page, see *Express and Star*, August 25, 1951.
117 Census of England and Wales, 1901, RG13/1200/42; RG14/PN/17024.
118 Census of England and Wales, RG14/PN/16979.
119 Census of England and Wales, RG14/PN/16979.
120 www.localhistory.scit.wlv.ac.uk/Museum/Other Trades [March 2012].
121 For the links between football and Conservatism in Wolverhampton, see Lawrence, 'Class and Gender'.
122 *Kelly's Directory of Staffordshire*, 1896, p. 370; *London Gazette*, August 5, 1913; April 4, 1916; March 15, 1935; *Express and Star*, December 1, 1962.
123 Hunter, *The First £100 Million*, p. 1.

Part III
SACRIFICE

5 'THE THING TO DO': CLASS, PATRIOTISM AND PREPARATION

Losses and laments

1914 marked a turning point in Gerald's life, as in the lives of millions and millions of others in Britain, Europe and beyond. He began the year a provincial solicitor enjoying the sort of safe, secure and comfortable existence that one associates with such a career. Approaching his thirty-fourth birthday, he had much to be thankful for and much to look forward to. An Old Etonian and Cambridge Blue, he lived with his parents in an impressive home on the Shropshire-Staffordshire border. A partner in one of Wolverhampton's best known legal practices, he managed, easily it seems, to combine his professional commitments with his sporting interests. Playing his golf at the prestigious South Staffordshire Golf Club and his cricket at Wolverhampton Cricket Club, he had a significant local profile. Selected a few years earlier to play cricket for Staffordshire, he had turned out the previous summer for the Free Foresters, and was preparing for his third season as captain of Wolverhampton.

Two years later Gerald Howard-Smith was dead. He was not the only one, of course: the First World War claimed, in Britain alone, more than 700,000 lives, not to mention the 2 million or so who were 'wounded in body or in mind, their lives never to be the same again'.[1] The causes and consequences of such appallingly heavy casualties became, of course, a matter of regret and recrimination, of comment and conjecture.[2] 'The loss sustained by the war can only be described as the wiping out of a generation', lamented the Bishop of Worcester in 1922.[3] Three-quarters of a century later, the historian Peter Clarke attempted, like so many others, to put the conflict into some kind of perspective:

> The casualties were horrific. It is the sheer cumulative impact of the losses, week by week and month by month, which is staggering... It is not the demographic but the human impact of the losses which burned so deep. Bereavement was a more common experience anyway in the early twentieth century, but that does not rationalize away the poignancy of parents burying sons, or of wives and lovers losing young men in their prime.[4]

Yet in death as in life, in war as in peace, class reared its head. There was, there still is, a widespread and deeply entrenched view that it was young (and youngish) men like Gerald who suffered the most, who sacrificed the most.[5] The aristocracy and upper middle class, it is said, were particularly patriotic, their losses, it is believed, the greatest of any social group. 'Half the great families of England, heirs of large estates and wealth, perished', claimed C.F. G. Masterman in 1922.[6] According to this reading of events, the country was to pay the price for years to come. 'Casualties were about three times heavier in proportion among junior officers than with common soldiers', explained A. J.P. Taylor in 1965. 'The roll of honour in every school and college bore witness to the talents which had perished – the men of promise born during the eighteen-nineties whose promise was not fulfilled.'[7] As the head of British Steel remarked twenty years later, 'even today we have not fully replaced the dynamism and leadership qualities of the generation that we threw away in the First World War.'[8]

Such views retain their potency. In one of the first major publications timed to coincide with the centenary of the outbreak of the war, Anthony Seldon and David Walsh produced an extended study of – some might say an extended apologia for – the *Public Schools and the Great War*. 'Public schoolboys', they explain at the very outset, 'were to die at almost twice the average for all those who served. Whereas some 11 per cent of those who fought overall were to die as a direct result of the fighting, the figure for public schoolboys was over 18 per cent. Those who left school between about 1908 and 1915 were to die at even higher rates, as they were the most likely to serve in the front line as junior officers, and as pilots in the Royal Flying Corps, which saw very high casualties.'[9]

This slaughter of the middle and upper middle classes, Seldon and Walsh suggest, can be attributed to a number of factors: some ideological, some social, economic and structural. The middle and upper middle classes, it is said, were more patriotic than other classes and more likely therefore to volunteer for military service.[10] They were healthier than other classes and more likely therefore to be accepted when they volunteered and, once accepted, more likely to be allocated to frontline duty. They were, of course, more socially acceptable than other classes: and this meant that they were more likely, especially during the early years of the war, to be commissioned as officers – and officers' casualty rates were a great deal higher than those of men serving in other ranks. So it is that Seldon and Walsh quote with approval the conclusions reached by the American historian Jay Winter:

> The higher up the social scale a man was, the greater were the chances that he would serve from early in the war and that he would do so in a combat unit ... Casualty rates among officers were substantially higher than the men in other ranks and the most dangerous rank in the army, the subaltern, was recruited through much of the war from current pupils or old boys of the public schools and ancient universities.[11]

Nevertheless, one cannot help harbouring some doubts. Did breeding, background and upbringing play quite such a decisive role in determining attitudes and behaviour during the course of the war? Is the evidence for middle- and upper middle-class patriotism and sacrifice really as clear and compelling as scholars such as Seldon, Walsh and Winter suggest? Is it unduly cynical to suspect an element (and more) of special pleading in their interpretation of events? These are complex and contentious issues and it is the aim of this chapter, covering the penultimate year of Gerald Howard-Smith's life, to make some contribution towards determining the truth of the matter. It will consider two key components of the case that can be made for the disproportionate scale and intensity of middle- and upper middle-class patriotism and sacrifice. It will examine the reasons that Gerald Howard-Smith (and men like him) volunteered to fight in the war; it will then explore the possibility that Gerald (and men like him) coped better than those from other classes with the training and preparation which they were required to undertake before leaving for the Western Front.

The call to arms

What then of the claim that Gerald Howard-Smith and men like him were particularly patriotic, and particularly responsive therefore to the call to arms when it came in the summer of 1914? Two cautions need to be entered at the outset: one conceptual, the other contextual. First, it is never easy to identify attitudes, let alone to trace the relationship between attitudes and behaviour; and it is a mistake to assume that similar attitudes necessarily produce similar behaviour or that similar behaviour is necessarily the product of similar attitudes. Second, it is important to bear in mind the response to the call to arms that came from men much less privileged than Gerald Howard-Smith. He and his privately educated contemporaries were far from alone in their willingness to fight for king and country. 'There was never a volunteer army like it before', claims W.J. Reader. 'It seems safe to say there never will be again ... Men in millions came forward to enlist, not only the most numerous but probably the most enthusiastic volunteers the world has ever seen and, as their fighting record shows, brave and enduring also.'[12]

The implications for this study are obvious. Nothing can be taken for granted; and it is a great deal more difficult to understand Gerald Howard Smith's – and his privately educated contemporaries' – reactions to the outbreak of war than some have assumed. As Gerard J. DeGroot reminds us, the 'great rush to the colours might seem an enormously unselfish response by citizens of all classes to their country's call. But it is important to realise that these men did not share a common will to serve. Only by studying the various motivations for volunteering can we understand the type of army which eventually evolved and the effect which war had upon those who served.'[13]

DeGroot is right. And we must recognise too the difference between what is knowable and what is not. It is exceptionally difficult to attribute motivation, to disentangle the complex, often unarticulated balance of propaganda and patriotism, duty and dissatisfaction, local ties and national concerns that drove so many from comfortable upper middle-class backgrounds to participate willingly, and apparently eagerly, in the national war effort. A biography like this, with no personal papers or recollections to draw on – written from the outside in rather than from the inside out – can hope only to come to conclusions that are speculative rather than definitive, preliminary rather than conclusive. We will restrict ourselves therefore to two deceptively simple questions. Why did Gerald Howard-Smith volunteer? And why did he volunteer in September 1914, rather than earlier or later?

Why did Gerald volunteer? If one goes along with much of the existing literature, this may seem an obvious question with an obvious answer. His decision to enlist, one would think, was virtually preordained: force-fed a diet of military, nationalistic and imperialist propaganda at prep school and public school, Gerald (and those like him) flocked to the colours in a blaze of innocent, unthinking enthusiasm. The public schools of England, claims Niall Ferguson, inculcated precisely the right qualities for war: 'loyalty, honour, chivalry, Christianity, patriotism, sportsmanship and leadership. Eton, Winchester, Harrow, Shrewsbury: these were the gateways to the trenches in 1914–15'.[14]

There were other aspects, too, of Gerald's background, upbringing and circumstances that may have encouraged him to think of enlisting. He was single, of course, with no wife or children to consider. And although there was no military tradition in the family, he was well off and healthy – and both wealth and health, it has long been suggested, were likely to prove potent recruiting sergeants. So although the better off had more to lose than the poor by volunteering, they and their families had greater resources on which to fall back.[15] Bigger, stronger and taller than those from the working class, they usually had no trouble meeting the military's physical requirements. When the war began, the army set a minimum height standard of five feet three inches (1.6 metres), which it raised in September 1914 to five feet six inches (1.68 metres), before returning it two months later to the original five feet three inches. Indeed, the authorities began recruiting 'bantam' units of – predominantly working-class – men who were unable to meet even this seemingly modest height requirement.[16]

As befitted someone from his privileged background, Gerald was a healthy, well-nourished boy and grew into a tall, well-built man. (Public schoolboys in Edwardian Britain were an average five inches (thirteen cm) taller than those attending state schools.)[17] So it was that when Gerald left home for Temple Grove a few months before his tenth birthday, he already weighed five stones four pounds (thirty-four kg) and measured four feet eight inches (1.42 metres) tall.[18] By the time he enlisted in Eton's Officers Training Corps at the age of fifteen, he had leapt up to five feet nine inches (1.75 metres) tall.[19] With several years further growth ahead of him, he was already six inches beyond the minimum height standard that many working-class men, even when fully grown, struggled to meet at the outset of the war.[20]

Gerald's physical advantages were reinforced, we can be sure, by his fitness and enthusiasm for sport. An outstanding athlete, a keen footballer and a fine cricketer, he continued to compete long after many of his contemporaries had abandoned such activities for more sedentary interests. Training may have been lax by modern standards, but he continued to compete at a high level, turning out for the London Athletic Club when he was in his mid-twenties and playing football for the Old Etonians until he was nearer to thirty. Cricket, of course, was less physically demanding than football and athletics and Gerald was selected to represent Staffordshire when he was thirty years old, and made captain of Wolverhampton Cricket Club two years later at the age of thirty-two.

It was not just those with a vested interest in public school education and military training who saw benefits in competitive sport. The *Cambridge Chronicle* was confident, it will be recalled, that 'Men trained in the athletics field can be turned into first class soldiers in a much shorter time than those whose nerves and sinews have not been hardened by constant and regulated practice.'[21] Even those critical of professional football's refusal to shut down when war was declared paid lip service, if nothing else, to the role that the sport played in fostering physical capability. 'Football is an excellent thing, even in time of war', stressed the historian A.F. Pollard in November 1914. 'Armies and navies can only be maintained so long as the community fulfils its function of producing the means for their support; and healthy recreation is essential for efficient production.'[22]

Gerald's social and educational background set him apart, of course, from the vast majority of footballers in the country. It may also have encouraged him to look less askance than most of his fellow players at the possibly of enlistment. Whether or not he had been subjected to torrents of patriotic propaganda from his schoolmasters and tutors, Temple Grove, Eton and Cambridge must inevitably have left their mark. His years of boarding meant that he was used to living away from home, was familiar with coping in all-male environments, and was accustomed to negotiating his way through rigidly hierarchical structures.[23]

His two or three years as a member of the Eton Officers Training Corps meant too that he had been introduced to the rudiments at least of military discipline, tactics and leadership.[24] Perhaps also, however, it had given him an unrealistically optimistic picture of what an officer's life might be like. The 'young Eton Volunteers go to Camp', observed a correspondent to the *Eton College Chronicle* during the time that Gerald was a cadet, 'and are supposed to be going to rough it, but yet, as I am told by a friend who was there, they have seven course dinners, and everything else on the same scale'.[25]

Whatever Gerald's privileged background, whatever his physical attributes, whatever he had been taught at school and whatever he had been led to believe about military life, there was certainly great pressure on him – as on millions of others – to enlist in the late summer and autumn of 1914.[26] These responsible for recruiting made explicit efforts to target the middle class as

102   *Sacrifice*

well as the working class. In London, Sir Henry Rawlinson met Major the Hon. Robert White at the Travellers' Club in Pall Mall to ask him to collect the names and addresses of the 'many City employees who would be willing to enlist if they were assured that they would serve with their friends'. In Bristol, the chairman of the city's Citizens' Recruiting Committee drew up a form 'in connection with the better class young men ... appertaining to a Citizens' Battalion'.[27]

In Wolverhampton, too, recruiting began immediately war was declared, with volunteers sought for two bodies: the 6th Battalion, South Staffordshire Regiment, a territorial unit which had been in existence since 1908; and the 3rd (Reserve) Battalion, South Staffordshire Regiment, a new body whose members would serve in the regular army.[28] Recruiting began, barely a week into the war, with a well-attended meeting at Wolverhampton drill hall. When one of the speakers stressed that he 'appealed not only to the working classes, it was not a time when there should be any distinction between rich and poor', his words, it was noted, were met with cheers.[29] The campaign conducted over the following few weeks continued to concentrate, in part at least, on attracting middle-class support. The *Express and Star* announced the formation at the end of August of 'special service companies' of the 6th Battalion, South Staffordshire Regiment that were designed to accommodate recruits from clerical and professional backgrounds.[30] A number of meetings were organised: one early in September targeted former pupils of Wolverhampton Grammar School and the town's private Tettenhall College.[31] Another, held a few days later and addressed by the headmasters of both schools, was attended, it was reported, by more than one hundred ex-public school boys.[32]

There is no knowing, of course, the impact that such appeals had on Gerald. But nationally they provoked an astonishing response. Enthusiasm was at its height, perhaps not surprisingly, during late August and early September.[33] Whatever caveats one enters, the recruitment figures were extraordinary. Within eight or nine weeks of the declaration of hostilities, more than three-quarters of a million – *three-quarters of a million* – men had volunteered to serve either in the regular army (including the New Army) or in the Territorials. Over 298,000 took the oath of allegiance in August; another 462,000 did so in September.[34] It was the beginning, as W.J. Reader reminds us, of 'one of the most extraordinary mass movements in history: the surge of volunteers – more than 2½ million – into the British army during the first sixteen months of the Great War'.[35]

In Staffordshire, as in the rest of the country, the campaigns to recruit the middle class (along with the upper middle class and the aristocracy) had their effect. A meeting held at Wolverhampton town hall in the middle of August produced thirty to forty applications from men seeking commissions – including one from the son of Lord Lichfield and another from the second son of Lord Dartmouth, scions of two of the most influential families in the area.[36] A couple of weeks later, the first contingent of 'non-manuals' recruited for the new territorial 'special service companies' paraded outside the offices of the

Express and Star, before marching to the town hall to be medically examined and attested.[37] 'Non-manual Workers Answer the Roll Call', ran the paper's predictably patriotic headline.[38] This was far from mere hyperbole. According to the historian of volunteering in the county, 'the specific targeting of middle class recruits to enlist in separate companies within the battalions' was one 'notable recruiting initiative that was to benefit the Territorial Force infantry units in Staffordshire'.[39] Wolverhampton's clerical, non-manual workers and professional men – its middle and upper middle classes – responded eagerly, a good number of them, to the call to arms in August and early September 1914.[40]

Gerald volunteered too, but probably not until the middle of September. Although his commission was announced in the *London Gazette* on 9 October, this does not tell us when he enlisted.[41] Territorial commanders retained considerable discretion over the appointment of officers: securing a commission, points out Keith Simpson, 'was something of an uncertain business, with qualifications, luck and influence all playing a part'.[42] The poet Robert Graves recalls the way in which he was recruited: 'The Harlech golf club secretary suggested my taking a commission instead of enlisting. He rang up the nearest regimental depôt – the Royal Welch Fusiliers at Wrexham – and told the adjutant that I had served in the Officers Training Corps at Charterhouse. The adjutant said: 'Send him right along.'[43]

Commanders exercised significant autonomy, too, in the matter of how much training potential officers should receive between enlisting and being awarded their commissions.[44] It was a process which, until it was regularised in 1916, normally seems to have taken some three to four weeks when joining the territorials.[45] If we err on the side of caution and assume that Gerald's elite education, military training and social standing did nothing to expedite his progress through the system, we are left with the conclusion that he probably enlisted in the middle, or perhaps towards the end, of September.

If this calculation is correct, Gerald enlisted six weeks or more after war broke out, six weeks or more into the barrage of pro-war propaganda that was directed at those wondering whether or not to join up. Why then did he not volunteer sooner? Why was he less patriotic and committed than some of his contemporaries? Or to put it the other way round, why was he more cautious, sceptical and sensible than other prospective middle- and upper middle-class recruits? Of course, posing the question in either of these ways is to load the dice, to shape the subsequent discussion for or against the stance that Gerald took in the late summer and early autumn of 1914.

It is important to avoid judging Gerald – or anybody else – against some *post-hoc*, idealised standard of thinking and behaviour. This is difficult to do but when it is, it can be seen that there were good reasons why Gerald – and those like him – might decide to enlist in September rather than earlier or later. Motives, no doubt, were mixed, and the reasons individuals gave for their actions likely to be self-serving, confusing and perhaps contradictory. In Gerald's case, we have no direct evidence at all on which to draw. However, it seems likely that age, professional commitments and peer pressure all played a part in his decision to join up when he did. Gerald's age and professional commitments discouraged him perhaps from enlisting immediately war broke out. But as time went by, the pressure exerted by friends, colleagues, acquaintances – and the wider community – built up, one imagines, until it became difficult to ignore.

Age was certainly a factor. Gerald was over thirty-four years old when war broke out. And as we saw in the previous chapter, it was not unusual in the early years of the twentieth century to regard even one's early thirties as marking the onset of middle age.[46] In such a climate, it is scarcely surprising that the government's first appeal for volunteers on 7 August stipulated that recruits should be aged between nineteen and thirty.[47] It was a requirement that was reiterated at the first major recruitment meeting held in Wolverhampton a few days later: men in their thirties, it was made clear, were too old to serve.[48] Indeed, it was felt well into the war that there were plenty of young 'slackers' loafing around on the home front who should do their bit before calling on those who were in their thirties and forties.[49]

Important, too, was the fact that Gerald had business to attend to.[50] The 'very first rush of recruits', notes DeGroot, 'was dominated by the sort who had always volunteered for the army, namely the young, unskilled, unemployed and desperate'.[51] Gerald, of course, was neither young, nor unskilled; neither unemployed nor desperate. He was thirty-four years old and he had responsibilities. Although he had no wife or children to support, he was a partner in one of Wolverhampton's leading legal practices: his former principal James E. Underhill was now eighty years old and one of the other partners in the firm was in his very late sixties.[52] It was easy, no doubt, for someone in Gerald's position to believe – or to persuade himself – that he was irreplaceable, that his business and career would suffer irretrievably were he to abandon them. It was a view for which some contemporaries expressed a surprising amount of understanding. 'Although never stated explicitly', concludes Ugolini, 'it is clear that such sympathy applied to middle-class businesses and careers, rather than to working-class trades or job prospects.'[53]

Whatever sympathy there was for those with work (and domestic) commitments, the pressure to enlist intensified during the late summer and autumn of 1914. Gerald, like everybody else, would be aware of the news from France, the claims that the British were heavily outnumbered and suffering severe losses.[54] He would be aware, too, of the successful efforts being made to enrol middle- and upper middle-class recruits. The meeting held at Wolverhampton town hall in the middle of August resulted, it will be recalled, in thirty to forty of those present applying for commissions. By the end of the month, we have seen, the 3rd (Reserve) Battalion, South Staffordshire Regiment had acquired a complement of twenty-four officers; and a week or so later, Wolverhampton's 'non-manual' workers were marching off to join the special units attached to the 6th Battalion, South Staffordshire Regiment.

Some idea of the pressure placed on professional men like Gerald in the summer and autumn of 1914 can be gleaned from the memoirs of Philip

Class, patriotism and preparation 105

Highfield-Jones. A trainee solicitor in Wolverhampton when war broke out, he became an officer in the 6th Battalion. Seconded to recruiting duties in the town centre, he was well placed to judge contemporary attitudes towards the war. Looking back later, Highfield-Jones was surprised at his – and his contemporaries' – decision to enlist:

> From the first day of the war, people who considered themselves fit (mentally) began to try and get commissions. I have often wondered why people went into the Army. Just a few, I suppose, went in because they liked excitement. I believe that the majority of officers, at any rate, went in because it was the thing to do. I am afraid that was my reason.[55]

Whether or not it was the thing to do to enlist, it was certainly the thing to do for men like Gerald to apply for a commission. And as we have seen, it was not difficult for someone with his upbringing, education and connections to get what he wanted. Gerald and the commanding officer of the 6th Battalion, South Staffordshire Regiment, Lieutenant-Colonel Thomas Francis Waterhouse, moved in the same sorts of circle. Both were Wolverhampton solicitors; and both were members of the South Staffordshire Golf Club, where Gerald had become involved in shaping policy towards Sunday opening and Thomas had served a term as honorary secretary.[56] In the unlikely event that Gerald and his prospective commanding officer did not know each other personally, they knew some of the same people and must have known about the other's existence.[57]

Whatever the balance of birth and breeding, education and experience in the army's procedures, Gerald's application was accepted. His commission as a second lieutenant in the 6th Battalion, South Staffordshire Regiment was announced, with due solemnity, in the *London Gazette* on 9 October 1914. The entry detailing his appointment drew attention, in just a few words, both to his privileged background and to his military experience (such as it was): 'Gerald Howard Smith (late Cadet Lance-Serjeant, Eton College Contingent, Junior Division, Officers Training Corps).'[58]

The 6th Battalion, South Staffordshire Regiment was a territorial unit and the territorials, like their predecessors the Volunteers, drew heavily on local ties and local loyalties.[59] Although Gerald had lived in the West Midlands for fewer than ten years, he had integrated successfully, we have seen, into local legal, sporting (and, no doubt, social) circles. It is no surprise then that Gerald, along with a number of other ex-public schoolboys, local solicitors, golfing enthusiasts and teammates from Wolverhampton Cricket Club, joined the 6th Battalion. Gerald was one of six second lieutenants whose commissions to the 6th Battalion were announced in the *London Gazette* on 9 October.[60] Two of the six (Gerald and Herbert Leslie Graham) were Old Etonians, one (Arthur Richard Anson Dickins) had been to Shrewsbury School and one (Howard Vivian Mander) had recently left Wellington College.[61] Of the other two, one (Harold Bantock Sankey) had been Cadet Colour-Sergeant at

Wolverhampton Grammar School, and one (Arthur Cyril Finnis) had played alongside Gerald in the first team at Wolverhampton Cricket Club.[62]

We will never know for sure whether Gerald, Herbert, the two Arthurs and the two Harolds volunteered to fight from patriotic conviction, from a desire for excitement, from a feeling that it was the thing to do – or from a mixture of all three motives. Whatever their reasons, they chose to enlist at the same time, to apply for commissions at the same time and, quite possibly, to apply for commissions in the same regiment. Moving in the same, or similar, professional, sporting and social circles before the war, they found, we shall see, that these overlapping ties, contacts, and friendships were to serve them well in the years ahead.

The demands of war

What then of the idea that once enlisted, Gerald and men like him coped better than those from other classes with the demands of war – not to mention the demands of the army? It is claim that has a good deal to commend it. This, it must be stressed, is not because of any innate superiority on the part of the officer class, but because of the way in which Gerald and those like him had been brought up. Gerald's background meant that he, like many of his fellow officers, was used to living away from home, was familiar with hierarchical, all-male organisations and had been introduced to the rudiments at least of military discipline and training.

The trouble is that in assessing how Gerald and those like him coped once they had enlisted, we are forced to rely heavily – much too heavily – on a single source, *The War History of the Sixth Battalion the South Staffordshire Regiment*. Published in 1924 by 'A Committee of Officers who Served in the Battalion', it has the merits and demerits one would expect of volume of its type.[63] Fortunately, however, it is more revealing than either its title suggests or its compilers probably realised. Although never reluctant to stress the courage and resilience of the officer class who put it together, the *War History* exposes – seemingly unselfconsciously – a sense of the elitist atmosphere that Gerald and the others managed to preserve both in training and in combat. It supports the view that Gerald and those like him were able to recreate in the officers' mess, as they had in their colleges and sports clubs, something of the separate, enclosed boarding school and university world in which many of them had been brought up.[64]

It will be suggested more specifically that Gerald and his fellow officers were men who knew how to make the best of things.[65] So although they probably found the time they spent training in England during the autumn and winter of 1914–15 both physically demanding and emotionally draining, they dealt well, it seems, with the changes and adjustments that their new regime demanded. It was a transition that was eased, no doubt, by the fact that the army permitted, in fact encouraged, the officers' mess to maintain the social distance and many of the social distinctions with which its members were familiar.

By the time Gerald was commissioned in October 1914, the war was two months old and the 6th Battalion, South Staffordshire Regiment had begun to get itself onto a war footing. After cutting short its annual training in Wales when war was declared and returning to Wolverhampton, it moved, via Burton-on-Trent and Bishops Stortford, to Luton which it reached in the middle of August.[66] Joining up with troops from Derbyshire, Leicestershire, Lincolnshire and Nottinghamshire to form the 46th (North Midland) Division, the Battalion, along with the other territorial units in the town, took on two major responsibilities: guarding the northern outskirts of London from enemy attack; and completing the training that was deemed necessary before they could be posted to France.[67]

Although the 6th Battalion was settled in Luton with a full complement of a thousand or so men (commanded by twenty to thirty officers),[68] there was, inevitably perhaps, something of the phony war about the Battalion's preparations during the course of August and September.[69] However, by the time Gerald was commissioned in early October, the training was becoming more serious, the emotional and physical demands it placed on the Battalion more taxing and unsettling.[70] It was at the end of October, for instance, that Gerald made his will (leaving everything that he had to his brother Charles).[71]

It was in October, too, that officers and men were pitched into a challenging round of training activities. Whether the weather was good or bad, whether or not they had the equipment they needed, the members of the Battalion took part in drills and inspections, field days and physical training, route marches and trench digging, mock battles and musketry instruction.[72] The *Luton News* was impressed, noting admiringly in the middle of the month that the troops based in and around the town were put to three days 'of very hard work' digging trenches; they then bivouacked overnight, before getting up after 'only a few hours sleep' in order to take part in 'a big battle at dawn'.[73]

A month later, the Battalion was on the move. After marching the twenty miles or so from Luton to Hertford, it set off the next day for Bishops Stortford, a further fifteen or so miles.[74] The 6th Battalion was part of a much larger military influx, an incursion which saw a market town of 7,000 people double in size in just forty-eight hours. As might be expected, the authorities, both military and civil, struggled to keep control of the situation. There was discipline to maintain, buildings to commandeer, billets to arrange, leisure activities and sanitary provision to see to.[75] Washing facilities, for instance, were in desperately short supply. The very least that was needed, suggested Bishop Stortford's highways and sanitary committee, were four new baths, a boiler, a twenty-gallon cold water tank and a one hundred and thirty-gallon hot-water tank.[76]

The autumn and winter of 1914–15 continued to be emotionally as well as physically draining. The Battalion faced constant uncertainty as to what they would be doing next, where they would be going next. Although it did not leave for France until the following March, there was no shortage of rumours:

> You want to know what is to become of us? I will tell you, on absolutely reliable information. We are going to Cherbourg, to stand by as a reserve force; to Paris, to act as a protection against surprise attacks; to Ostend, to relieve the casino; to Antwerp, to resist the Zeppelins; to the French frontier, to guard lines of communication; to Leicester to guard German prisoners.[77]

On one occasion at least, the rumours appeared to have a solid basis in fact. A conference of senior North Midland Division officers was told in the middle of October to prepare to sail for France at the end of the month.[78] Officers and men went home on special leave, they were made a fuss off, they said their farewells. Then the next weekend, they were back home again on leave.[79]

Unsettling, too, was the upheaval of relocating from base to base. In August alone, the Battalion visited, sometimes very briefly, Luton, Hertford and Burton-on-Trent. It was on the move again at the beginning of December, this time leaving Bishops Stortford for nearby Saffron Walden, where it was to remain until it left England early the following March. As they moved from place to place, Gerald and the other officers found themselves billeted in halls and a school or, when they first arrived in Luton, in the town baths (until they were 'removed by the Public Authorities').[80] Saffron Walden was not much liked. It was a town, recalled a private from London, whose inhabitants 'were mostly Quakers, who kept their daughters out of sight. We hardly saw a young girl all the time we were there.'[81] Christmas Day was particularly dispiriting. Clustered around their schoolroom's 'old Yule Hot-Water Pipe', the Battalion's officers spent the afternoon either asleep, daydreaming, darning socks or, in the case of the commanding officer, sitting at the bridge table 'in an authoritative, relentless silence'.[82]

One feature of the Battalion's training that made a particular impression was the sight of officers working alongside other ranks in tasks that, in other circumstances, they would never have considered undertaking. So when the *Luton News* published its report of trench digging training in the middle of October, it was taken aback not just by what the officers were doing but also by their apparent acquiescence – and even satisfaction – in what was being asked of them:

> [I]t was a very interesting sight to see the officers as well as the men with their tunics off and shirt sleeves rolled up, slogging away at the job for all they were worth. Many a smooth palm became rough and sore during the making of these trenches, but afterwards the hands were regarded as something worth showing – and so they were.[83]

Although such challenges to traditional class roles obviously raised a number of unsettling questions, and although the territorials enjoyed a reputation for relatively relaxed relations between officers and men,[84] class boundaries were maintained tightly and rigidly. This was made easier, of course, by the homogeneity of the mess that Gerald joined.[85] With work, sporting and social ties in Wolverhampton overlapping as closely as they did, he already knew some of his fellow officers very well indeed. Edward Arthur Cresswell, for example, not only worked with Gerald at Underhill, Thorneycroft and Smith but was also match secretary at South Staffordshire Golf Club, in whose affairs, we have seen, Gerald took an increasing interest.[86] Edwin Read Collinson had been articled, like Gerald, at Underhill, Thorneycroft and Smith and was, again like Gerald, one of the leading figures at Wolverhampton Cricket Club.[87]

Other members of the mess shared Gerald's love of the game: aside from Arthur Finnis who had been commissioned with Gerald, four others, Percival Samuel Bayliss, Clifford Howl and Harold Aston Page, had been playing alongside Gerald for the Wolverhampton first eleven just a few short months before.[88] Indeed, it turns out that at least two of the Battalion's thirty-one officers in November 1914 were solicitors in Wolverhampton; that at least three (including their commanding officer Lieutenant-Colonel Waterhouse) were members of South Staffordshire Golf Club; and that at least seven were members of Wolverhampton Cricket Club.[89]

Gerald and his fellow officers managed to recreate in their mess some elements of the world that they had been able to take for granted just a few short months before. Officers, it goes without saying, ate, slept and socialised separately from the men they commanded. They dressed the part: even though they never knew how long they would be staying in a particular place, some members of the mess continued to buy their clothes on credit from specialist tailors in the time-honoured middle- and upper middle-class fashion.[90] When the Battalion left Luton in November, the *War History* reveals, 'the local tailor was up and about before dawn, collecting his unpaid accounts'.[91]

The officers' efforts to replicate the comforts and pleasures they had known before the war were helped, of course, by the hierarchical structure of the army, by the fact that they had servants to look after them.[92] This right to a servant set officers and other ranks sharply apart. It is an issue that raises strong feelings, an issue that many of us have been introduced to, for better or worse, by the television series *Blackadder Goes Forth*.[93] The scholarly consensus suggests, not surprisingly, that at their best, relationships between officers and servants replicated the intimacy and mutual respect that sometimes existed between masters and men before the war at home or in the club. At their worst, they degenerated into friction and resentment, cruelty and bullying, insolence and insubordination.[94]

It was easiest, it has been said, for men like Gerald. Used to dealing with servants, they felt comfortable with them, knew what was expected and so got the best out of the relationship.[95] Insofar as one can judge from the history of the 6th Battalion, Gerald and his fellow officers either took their servants for granted or regarded them – at least after the war had ended – with paternalistic affection/appreciation.[96] Individual servants were picked out for particular mention. Gerald's batman, Private Keene, noted the *War History*, acquired a certain reputation.[97] So, too, did 'Private Bould, who, in pre-war days, had been familiar to many of us as a billiard marker at the Wolverhampton Conservative Club, and whose war record is largely associated with the Hqrs. Mess, of which he was corporal'.[98]

110   *Sacrifice*

This combination of class awareness and class superiority permeated the Battalion's *War History*. The officers who put the volume together could not but be aware of their class identity and class advantages.[99] They noted that the 6th Battalion's recruits came 'from all classes' of society.[100] They recognised that some working-class recruits brought with them skills and qualities that proved of immense value to the war effort. Sergeant W. Postance was one such: 'In civil life', the *War History*, reported, 'he had been a first-class artisan, employed by the Sunbeam Motor Company, Limited, in their Wolverhampton works. His efficiency was always equalled by his industry, and probably he knew as much as any man, eventually, of the improving and constructing of "dug-outs," as well as in the front as elsewhere.'[101]

The officers compiling the *War History* were struck particularly forcibly by the linguistic indicators of class, by how differently the middle-class and working-class members of the Battalion expressed themselves. Attempting to reproduce what they heard when they listened to their Black Country subordinates, they resorted to what sounds suspiciously like cod Cockney.[102]

> Thus, among the good old 'B' Company type you will hear: "Ere Bill, where's me pull-through?' 'I ain't seen your ruddy pull-through.' 'You'm a liar: you've bin and took it.' 'Get off with yer, I ain't. If yer want a ruddy pull-through, why don't yer pinch Joe's ruddy Pull-through? 'E's away on guard.'[103]

Meanwhile, according to the *War History*, in 'H' Company, the home of the 'non-manuals', the language – and the morals – were strikingly different:

> 'Angus, have you seen my pull-through anywhere?' 'No, Gerald, I have not.' 'You are sure you haven't taken it by mistake?' 'I assure you I have not. But if you want a pull-through, I am sure Clement would not mind your borrowing his temporarily.'[104]

Ready to fight

By the time the Battalion set sail for France in March 1915, it was ready, the *War History* was sure – or affected to be sure – for anything that it might face in the months and years ahead. Whatever their class backgrounds, whatever their reasons for enlisting, however quickly or slowly they adapted to the demands of military life, the officers and men of the 6th Battalion, South Staffordshire Regiment had been moulded, we are assured, into a cohesive and committed fighting force.

> The Battalion was very different from the one that marched forth from Wolverhampton, in August, or even from Luton, in November, 1914. The unit that entrained on 1 March at Audley End station for Southampton was no territorial 'lot' going to camp, but a quasi-regular Battalion 'proceeding' to destination.[105]

Notes

1. Anthony Seldon and David Walsh, *Public Schools and the Great War: The Generation Lost* (Barnsley: Pen & Sword, 2013), p. 1. Also Ian Beckett, 'The Nation in Arms, 1914–18', in Ian F.W. Beckett and Keith Simpson (eds), *A Nation in Arms: A Social Study of the British Army in the First World War* (London: Tom Donovan, 1990), p. 27.
2. J.M. Winter, 'Britain's "Lost Generation" of the First World War', *Population Studies*, 31, 3, 1977, p. 449. Also J.M. Winter, *The Great War and the British People* (London: Macmillan, 1985).
3. Seldon and Walsh, *Public Schools*, p. 234.
4. Peter Clarke, *Hope and Glory: Britain 1900–1990* (London: Penguin, 1996), pp. 80–81.
5. J.M. Winter's analyses of the class distribution of military mortality remain essential reading. See Winter, 'Lost Generation'; J.M. Winter, *Great War*; J.M. Winter, 'Some Aspects of the Demographic Consequences of the First World War in Britain', *Population Studies*, 30, 3, 1976.
6. Seldon and Walsh, *Public Schools*, p. 238.
7. A.J.P. Taylor, *English History 1914–1945* (London: Penguin, 1975 edition), p. 165.
8. Seldon and Walsh, *Public Schools*, p. 245.
9. Seldon and Walsh, *Public Schools*, p. 1.
10. Gary Sheffield reminds me that after the introduction of conscription, the middle and upper middle class were also more likely to be called up than working-class men in key industries.
11. Seldon and Walsh, *Public Schools*, pp. 238–9.
12. W.J. Reader, *At Duty's Call: A Study in Obsolete Patriotism* (Manchester: Manchester University Press, 1988), p. 2. See, too, Richard Holmes, *Tommy: The British Soldier on the Western Front 1914–1918* (London: HarperCollins, 2004), p. 89; Peter Simkins, *Kitchener's Army: The Raising of the New Armies 1914–1916* (Barnsley: Pen & Sword, 2014), part 1.
13. Gerard J. DeGroot, *Blighty: British Society in the Era of the Great War* (London: Longman, 1996), pp. 43–4.
14. Niall Ferguson, *The Pity of War* (London: Penguin, 1998), p. 201. See too DeGroot, *Blighty*, pp. 44–6; Winter, 'Lost Generation', pp. 449–50; John M. Mackenzie (ed.), *Imperialism and Popular Culture* (Manchester: Manchester University Press, 1986); Laura Ugolini, *Civvies: Middle-Class Men on the English Home Front, 1914–18* (Manchester: Manchester University Press, 2013), p.124.
15. Helen Jones, *Health and Society in Twentieth-Century Britain* (London: Longman, 1994), p. 50.
16. DeGroot, *Blighty*, p. 46. See Norman Brooke, *Half-Pint Heroes: The Bantams of World War One* (London: Janus Publishing, 2002).
17. John Lewis-Stempel, *Six Weeks: The Short and Gallant Life of the British Officer in the First World War* (London: Orion, 2010), p. 14.
18. East Sussex Record Office, Temple Grove School, TGS2/2/2, Admissions Book.
19. Eton College Archives, SCH/CCF/2/2, Eton College Officers Training Corps, Corps Records, 1895.
20. See E.M.R. Clements, 'Changes in the Mean Structure and Weight of British Children over the Past Seventy Years', *British Medical Journal*, October 24, 1953.
21. *Cambridge Chronicle*, April 6, 1900.
22. Tony Mason, *Association Football & English Society 1863–1915* (Brighton: Harvester, 1981), p. 251.
23. See, for example, Hamish Telfer, 'Luddism, Laughter and Liquor: Homosocial Behaviour in Late- Victorian Scottish Harriers Clubs', in Mike Huggins and

112 *Sacrifice*

      J.A. Mangan (eds), *Disreputable Pleasures: Less Virtuous Victorians at Play* (London: Cass, 2004).
24 See G.D. Sheffield, *Leadership in the Trenches: Officer-Man Relations, Morale and Discipline in the Era of the First World War* (London: Macmillan, 2000), pp. 34–7.
25 'One Who Would Have Come', to *Eton College Chronicle*, October 10, 1896. See also L.S.R. Byrne and E.L. Churchill, *Changing Eton: A Survey of Conditions based on the History of Eton since the Royal Commission of 1862–64* (London: Cape, 1937), pp. 220–24. For the effectiveness generally of the Officers' Training Corps, see Sheffield, *Leadership*, pp. 35–7; Seldon and Walsh, *Public Schools*, pp. 24–7.
26 Wolverhampton Archives, MISC/18, 'Recruiting Committee Minute Book No. 1', 1914–15.
27 Simkins, *Kitchener's Army*, p. 83.
28 *Wolverhampton Chronicle*, August 12, 26, 1914.
29 *Wolverhampton Chronicle*, August 12, 1914. See Andrew Thornton, 'Recruiting for the Territorial Force in Staffordshire, August 1914–December 1915', *Journal of the Centre for First World War Studies*, 1, 2, 2004, pp. 5–6.
30 Thornton, 'Recruiting', p. 16.
31 *Wolverhampton Chronicle*, September 9, 1914.
32 *Wolverhampton Chronicle*, September 16, 1914. Also August 19, 1914.
33 Simkins, *Kitchener's Army*, p. 104.
34 Reader, *At Duty's Call*, p. 107; Beckett, 'Nation in Arms', p. 8.
35 Reader, *At Duty's Call*, p. viii. See *Wolverhampton Chronicle*, August 26, 1914.
36 *Wolverhampton Chronicle*, August 12, 1914.
37 Thornton, 'Recruiting', p. 16.
38 *Wolverhampton Chronicle*, September 9, 1914. See Committee of Officers, *War History*, p. 7.
39 A. Thornton, 'The Territorial Force in Staffordshire 1908–1915' (MPhil thesis, University of Birmingham, 2004), p. 81.
40 R.D. Williams, 'A Social and Military History of the 1/8th Battalion, the Royal Warwickshire Regiment in the Great War' (MPhil thesis, University of Birmingham, 1999).
41 *London Gazette*, October 9, 1914.
42 Keith Simpson, 'The Officers', in Beckett and Simpson, *A Nation in Arms*, p. 73.
43 Robert Graves, *Goodbye to All That* (London: Penguin, 1960), p. 62.
44 Simkins, *Kitchener's Army*, pp. 222–5.
45 Information from Spencer Jones; Sheffield, *Leadership*, pp. 34–40, 53.
46 John Benson, *Prime Time: A History of the Middle Aged in Twentieth-Century Britain* (London: Longman, 1997), p. 9.
47 Reader, *At Duty's Call*, p. 105.
48 *Wolverhampton Chronicle*, August 12, 1914. The age was raised to forty in the spring of 1915.
49 Ugolini, *Civvies*, p. 110.
50 Simkins, *Kitchener's Army*, p. 170.
51 DeGroot, *Blighty*, p. 47.
52 Census of England and Wales 1911, RG11/2788/60/15; RG14/17002/10/50.
53 Ugolini, *Civvies*, p. 135.
54 I am grateful to Spencer Jones for his advice on this aspect of recruitment. See Denis Winter, *Haig's Command: A Reassessment* (London: Penguin, 1992), pp. 34–5; Simkins, *Kitchener's Army*, p. 171.
55 Cited in Thornton, 'Territorial Force', p. 99. Also Graves, *Goodbye*, p. 62; Thornton, 'Recruiting', pp. 13–14.
56 www.southstaffordshire.csiwebsites.com/Page.aspx?pid=25577 [November 2014]; Census of England and Wales, 1911, RG14/17007/10/50.

Class, patriotism and preparation 113

57 Both featured regularly in the pages of the local press.
58 *London Gazette*, October 9, 1914.
59 Reader, *Duty's Call*, p. 81; Thornton, 'Volunteer Force', p. 48; K.W. Mitchinson, *The Territorial Force at War, 1914–1916* (London: Palgrave Macmillan, 2014), p. 197.
60 *London Gazette*, October 9, 1914. See Percy Hurd, *The Fighting Territorials*, vol. 2 (London: Country Life and George Newnes, 1915), pp. 9–10.
61 *London Gazette*, October 9, 1914; www.cricketarchive.com/Archive/Players/249/249260.html [September 2014].
62 *London Gazette*, October 9, 1914; John Benson, 'Sport, Class and Place: Gerald Howard-Smith and Early Twentieth-Century Wolverhampton', *Midland History*, 37, 2, 2012, p. 220.
63 See Tim Cook, '"Literary Memorials": The Great War Regimental Histories, 1919–1939', *Journal of the Canadian Historical Association*, 13, 1, 2002.
64 Holmes, *Tommy*, pp. 356–62; Mitchison, *Territorial Force*, pp. 7–8.
65 See, for instance, Michael Roper, *The Secret Battle: Emotional Survival in the Great War* (Manchester: Manchester University Press, 2010).
66 See, for example, *Express and Star*, September 12, 1914; David Clare, Carolyn Downing and Sarah Turner, *Bishop's Stortford in the First World War* (Stroud: Amberley Publishing, 2014), ch. 5.
67 www.1914–1918.invisionzone.com/forums/index.php?showtopic=35410 [November 2014]; R.E. Priestley, *Breaking the Hindenberg Line: The Story of the 46th (North Midland) Division* (London: Fisher & Unwin, 1919); Mitchison, *Territorial Force*, p. 194.
68 A Committee of Officers who Served with the Battalion, *The War History of the Sixth Battalion the South Staffordshire Regiment* (London: Heinemann, 1924), p. 8.
69 See, for instance, *Luton News*, August 20, 24, 1914.
70 Committee of Officers, *War History*, pp. 1–2.
71 Wills and Administrations, 1916, p. 260.
72 Staffordshire Regiment Museum, 5575 (31/6163); 'Battalion War Diary', February 1915; Committee of Officers, *War History*, pp. 3–20. See also W.C.C. Weetman, *The Sherwood Foresters in the Great War 1914–1919 1/8th Battalion* (Nottingham: Thos. Formand & Sons, 1920).
73 *Luton Times*, October 15, 1914.
74 Committee of Officers, *War History*, p. 10.
75 Simkins, *Kitchener's Army*, pp. 198–207.
76 Clare, Downing and Turner, *Bishops Stortford*, pp. 34–6.
77 Committee of Officers, *War History*, p. 8.
78 www.1914–1918.invisionzone.com [March 2015]; Committee of Officers, *War History*, pp. 14–15.
79 Committee of Officers, *War History*, pp. 14–15.
80 Committee of Officers, *War History*, p. 3.
81 Simkins, *Kitchener's Army*, p. 246.
82 Committee of Officers, *War History*, p. 16.
83 *Luton News*, October 15, 1914.
84 I have discussed this point most helpfully with Gary Sheffield.
85 Keith Simpson, 'The Officers', in Beckett and Simpson (eds), *A Nation in Arms*. See Hurd, *Fighting Territorials*, pp. 9–10; Mitchison, *Territorial Force*, p. 300.
86 Thornton, 'Territorial Force', p. 50.
87 Staffordshire Regiment Museum, Book 59, unattributed press cutting, October 23, 1915.
88 Benson, 'Sport, Class and Place', p. 221.
89 Committee of Officers, *War History*, p. 5. There was also, it will be recalled, 'a large contingent of volunteers from the Wolverhampton Cricket Club, a

magnificent contribution to the ranks, but the devil for officers, some short of experience, to rule'.
90 *Field Service Manual, 1914. Infantry Battalion. (Expeditionary Force.)*. See Laura Ugolini, *Men and Menswear: Sartorial Consumption in Britain 1880–1939* (London: Ashgate, 2007), ch. 3.
91 Committee of Officers, *War History*, p. 10.
92 Sheffield, *Leadership*, pp. 61–2.
93 See, for example, the dispute between Michael Gove, the then Education Secretary, and Tony Robinson, the actor who played Baldrick. *Daily Mail*, January 2; January 6, 2014. Also Gary Sheffield, *The Chief: Douglas Haig and the British Army* (London: Aurum Press, 2011), Introduction.
94 See Holmes, *Tommy*, pp. 359–61.
95 Holmes, *Tommy*, pp. 359–62. See Graves, *Goodbye*, p. 65.
96 Committee of Officers, *War History*, pp. 49, 101, 106; Thornton, 'Volunteer Force', p. 136.
97 Committee of Officers, *War History*, p. 49.
98 Committee of Officers, *War History*, p. 106.
99 John Benson, *Affluence and Authority: A Social History of Twentieth-Century Britain* (London: HodderArnold, 2005), pp. 193–7.
100 Committee of Officers, *War History*, p. 7.
101 Committee of Officers, *War History*, pp. 13–14.
102 This is another point that I owe to Gary Sheffield.
103 A pull-through was part of the equipment used for cleaning rifles.
104 Committee of Officers, *War History*, p. 7.
105 Committee of Officers, *War History*, p. 19.

6 'LARGE, GALLANT, AND LOOSE-LIMBED': CLASS, PATRIOTISM AND SACRIFICE

Hopes and plans

The past, of course, is not necessarily a guide to the future. So the fact that Gerald Howard-Smith and his fellow officers managed to maintain their class privileges while training in England does not mean that they would be able to do so when the Battalion finished its preparations, moved to France and was sent to the frontline. Indeed, there are good reasons for supposing that they would find it extremely difficult to do so. Whatever the strength of Gerald's and his colleagues' class awareness, class isolation and sense of class superiority, they were bound to disintegrate, one would have thought, amid the carnage of war. Once at the front, the members of the Battalion would surely all be in it together, would surely all be confronted, whoever they were, by the misery, the indignities, the horrors of trench warfare.

It has been suggested, after all, that one of the few redeeming features of the First World War was its loosening of social barriers. 'During the war years', explains Gary Sheffield, 'there was much talk among civilians about the positive effects of war service on social cohesion. In 1916 the Bishop of London spoke of a "brotherhood" being "forged of blood and iron" in the trenches, which should be maintained into peacetime thus ending the class war between "Hoxton" and "Belgravia".'[1]

There is also the impact that the war, it is believed, had on 'one-nation' Conservative politicians such as Anthony Eden and Harold Macmillan. It has been said indeed that the events of 1914–18 were to influence British prime ministers for getting on for three-quarters of a century.[2] Macmillan, for example, believed that, in his case, the major legacy of the war was the increased understanding that it gave him about the lives of those from backgrounds different from, and much less privileged than, his own. It was an understanding that proved, it has been claimed, of national, as well as personal, significance, informing in particular Macmillan's commitment to tackling the unemployment of the inter-war years.[3]

It is a reassuring argument. By providing the hope that good can come from evil, that unintended consequences can be benign as well as malignant, it enables us to hang onto the idea that the slaughter of the Western Front

116 *Sacrifice*

was not in vain. Certainly, by the end of the war, there was a widespread commitment to building a better and more equal society. As the war cabinet had commented when the Ministry of Reconstruction was established in 1917, it was 'not so much a question of rebuilding society as it was before the war, but of moulding a better world out of the social and economic conditions which have come into being during the war.'[4] Old Etonian Gilbert Frankau put such contemporary hopes for a less class-bound future into verse:

> And this England they saved shall endure,
>
> She shall neither dwindle nor pass,
>
> Her feet shall be virile and pure;
>
> She shall stamp on the creed impure –
>
> The creed of class-against-class.[5]

Reassuring though such hopes and plans may have been, were they anything more than empty rhetoric? Did they ever amount to anything? Can it really be shown that the shared experience of fighting together against a common enemy changed, or helped to change, the ways in which members of the different classes regarded one another? It is the aim of this chapter, covering the final twelve months of Gerald Howard-Smith's life, to make a contribution to this complex and contentious debate.

It will do so in two stages. The first will attempt to provide a flavour, however partial and inadequate, of what Gerald Howard-Smith went through between leaving England for France in March 1915 and his death almost exactly a year later. This is more difficult than one might think. It is not at all easy to discover precisely where Gerald – or any other individual – was at any given time, what he was doing, what was happening to him. For despite the mass of primary source material and the overwhelming volume of scholarly and popular works on the First World War, it can be frustratingly difficult to move from the general to the particular, to isolate the experiences of any particular combatant. In Gerald's case, one is again forced to rely much more than one would wish on the Battalion's war diary and, as in the previous chapter, on *The War History of the Sixth Battalion the South Staffordshire Regiment*.[6]

The second, more substantial, stage of the process will ask whether the twelve months that Gerald spent in France between March 1915 and March 1916 changed the way in which he and his fellow officers regarded those whom they were commanding. It will begin by considering whether Gerald and his fellow officers wished – and were able – to maintain the class distinctions and class benefits that they had enjoyed while training in England. It will then ask if it is really possible to show that in the short term (never mind the long term), the officer class (never mind the middle and upper middle class as a whole) changed the ways in which it viewed the working-class and lower middle-class men (and women) with whom it came into contact.

Posing the questions to be addressed in such stark terms underlines, of course, the sensitivity and complexity of the task ahead. There are two major constraints. The first is that Gerald died in March 1916, less than halfway through the war, which makes it difficult to use his experiences as a conduit through which to analyse even short-term trends in class identity, class awareness and class consciousness. The second is that he left no personal papers. Although this problem has been pointed out time and again during the course of the book, it bears repeating. It means that the empirical basis for the analysis of this – and many of the other – issues which it addresses can be flimsy in the extreme. The result is that some of the conclusions of a biography like this, written from the outside in rather than from the inside out, are always likely to remain open to refinement and reappraisal.

The Western Front

The 6th Battalion, South Staffordshire Regiment, received its long expected instructions to prepare for mobilisation towards the end of February 1915.[7] This marked the beginning, it hardly needs saying, of a period of profound change and adjustment for Gerald and everybody else connected with the battalion. Twelve months before, Gerald had been a successful provincial solicitor, living with his parents and looking forward, no doubt, to captaining Wolverhampton Cricket Club as it prepared for the forthcoming season. Now in the late winter of 1915, he found himself subject to military discipline, messing with his fellow officers and preparing, not to play cricket, but to fight and perhaps die in the service of his country. Empathy is all very well, but one cannot even begin to put oneself in Gerald's position. It would be impertinent to try to do so.

What one can do is try to plot what happened between Gerald's departure from England and his death a year later. The 6th Battalion's task, along with a number of other territorial divisions, was to reinforce the British Expeditionary Force which had become bogged down on the Western Front (the four hundred-mile line that ran from the Belgian coast down to the Swiss border).[8] Neither Gerald nor those who went to France with him knew it, of course, but the Western Front was to become, and remains to this day, a byword for misery, death and disability. Indeed, it is the costliest theatre of war in which British troops have ever been involved: of the 4 million or so English, Welsh, Scottish and Northern Irish soldiers who fought along it between 1914 and 1918, almost 1¾ million were killed, wounded or reported missing.[9] 'What distinguishes the Western Front', concludes Richard Holmes, 'is its dreadful combination of loss of life, qualitative misery and its sheer, mind-numbing scale, made somehow more strange by its "ridiculous proximity" to Britain'.[10]

It was distinguished too, as Gerald and thousands and thousands others would find out soon enough, by any number of irritations, annoyances and frustrations. Although individually these might be relatively minor, cumulatively they could become highly dispiriting. The delays, for example, began almost as soon as the Battalion left its base at Saffron Walden. Their train journey to Southampton was uneventful, but they were delayed at the coast for twenty-four hours, a hold-up which entailed a 'makeshift sojourn in the town'.[11] Then when one part of the Battalion set sail for France the following day, it had to wait on board ship for 4½ hours before it was able to head out into the Solent.[12] Eventually, after spending time under canvass on the outskirts of Le Havre, the Battalion boarded another train, this time to Nordpeene close to the frontline. Moving at no more than fast walking pace, it took thirty-six hours to travel one hundred and thirty miles – a demoralising average of less than four miles an hour.[13]

The 6th Battalion's experience was not unusual. The journey from training base in England to the frontline in France or Belgium was notoriously slow, frustrating and uncomfortable – an introduction to the realities of war that has been dubbed 'a locomotive and maritime marathon'.[14] There were any number of complaints. 'After two hours in an oily ship and then in a grimy train', claimed an officer from the Suffolk regiment, 'the "war area" was a haven of relief.'[15] Vera Brittain's brother Edward, a lieutenant in the Sherwood Foresters, took fifty-five hours to travel from London to Flanders. And fifty-five hours, he concluded, was 'not bad'.[16]

Fortunately for Gerald and the 6th Battalion, it was army policy to try to bed territorial troops in alongside regular army units before committing them to battle.[17] So unlike some of the units that followed them to France, the Battalion was not involved in any major operation until the autumn of 1915.[18] This, it must be stressed, is in no way to deny the tedium, the fear, the anxiety, the trauma of the following few months. It took another three days, for instance, for the Battalion to move the final thirty miles or so to its base just behind the frontline. The first stretch, a fifteen-mile march from Nordpeene to Borre, proved 'perhaps, one of the most tiring marches the Battalion had ever undertaken'; the second stretch, the fifteen miles from Borre to Sailly-le-Sec, thirty-five miles to the northwest of Paris, proved particularly frustrating. Finishing late at night, it exemplified, it was said, 'all the chaos and discomfort which is inseparable from the process of concentrating a mass of reserves immediately behind the battle line.'[19] They arrived on 11 March 1915, the day after the start of the first major British set-piece attack of the war, the battle of Neuve Chapelle, which took place one hundred and sixty or so miles to the north.[20] The Battalion was both too far south and too obviously inexperienced for it to be thrust into battle at this stage of its preparations.[21]

There was still a great deal to learn, a great deal to get used to. Passing ruined churches and the graves of French and English soldiers, the Battalion marched on in the cold and the dark. 'We were hardened by training', noted the *War History*, 'but new to this sort of thing. By the time the officer had got his dead-beat men nourished and stalled, he was more than dead-beat himself.'[22] Officers and men spent several more weeks undergoing the training

Class, patriotism and sacrifice 119

designed to prepare them for what lay ahead. Their preparations culminated at the end of March when they were sent to Armentières to learn what was involved in occupying a section of the frontline. Deployed alongside regular troops, a little over three hundred metres from the enemy, they were taught, for instance, how to dig and repair trenches, how to carry out wiring and how to conduct listening patrols in 'no-man's land'.[23] This brief period at the front made, as might be expected, an intense impression. 'Every officer and man living today', concluded the *War History*, 'probably remembers with the liveliest gratitude the welcome and care shown by his individual opposite number, the grasp of whose hand, upon arriving out of the endless mud of a pitch dark night into the actual trench, was something sent from God!'[24]

Finally, at the beginning of April, Gerald and the rest of the Battalion were deemed to be ready for action. They recognised the significance of the moment. 'Mobilised for action early in August, 1914', the *War History* reflected, 'the Battalion had arrived – by devious and dilatory ways after many false alarms and excursions – to within three hundred and fifty yards of the enemy.'[25] Although the Germans were in the ascendancy, the Battalion's introduction to the frontline proved relatively benign.[26] Deployed along with the rest of the North Midland Division, they were posted to the Wulverghem sector, a 2,000 metre-long stretch of the line facing the German forces, who were dug in on the Messines Ridge (the scene two years later of a famous British victory).[27]

The intensity of fighting varied from sector to sector and, fortunately for Gerald and the Battalion, Wulverghem enjoyed the reputation of being one of

Figure 6.1 Gerald Howard-Smith (far right) and fellow officers of the 6th Battalion, South Staffordshire Regiment, three miles southeast of Ypres, March 1915. (Reproduced by permission of the Imperial War Museum)

the least dangerous. Alternating four days in the line with four days in 'rest billets' behind them: 'Our formal entry into firing-line business', conceded the *War History*, 'was probably on the comfortable, well-ordered side'.[28] Indeed, they were sent initially not to the trenches but to one of the billets behind the frontline. Bulford Camp, as it was known, 'was not a pretty camp, maybe', the *War History* went on, 'but it was a good camp. And each time that we subsequently returned to it, after four days in the trenches, we thought better of it. A number of decently clean huts, well sited and affording adequate accommodation; conveniently near to Bailleul; a not too distant march to trenches, whether for going in or coming out, or making interim excursions for fatigues; we knew from the start that we could, and should, do worse than this.'[29]

Nevertheless, the Battalion had more than enough to contend with. The Western Front was synonymous, of course, with trench warfare. And trench warfare, no matter how benign the stretch of the line to which one was posted, was never less than grim, uncomfortable and unnerving. Conditions had been particularly difficult during the previous winter and even though improvements were made (at Wulverghem and elsewhere) during the year that Gerald spent at the front, they did not generally amount to much: 'Sandbags provided an extra measure of protection, "duckboards" lined the trench floor and the front and rear walls of the trench were bolstered with timber or similar material.'[30] Those who were in the trenches never forgot about it. 'The night is the time best remembered', recalled one of Gerald's fellow officers. 'The trudging and slithering along muddy tracks, partly boarded and partly not, from bay to bay, pausing to stand by the sentry, gaze into the black night, and help him in his endless task of keeping awake by talking to him.'[31]

The Battalion, it was reminded all the time, was at war. 'In all sectors, active or cushy', Gary Sheffield confirms, 'danger was ever present. A shell, mortar bomb or sniper's bullet could snuff out a life in a "quiet" period just as effectively as in a major battle.'[32] The risks hit home soon enough, the Battalion suffering its first fatality within a week of embarking on active duty. Twenty-year old lance corporal George Butler was killed on 7 April, followed in quick succession by twenty-two year old Arthur Coomes, nineteen-year old Godfrey Rickets and seventeen-year old Frederick Lowley. By the end of April, the Battalion's death toll stood at twelve, infinitesimal, of course, by the standards of the war, but sobering and shocking, one can be sure, for those new to the frontline.[33]

As the death toll mounted, so too did the numbers of those who were injured: three men wounded on 18 April, two more on 21 April, an officer and five 'other ranks' on the 26 April.[34] Those not injured or killed had to live, of course, with tiredness, the threat of sickness and the constant anxiety as to what might happen to them.[35] The fear of death, injury and mutilation was epitomised most graphically, perhaps, by the horror provoked by the introduction of poison gas, the dreaded 'devil's breath'. Indeed, the Battalion's arrival at the frontline coincided almost exactly with the Germans' introduction of chlorine gas during their spring offensive at Ypres to the north.[36] Although the Battalion was not directly affected, they saw – or heard about – the effects that gas could have when victims were evacuated to nearby casualty clearing stations. Gerald's batman, like the rest of the Battalion, apparently talked of little else.[37]

Gerald did not fall victim to gas, but he was one of the sixty or so members of the Battalion to be injured during the two-and-a-half months that they spent on the Wulverghem sector of the line. Sometime during the first three weeks of May, he was wounded by 'a bullet grazing his knee-cap while he was out on a working party'. We do not know the seriousness of the injury – much depends, of course, on what is meant by 'grazing' of the knee. However, the wound was sufficiently serious – and/or Gerald was sufficiently prominent in the Battalion – for it to be mentioned at least twice: in the *War History* and in one of his colleagues' letters home.[38] Yet however severe Gerald's injuries, he had got off relatively lightly. By the time the 6th Battalion left the Wulverghem sector on 19 June, they had buried twenty-six officers and other ranks – virtually one death every three days.[39]

The Battalion was sent north to Ypres. This was a very different proposition. The Ypres Salient, which by this time was surrounded on three sides by German forces, had changed hands a number of times during the course of the war. Although Gerald and his colleagues were not involved in any major battles during the fifteen weeks they spent there, this was one of the most dangerous and disagreeable sectors of the entire Western Front. 'My chief impressions of the Ypres line', explained one officer at the time, 'are woods full of shell-scratched trees, long huts, rotting sandbags, smells, flies, old rifles and equipment, tins, the smell of chloride of lime, very deep fire trenches, the tired whisper of approaching crumps, everywhere the great untidiness and wastefulness of the Army, the fearsome echoing of a bombardment in the woods'.[40]

The longer they were on the line, the worse it got. The pressure was cumulative, of course. One aggravating factor was the reduction in the time allocated for rest and recuperation. When they arrived at the end of June, they alternated six days at the front with six days of rest (in bivouacs) behind the line; by the time they left at the beginning of October, this had been rescheduled so that they spent six days in the trenches, six days in support and then (and only then) six days of rest.[41] More important was the increased dangers that they faced. During their first six days in the line, for instance, two officers and two men were killed and another thirty-five men wounded. Even peaceful periods, as we saw above, could be disconcertingly deadly: the Battalion, it was reported, suffered less 'in casualties from the organised bombardments than from the incidental bullets and shells of the "quiet intervals"'.[42]

It was Gerald and the officers who had to deal with the disciplinary, organisational and other consequences of the Battalion's fatigue and anxiety, its fatalities and injuries. The mess itself had been reduced, they felt, to the barest of bare bones. Taking stock after one particularly onerous turn at the front, they analysed the manpower situation in which they found themselves. The 6th Battalion set out the summer before, it will be remembered, with a complement of thirty or so officers. Two of them were now dead; five had been injured and six were being treated in hospital. Three more had been repatriated (permanently or temporarily) back to England, while others were on leave or had been seconded to staff duties. This left just Gerald and four other officers (reinforced by five newcomers) to take on everything that had to be done.[43]

Gerald now had new responsibilities. Appointed Battalion Bombing Officer earlier in the summer, he had exchanged regular platoon leadership for membership of the Battalion's seven-man headquarters staff.[44] Each battalion had a platoon of bombers, consisting initially of an officer, a sergeant and thirty-two other ranks, whose job it was to attack the enemy with hand grenades. It had its attractions, some believe: 'Lobbing a grenade from a shell-hole into a trench was a very effective way for the individual soldier to bring firepower to bear on the enemy.'[45] Unfortunately, it also had the gravest possible disadvantages. Bombing was dangerous even by the standards of the frontline.[46] Gerald's predecessor, Lieutenant Leonard Joynson, himself only recently appointed Brigade Bombing Officer, had been killed early in May when a grenade he was holding exploded, not in the heat of battle, but during a demonstration he was giving some distance behind the lines.[47]

Anything to do with hand grenades was highly risky. 'For the first eighteen months of the war', explains Richard Holmes, 'private ingenuity vied with official manufacture as the army struggled to produce grenades that were both lethal to the enemy and safe to their users.' It proved a difficult balancing act. 'Some early versions were so delicate or unstable that their users – "bombers", first grouped as a platoon within the battalion, and eventually spread more widely so as to constitute "a nucleus of one officer and eight men" per company – shared with the crews of early trench mortars the discouraging nickname "Suicide Squad".'[48]

'Discouraging' was hardly the word. In spite – or more likely because– of the dangers they faced, one of the ways that members of 'suicide squads' coped was to claim, at least to their loved ones, that what they did was all in a day's work. Private Arthur Dean of the North Staffordshire Regiment was one of the early bombing trainees. In a letter home to his family earlier in 1915, he explained what his duties entailed: 'Our job is to work along a captured trench and drive the enemy out by throwing these bombs, two of us going ahead of the throwers with fixed bayonets to finish off any who may survive the effects of the bomb. Also, in case of attack, we hurl bombs into the middle of the enemy. The rest amuse themselves with telling us how risky the work is, but it is no worse than any other infantry work.'[49]

Gerald threw himself into the job. Indeed, according to the only detailed account we have of him during this period of the war, he became obsessed by his new responsibilities. Even before his appointment as Bombing Officer, he would regale his colleagues on the 'black arts' of bomb making.[50] Once appointed, he began taking unnecessary risks, seizing every opportunity he could, it was said, to go 'out for a nocturnal stroll with a handful of bombs, seeking a little pleasure over the way'.[51] Even his appearance began to change. 'For some time past', it was explained when he was killed a few months later, 'his cap had assumed an aggressive angle, and his eyebrows grow hourly more ferocious.'[52]

The Battalion's task in the autumn of 1915 was to participate in the attack by the 46th (North Midland) Division on what they, and everybody else, regarded as 'the strong position in the German line', the notorious Hohenzollern Redoubt.[53] The attack, the final stage of the Battle of Loos, was set for early/mid-October – almost exactly a year since Gerald had enlisted, almost exactly six months since he and the Battalion had set sail for France. It was a meticulously planned operation, the orders the Battalion received detailing everything from what they should wear to the allocation of communication trenches, everything from the lines of attack they should follow to what they should do with any prisoners of war that they managed to capture.[54]

Gerald and his bombers had a key role to play. With military tacticians coming to the view during 1915 and 1916 that grenades might provide a solution to the deadlock of trench warfare, he and his bombers were central to the 6th Battalion's final preparations.[55] Gerald was involved presumably in providing the 'instruction in bomb throwing' which was given during the week or so leading up to the attack. He was certainly involved two days before the attack when he paraded the Battalion bombing parties for final, 'special instruction'.[56] The bombers, like everybody else, received detailed orders as to what they were to do when the assault got under way. Their job was to target specific enemy dug-outs, to clear them out (taking 'the greatest care ... that none are left unsearched') and when this was done to mark the positions of the trenches they had captured by displaying red flags eighteen inches square.[57]

The planning came to nothing. The 6th Battalion comprised the third wave of troops to attack, and as they advanced – over the bodies of those who had gone before them – they were mown down at close range.[58] 'As soon as the battalion started to get out of the trenches the machine guns played on them', recalled Lance-Corporal Walter Shotton. 'We in the rear scrambled out of our trenches, and five yards away lay down until we were all ready. We had our coats rolled on our backs, but most of us threw them away so we could run faster. We made our first rush of twenty yards or more, and as we did so the machine gun bullets struck many of us. Then we had another rush to the second line of trenches. The machine guns were effective again.'[59]

Unable to achieve the objectives he had been given, Gerald, together with two sergeants, led his men in support of the attack taking place on a trench known as Big Willie, 'the only barrier between the two sides'.[60] Embroiled in fierce fighting, their efforts were hampered not only by a shortage of bombs, but by the fact that the narrow communication trenches along which they needed to move had become clogged up with the bodies of casualties.[61] It was here that Gerald was injured for a second time (although again only relatively

124 Sacrifice

slightly).[62] It was here, too, that he earned the military cross that he would be awarded in the New Year's Honours List of 1916, a decoration that was conferred for gallantry in the presence of the enemy.[63]

The attack on the Hohenzollern Redoubt was a disaster, a bloodbath. The 46th (North Midland) Division suffered more than 3,600 casualties, the majority of them during the first ten minutes of the assault.[64] The 6th Battalion lost eighteen officers along with almost four hundred other ranks. The *War History*'s conclusion is telling in its simplicity: '[I]n the short space of ten minutes a valuable fighting force received a blow from which it was destined to recover only slowly.'[65]

One cannot begin to imagine the impact of death and destruction on such a scale (unexceptional though it might have been by the standards of the war). The attack on the Redoubt left hundreds of men dead (hundreds more injured), and hundreds of families bereaved. Gerald was one of those injured (albeit only slightly).[66] He had also lost many of his colleagues (and friends): a quarter – perhaps a third – of the officers with whom he had been living and working just a couple of days before were now dead.[67] Reinforcements were brought in. But they were not – they could not be – like-for-like replacements. They were newcomers who may have heard about – but had not seen or been through – the carnage that Gerald and the rest of the Battalion had experienced:[68]

> [I]t was impossible to replace men such as those who were already in the Battalion at the outbreak of war, or those who joined shortly afterwards. They were the best type of civilian soldier, and having been trained in the traditions of the Battalion, it is safe to say, without disparagement of their successors, that their loss could never be made good.[69]

It is telling therefore that that when the author of Britain's official history of military operations during the war circulated his draft chapters dealing with the attack on the Redoubt, a number of officers asked him to remove the expression, 'a certain demoralisation set in'.[70]

Rest, recuperation and death

Demoralised or not, the Battalion regrouped for two weeks before being sent to support an imperial brigade. 'In casualties, maybe, this trench line was a welcome contrast to recent experiences', conceded the *War History*; 'but being practically waterlogged and having only a three-foot-six parapet constructed by the Indians, in the matter of discomfort it surpassed everything that had gone before.'[71] As so often, physical discomfort was compounded both by past suffering and by uncertainty as to the future. There were constant rumours as to where the Battalion would be posted to next, rumours that were fuelled, not surprisingly, when they were given a lecture early in December on 'Duties on board ship'.[72]

The gossip was not without foundation. Gerald and his colleagues set out on Christmas Day for the port of Marseilles, a two-day journey 'through

Class, patriotism and sacrifice 125

some of the finest scenery in France'. They stayed for a week on the coast, 'in a sunny camp, pitched on the side of a hill and overlooking the blue Mediterranean and the occasional outward-bound liner going east with troops'. 'Marseilles', the Battalion history concluded contentedly, 'proved to be a place above criticism. Parades were perfunctory and soon over; sea bathing and other amusements were continuous.'[73]

No doubt, the Battalion would have liked to have remained much, much longer. But it was not to be, the New Year seeing it set sail from Marseilles. They were not told until their second day at sea that their destination was Alexandria, on the north coast of Africa, which they reached just under a week later. Believing mistakenly that they were en route for the Dardanelles, they waited at sea for a day before being told to disembark and take the train to the Suez-side base of Shaluffa. They still did not know what their mission was to be, whether they would be staying in Shaluffa or whether they would be moving on somewhere else.[74]

In the event, they spent two weeks at Shaluffa. It is a commentary, of course, on what they had been through that even the threat of scurvy, heat stroke and septic sores did not stop the Battalion regarding its time in North Africa as a comfortable interlude.[75] So although there were lectures on heliography, night marching, flag signalling and lamp signalling, some, perhaps most, of the men had other priorities. The army hierarchy, we know, was becoming increasingly aware of the positive role that sport could play.[76] The members of the Battalion needed little persuading: 'The cricket season had begun, and officers were sending home "Urgent priority" messages for polo sticks.' Everybody was in a more relaxed mood: 'the period of its war history from 10th to 26th January, 1916, was little concerned with war, and was far more cheerfully illuminated with prospects of a long siesta, so to speak, in the Near East – with such occasional undertakings as might be necessary to justify the uniform and make for permanence in this healthier country.'[77]

It was over all too soon. By the end of the month, the Battalion was on the move again, this time back to France. 'The Egyptian excursion ended all too suddenly and soon', concluded the *War History*: 'Thus, by a zigzag course made essential by the presence of submarines; thus, in perfect weather, with occasional glimpses of the Italian coast, and a day's cruising about Malta; thus after mornings spent in drill and lectures, afternoons spent in boxing-matches and ship's games, evenings spent in amateur concerts and nights spent in lifebelts; thus, back to France!'[78]

Meanwhile, Gerald's military career was flourishing. He had seen conflict, he had survived two minor injuries and, most crucially perhaps, he had managed to stay alive. Awarded the military cross in the New Year's Honours List, he was promoted from Second Lieutenant to Temporary Lieutenant in the middle of January.[79] He therefore played a leading part, one assumes, in organising the Battalion's preparations between the middle of February and the beginning of March. 'Back in the battle area, the unit's movements seemed to the men to be oddly numerous and uncertain ... To the Battalion the only thing evident was an incessant need of changing billets.'[80]

Eventually on 11 March 1916, an advance party (including the bombers) set out for Neuville St Vaast, just north of Arras, where the Battalion was due to resume its duties at the front.[81] It was a bleak and depressing section of the line. The *War History* presents a grimly stark picture: 'The stretch of trenches in question ran through the centre of what had once been a considerable township, now levelled to the ground. Not many weeks before the occupation by the Battalion it had been in German hands. From them it had been wrested by the French a few days previously. The line showed every sign of hard battle. Parts of it had actually been blown up by large mines, and everywhere were the evidence of continual and relentless pressure.'[82]

There was no particular pressure for a couple of weeks. But then in the late evening of 27 March, the 'enemy commenced heavy fire with mortars', noted the war diary: 'Field Guns, rifle grenades, and machine Guns'. The Battalion responded with its own field guns, whereon it remained reasonably quiet until the following morning when the Germans opened fire with their heavy trench bombs.[83]

The next day, 29 March, saw a further escalation of hostilities, with the Germans shelling the British trenches in the early afternoon. The Battalion responded with an artillery barrage, and then in the early evening 'sprang a mine which formed a crater', that it 'occupied and partly consolidated.' This was followed by yet another exchange. 'Intermittent artillery fire continued till 8p.m.', reported the war diary, 'and from that time the situation was quiet, and the work of repairing and consolidating was pressed on.'[84] But there were casualties. 'In the chaos occasioned by the explosions of mines, rifle-grenades, and trench-mortars', reported the *War History*, 'Lieut. C.H. Pearson was killed, Lieut G.H. Howard Smith received fatal injuries, and Captain Harold Page was wounded.'[85]

Gerald Howard-Smith was thirty-six years old when he died on Wednesday, 29 March 1916. It was a day that would never be forgotten by his parents, Philip and Mary, by his brother, Charles, or by members of his extended family. His memory lived on, too, as we see later, in the minds of friends and colleagues, of schoolmates and teammates and even, one suspects, of some who had known him only very slightly while he was alive.

Yet despite this book's focus on Gerald Howard-Smith, one must not lose one's sense of proportion. Harrowing though they were, the details of Gerald's death, injury and treatment do nothing to set him apart. 'His injuries were caused by a German bomb which almost shattered part of his leg. Amputation was resorted to with a view of trying to save his life, but without avail.'[86] He was just one of the men who did not return home from the war, one of more than 1¾ million men who were killed, injured or reported missing on the Western Front.

It was the way in which Gerald Howard-Smith died, the way his death was reported, that set him apart, and so fed the war's mythology of personal fortitude, regimental unity and cross-class collaboration. True or false, the reports of his death were all of a piece. It was said that even as the stretcher bearers were carrying him from the frontline to the military hospital where he was to be treated, he was heard singing 'It's a Long Way to Tipperary'.[87] It was said that even when he was in the military hospital, 'the last associations with him were of the usually merry kind. Even a few hours before the setting in of the fatal complications, the C.O., on his way to "leave in the U.K.," looked in at the hospital and took a jovial message from the wounded son to his people at home.'[88] Gerald Howard-Smith, recalled the *War History*, was 'large, gallant, and loose-limbed'.[89]

Distance and distinctions

Gerald, the officers and the men of the 6th Battalion, South Staffordshire Regiment had been through an enormous amount together. Some, like Gerald, had paid the ultimate price, and many more had been injured. But they had all suffered and paid their dues. They had all been separated from friends and family; had all been cold, wet and dirty; and had all seen (and no doubt done) terrible things. Everyone in the Battalion had been forced to live in close proximity to men they hardly knew, to put their lives on the line alongside those whom they would almost certainly never have met had it not been for the war. This coming together of the classes is a difficult and sensitive subject, and historians continue to debate whether it is sensible to speak of officers and men serving in the same battalion sharing a common experience.[90]

It is hoped that the remainder of the chapter will make some contribution to this debate. It will do so by considering whether Gerald and his fellow officers wished – and were able – to maintain on active service the class distance and class distinctions that had formed such a prominent feature of battalion life while they were training in England. It will consider too whether Gerald and his fellow officers' notions of class distance and class superiority were modified as they got to know, for the first time, large numbers of men whose class situation was so markedly inferior to their own. What is striking, it turns out, is not so much the persistence of class separation and the officers' notions of class superiority as their tendency to interpret class separation and class superiority in terms of cross-class cohesion and consensus

Class, class identity and class consciousness can be stubbornly powerful. There was a time, not so long ago, when such a claim would have been regarded as a statement more or less of the obvious. But not any longer. The long-running debate during the 1980s and 1990s concerning the merits and demerits of postmodernism led a number of historians to abandon class-based analysis – and many more to exercise considerable caution about making claims as to the centrality of class in British society.[91] This book reasserts the traditional view: that class analysis remains fundamental to the understanding of late nineteenth- and early twentieth-century (indeed the whole of modern) British history.[92]

However fierce one's commitment to class-based analysis, it would be a struggle, one might think, to make class, class identity and class consciousness defining features of the twelve months that Gerald Howard-Smith spent on or near the frontline. It turns out however that one does not have to dig too deep to uncover the evidence one needs to support such a stance. Even in the trenches, even as the Battalion, from the highest to the lowest, suffered indignity, injury and death, Gerald and his fellow officers enjoyed, and seemingly took for granted, many of the distinctions and privileges that they had enjoyed while training in England. So even though territorial regiments were supposedly less hidebound than regular units, they too subscribed to the view that distance, discipline and morale were all intimately entwined.[93]

Gerald and his fellow officers continued, so far as they were able, to travel apart, live apart, eat apart, sleep apart and socialise apart from those beneath them in the class/military hierarchy. They set the tone as they were leaving England. The journey the Battalion took from its training base to the frontline proved, it will be recalled, to be slow, frustrating and uncomfortable. It was slow and frustrating for everyone, but more for some than for others. In a reassuring reaffirmation of the status quo, Gerald and his fellow officers were spared the worst of it. Whereas they spent the interminable, thirty-six-hour train journey from Le Havre to Nordpeene in coaches, the men had to make do with cattle trucks. Yet at least one member of the mess was convinced that they were all in it together: 'I am afraid that the men will have found the long rail journey very much the "real thing", cattle trucks, thirty-seven men to a truck, with two trusses of straw!' But the officers, too, had it hard: 'We were no better off, eight to a small carriage, so that we could not lie down. You should have seen us shaving with drippings of hot water from the engine!'[94]

Whatever the rhetoric of shared discomfort and inconvenience, the Battalion continued to enforce whatever distinctions it could. Believing it essential that accommodation, for instance, should be strictly segregated, they started as they meant to continue. When the battalion arrived at Sailly-le-Sec in March 1915 for its first taste of life near to the frontline, the officers were billeted in a farmhouse – the men had to make to with the barns.[95] When the Battalion went into conflict a few weeks later, the practice, it will be recalled, was to alternate six days at the front with six days 'rest' at 'Bulford Camp. The *War History*'s comment, once again, is highly revealing. When the Battalion was in camp, it declared, 'The men are in much the same huts as ourselves, except that their huts are floor and roof, with no walls between them, and they are tightly packed rather than spread out.'[96]

This allocation of accommodation reinforced, as it was meant to, the officers' sense of separateness and superiority. However irritating they might find one another, they were among their own. One of the officers in the Battalion remembers spending his 'rest' time at Bulford alongside Gerald. 'Behind my valise, on the wall, hangs my little mirror, my web equipment, revolver and haversack, on a high ledge my boot brushes and shaving things, and my pack is my pillow. I sit on my valise, writing on the top of a biscuit tin.' Gerald, however, was as messy – and as unmilitary – as he had been as a schoolboy. 'Behind is Howard-Smith, whose valise is as untidy as the end of the world, reading a battered novel.'[97]

Neither did the officers give up their right to have servants when they left England for the frontline.[98] It was a system, as we saw in the previous chapter, that divides opinion, exasperating civilian (and other) critics and attracting enthusiastic military (and other) justification. Some do their best – not altogether successfully – to strike a middle way: 'The possession of a servant was a Country House prop to the gentlemanly lustre of the officer, but more meaningfully a servant freed his martial master from the petty cares of everyday living, so that the latter could concentrate on command.'[99]

So even in a territorial unit like the 6th Battalion, South Staffordshire Regiment, Gerald and the other officers enjoyed both the reassurance that conventional boundaries were being maintained and the support that those brought up with domestic help were accustomed to receiving. When, for example, the Battalion was moving from billet to billet in the spring of 1915, there were servants on hand to pack the officers' cases.[100]

One of the Battalion's best known soldier-servants, Private Bould, had worked before the war, as we saw in the previous chapter, as a billiard-marker at the Wolverhampton Conservative Club. He came into his own now as the waiter in the headquarters' mess. The *War History* printed a mock-celebratory account of Bould's and other servants' work which was conducted in 'the firing line'. 'The early *régime* of the one-course meal, consisting of the mere ration, soon gave way to an elaborate menu. Our servants even went to the length of discovering a potato-bury in the support trenches, and supplying us with *Pommes de Terre Nouvelles* long before the P.T.N. season should properly begin. We took to sitting on real chairs, eating off real tables.'[101]

Even when they got to the trenches, Gerald and his fellow officers did all they could to maintain pre-war standards and to enjoy whatever pre-war pleasures they could. May 1915, we have seen, was a quiet time on the Wulverghem section of the line.[102] The members of the mess took advantage, they, or more probably their servants, managing to put together a surprisingly pleasing meal. 'Just had a birthday lunch with Law, Page, Sankey, Howard-Smith, Adam', recalled one of Gerald's companions in a letter home:

> Cold pheasant, which lacked flavour as a pheasant, but served excellently as a cold chicken, and being the first poultry we've tasted these two months or more. Shortbread, washed down with a bottle of Benedictine, produced (from his machine gun?) by one Harold Page, in honour of the occasion. We sat over it long and comfortably, and agreed it was the best meal we had yet had in France.[103]

As this passage suggests, the Battalion's officers did their best to recreate aspects of the life they had known before the war, to remind themselves, albeit briefly, of the familiar and the comforting. 'With us, we begin to think less intently of the business of war', confirmed one of Gerald's colleagues, 'and to think a little more of the amenities of ordinary life with a view to reproducing a few of them in our daily round'.[104] It is telling therefore that when another

130 *Sacrifice*

member of the mess described (in a passage quoted earlier) the dreadful desolation that the Battalion encountered at Ypres, he concluded by comparing his response to the carnage of the Western Front to his reaction to the grandeur of his alma mater: 'that feeling which one used sometimes to have in the old buildings and quads at the 'Varsity, of being on the scene of "Great Days done".'[105]

The officers' sense of class difference and class superiority was confirmed not just by their educational advantages but by their day-to-day dealings with the men under their command. As we saw in the previous chapter, the way in which subordinates spoke left a particular impression. Although unhappy at having to censor the letters their men sent home from the frontline, they could not help but be struck by what they learned about the educational deficiencies of those writing them.[106] And although some of them had known private Bould before the war and saw him on a regular basis in the mess, they regarded him with something approaching anthropological fascination:

> If it interests you to study the native method of speech you will like to hear how our Mess Servant describes the little canvas bag he has just handed to me, as being the official issue of Emergency Ration Carrier, Military. 'What's this?' I ask him. He has no use for technical terms. 'To put summat in t'eat,' he says.[107]

Hopes, plans and repercussions

This chapter tackles some compelling and complicated issues. Despite the difficulties with which it has had to grapple, it has shown two things very clearly. It has provided some indication, it is believed, of the upheaval and trauma that Gerald Howard-Smith and the 6th Battalion, South Staffordshire Regiment, went through between leaving England for France in March 1915 and Gerald's death almost exactly a year later. The chapter has shown, too, that even when they were stationed in and near to the frontline, Gerald and his fellow officers managed to maintain a clear distance between themselves and the men they were commanding.

In other respects, it must be said, the chapter has struggled to meet its objectives. It has been much more difficult, as one would expect, to decide what Gerald and the other officers were thinking as opposed to what they were doing or what was being done to them. And it has proved impossible, again as one would expect, to form any judgement as to whether the ways in which Gerald and those serving alongside him were thinking changed during – let alone due to – their involvement in the first two years of the war.

What is striking is the way in which the committee of officers who compiled the *War History* in 1924 interpreted class relations in the battalion. It is true, perhaps, that a social historian (such as myself) is likely to find the issue of officer–man relationships more interesting and important than military historians familiar with, and immersed in, the ways of the British army at the

Class, patriotism and sacrifice 131

time of the Great War. But the issue is no disciplinary or ideological construct. The territorial officers of the 6th Battalion, South Staffordshire Regiment, not only kept their distance from the men they were commanding and accepted their superiority over them, but probably went along with, if they did not necessarily contribute to, the narrative of cross-class cohesion and solidarity presented in the *War History*.[108]

The sample, of course, is small: one year, one man, one mess, one battalion. But it is believed that the conclusions reached in this chapter may well be indicative of attitudes across the rest of the army and even perhaps across the rest of middle- and upper middle-class society. It is not without reason, it seems, that it is the second world war, rather than the first, which has been dubbed the 'people's war'.[109]

Notes

1 G.D. Sheffield, *Leadership in the Trenches: Officer–Man Relations, Morale and Discipline in the British Army in the Era of the First World War* (London: Macmillan, 2000), p. 125. Also Gary Sheffield, *Command and Morale: The British Army on the Western Front 1914–1918* (Barnsley: Pen & Sword, 2014), chs. 10, 11, 13.
2 Anthony Seldon and David Walsh, *Public Schools and the Great War: The Generation Lost* (Barnsley: Pen & Sword, 2013), p. 245.
3 Seldon and Walsh, *Public Schools*, pp. 249–50. See, too, Stephen Constantine, *Unemployment in Britain between the Wars* (London: Longman, 1980), p. 74; Peter Clarke, *Hope and Glory: Britain 1900–1990* (London: Penguin, 1996), p. 81.
4 Harold Perkin, *The Rise of Professional Society: England since 1880* (London: Routledge, 1989), p. 204.
5 John Lewis-Stempel, *Six Weeks: The Short and Gallant Life of the British Officer in the First World War* (London: Orion, 2010), p. 312.
6 A Committee of Officers who Served with the Battalion, *The War History of the Sixth Battalion the South Staffordshire Regiment* (London: Heinemann, 1924).
7 Staffordshire Regiment Museum, BV/75, Battalion War Diary, February 1915; Committee of Officers, *War History*, p. 19.
8 Gary Sheffield, *A Short History of the First World War* (London: Oneworld, 2014), p. 49.
9 Richard Holmes, *Tommy: The British Soldier on the Western Front 1914–1918* (London: HarperCollins, 2004), p. 13.
10 Holmes, *Tommy*, p. 14. Also Richard Holmes's foreword to Gary Sheffield, *Forgotten Victory: The First World War: Myths and Realities* (London: Headline, 2001), p. ix. For a more nuanced view, see Tony Mason and Eliza Riedi, *Sport and the Military: The British Armed Forces 1880–1960* (Cambridge: Cambridge University Press, 2010), p. 81.
11 Committee of Officers, *War History*, p. 20. Also Battalion War Diary, March 1915.
12 Committee of Officers, *War History*, p. 21. See K.W. Mitchinson, *The Territorial Force at War, 1914–1916* (London: Palgrave Macmillan, 2014), pp. 74–6.
13 Battalion War Diary, March 1915; Committee of Officers, *War History*, pp. 21–2.
14 Lewis-Stempel, *Six Weeks*, p. 70.
15 Lewis-Stempel, *Six Weeks*, p. 69. Also Mitchinson, *Territorial Force*, pp. 74–6.
16 Lewis-Stempel, *Six Weeks*, p. 70.
17 I am grateful to Spencer Jones for stressing this point to me.
18 Andrew Thornton, 'The Territorial Force in Staffordshire 1908–1915' (MPhil thesis, University of Birmingham, 2004), p. 123.

19 Committee of Officers, *War History*, pp. 22, 24; Battalion War Diary, March 1915.
20 Battalion War Diary, March 1915; Committee of Officers, *War History*, p. 23; Spencer C. Tucker, *The Great War 1914–18* (London: UCL Press, 1998), pp. 60–61; Gary Sheffield, *The Chief: Douglas Haig and the British Army* (London: Aurum, 2011), p. 104; Simon Peaple, *Mud, Blood and Determination: The History of the 46th (North Midland) Division in the Great War* (Solihull: Helion, 2015), p. 28.
21 Committee of Officers, *War History*, p. 23; Mitchinson, *Territorial Force*, pp. 79–80.
22 Committee of Officers, *War History*, p. 24.
23 Battalion War Diary, March 1915; Thornton, 'Territorial Force', p. 124.
24 Committee of Officers, *War History*, pp. 29–30; Michael Woods, '"Gas, Grenades and Grievances": The Attack on Hohenzollern Redoubt by 46th (North Midland) Division, 13 October 1915'. I am grateful to Michael Woods for allowing me to see this paper in advance of publication.
25 Committee of Officers, *War History*, p. 29.
26 During the first half of 1915, the territorials tended to provide additional labour rather than additional combatants. See Mitchinson, *Territorial Force*, pp. 98–9.
27 Committee of Officers, *War History*, p. 32; Peaple, *Mud*, p. 28.
28 Committee of Officers, *War History*, p. 33. Also Thornton, 'Territorial Force', p. 125.
29 Committee of Officers, *War History*, p. 33.
30 Sheffield, *Forgotten Victory*, p. 123. Also Committee of Officers, *War History*, pp. 39–40.
31 Committee of Officers, *War History*, p. 53.
32 Sheffield, *Forgotten Victory*, p. 126.
33 Battalion War Diary, April 1915; Mitchinson, *Territorial Force*, p. 113.
34 Battalion War Diary, April 1915.
35 Mitchinson, *Territorial Force*, pp. 92–5. A recent, well-reviewed study is Diana Preston, *A Higher Form of Killing: Six Weeks in World War I that Forever Changed the Nature of Warfare* (London: Bloomsbury, 2015).
36 Holmes, *Tommy*, pp. 418–26; Tucker, *Great War*, pp. 62–3.
37 Committee of Officers, *War History*, p. 49. Also pp. 47–8.
38 Committee of Officers, *War History*, p. 53.
39 Committee of Officers, *War History*, p. 56.
40 Committee of Officers, *War History*, p. 61.
41 Committee of Officers, *War History*, pp. 58, 61, 66.
42 Committee of Officers, *War History*, pp. 63, 69.
43 Committee of Officers, *War History*, pp. 79–80.
44 Committee of Officers, *War History*, p. 85. See Peaple, *Mud*, pp. 36–8; Mitchinson, *Territorial Force*, p. 85; Simkins, *Kitchener's Army*, pp. 286–7; Woods, 'Gas'.
45 Gerard DeGroot, *The First World War* (London: Palgrave, 2001), p. 169.
46 www.hellfirecorner.co.uk/Thornton/terriers5.htm, p. 4 [November 2011].
47 www.1914-1918.invisionzone.com, Great War Forum, Bombing Sections, p. 1 [June 2009].
48 Holmes, *Tommy*, p. 385.
49 Great War Forum, Bombing Sections, p. 1.
50 Committee of Officers, *War History*, p. 121.
51 Committee of Officers, *War History*, p. 120.
52 Committee of Officers, *War History*, p. 121.
53 Committee of Officers, *War History*, p. 82. See in particular Woods, 'Gas'. For the cult of the offensive, see Tim Travers, *The Killing Ground: The British Army, the Western Front and the Emergence of Modern War 1900–1918* (Barnsley: Pen & Sword, 2009), pp. 37, 50–51.

Class, patriotism and sacrifice 133

54 Committee of Officers, *War History*, pp. 86–96, esp. pp. 89–90. Also Woods, 'Gas'.
55 See Woods, 'Gas'.
56 Battalion War Diary, October 1915. See Peaple, *Mud*, p. 63.
57 Committee of Officers, *War History*, p. 90.
58 DeGroot, *First World War*, p. 38.
59 www.209.85.229.132/search?q=cache:_YJWRL140PcJ:1914–1918:invisionzone, Hohenzollern Redoubt, p. 4 [July 2009].
60 'hellfire-corner', p. 3. See Peaple, *Mud*, p. 66.
61 Bombing Sections, pp. 2–3; Woods, 'Gas'.
62 Unattributed press cutting, October 23, 1915.
63 National Archives, WO372/18/145923/24472, Medal Card of Gerald Howard-Smith.
64 Sheffield, *Short History*, p. 53; Woods, 'Gas'.
65 Committee of Officers, *War History*, p. 97. Also Battalion War Diary, October 1915. For reactions to the failure of the attack (including the removal of Major General the Hon. Stuart Wortley), see Travers, *Killing Ground*, pp. 20–21; Peaple, *Mud*, pp. 69–75, 196; Woods, 'Gas'.
66 Unattributed press cutting, October 23, 1915.
67 Thornton, 'Territorial Force', p. 147.
68 Thornton, 'Territorial Force', p. 148.
69 Committee of Officers, *War History*, p. 101.
70 Woods, 'Gas'.
71 Committee of Officers, *War History*, p. 101.
72 Committee of Officers, *War History*, p. 102.
73 Committee of Officers, *War History*, pp. 105–6.
74 J. Stirling, *The Territorial Divisions 1914–1918* (London: Dent, 1922), p. 22; Peaple, *Mud*, pp. 77–8.
75 Mitchinson, *Territorial Force*, p. 95.
76 Mason and Riedi, *Sport and the Military*, ch. 3.
77 Committee of Officers, *War History*, pp. 106, 108–9.
78 Committee of Officers, *War History*, p. 111.
79 *Supplement to London Gazette*, January 14, 1916.
80 Committee of Officers, *War History*, p. 112.
81 Battalion War Diary, March 1916; Peaple, *Mud*, p. 80.
82 Committee of Officers, *War History*, p. 113.
83 Battalion War Diary, March 1916.
84 Battalion War Diary, March 1916.
85 Committee of Officers, *War History*, p. 120. Also Battalion War Diary, March 1916.
86 *Temple Grove Magazine*, June 1916.
87 www.wolverhamptonswar.wordpress.com/2014/06 [February 2015].
88 Committee of Officers, *War History*, pp. 120–21.
89 Committee of Officers, *War History*, p. 65.
90 Sheffield, *Leadership*, pp. xxi, 125–8; Mitchinson, *Territorial Force*, p. 30.
91 For introductions to postmodernist criticisms of class-based analysis, see Keith Jenkins, *Rethinking History* (London: Routledge, 1991); and Alan Munslow, *Deconstructing History* (London: Routledge, 1997). R.J. Evans, *In Defence of History* (London: Granta, 1997) mounts a spirited counter-attack.
92 Nick Mansfield's forthcoming book, *Soldiers as Workers: Class, Employment, Conflict and the Nineteenth Century Military* (Liverpool: Liverpool University Press, 2016), argues that 'class is the single most important factor in understanding the British army in the period of industrialisation.'
93 Keith Simpson, 'The Officers', in Ian F. W. Beckett and Keith Simpson (eds), *A Nation in Arms: A Social Study of the British Army in the First World War* (London: Tom Donovan, 1985); Sheffield, *Leadership*, p. 140.

94 Committee of Officers, *War History*, p. 22. See Mitchinson, *Territorial Force*, pp. 68–70.
95 Committee of Officers, *War History*, pp. 24–5.
96 Committee of Officers, *War History*, pp. 38–9.
97 Committee, *War History*, p. 38.
98 Sheffield, *Leadership*, pp. 117–8.
99 Lewis-Stempel, *Six Weeks*, p. 160. Also Sheffield, *Leadership*, pp. 117–8.
100 Committee of Officers, *War History*, p. 26.
101 Committee of Officers, *War History*, p. 106.
102 Battalion War Diary, May 1915.
103 Committee of Officers, *War History*, p. 50. Cf. Graves, *Goodbye*, p. 141.
104 Committee of Officers, *War History*, p. 52.
105 Committee of Officers, *War History*, p. 61.
106 Committee of Officers, *War History*, p. 104.
107 Committee of Officers, *War History*, pp. 106–7.
108 Sheffield, *Leadership*, pp. 125–8.
109 Angus Calder, *The People's War: Britain, 1939–45* (London: Cape, 1969).

Part IV
COMMEMORATION

7 'IN LOVING MEMORY': CLASS AND COMMEMORATION, REPRESENTATION AND MISREPRESENTATION

A popular officer

It took two days for news of Gerald Howard-Smith's death to reach Wolverhampton. The local press was ready: the very next day the *Midland Counties Express* published a brief biography, along with a photograph that had been taken while he was training at Saffron Walden. The article, entitled 'A Popular Officer', explained that Gerald had been educated at Eton and Cambridge, before focusing on his sporting achievements, his work as a solicitor, his participation in the attack on the Hohenzollern Redoubt and his award of the military cross earlier in the year. 'Nine or ten days ago', it continued, 'it was announced that the gallant lieutenant had been wounded for the third time, and it is to these injuries that he has succumbed.' It went on to repeat the story of his bravery to the very end.

> An incident quite characteristic of Lieutenant Smith is narrated by one of his friends. After he had been wounded, and while being removed by stretcher bearers, he sang the refrain of 'It's a Long Way to Tipperary', which drew from one of the men the remark, 'How I could have loved him', a tribute from a soldier to an officer that speaks for itself and indicates the spirit of loyalty and comradeship which is such a conspicuous feature of the British Army.[1]

So began the process of mythologizing Gerald's personal bravery and integrating it into the regiment's – and the country's – narrative of cross-class integration. It is understandable, of course, that a Wolverhampton newspaper, published within a few days of Gerald's death and nearly two years into the war, should seek both to emphasise individual stoicism and to establish a link between the personal and the patriotic. But did other newspapers cover Gerald's death and, if so, did they adopt the same sort of stance? Did the many bodies and organisations with which Gerald had been connected commemorate his life and if so how did they choose to perpetuate his memory?

This, the final chapter of the book seeks therefore to explore two key aspects of the ways in which Gerald – and other members of the so-called 'lost generation' – were commemorated during and after the war. It will suggest, and suggest most strongly, that Gerald's class position did much to dictate the ways in which he, and, indeed, the officer class more generally, were remembered. It will suggest, too, that the ways in which Gerald and the officer class more generally were remembered provide but a partial guide to the lives that were being commemorated. It is almost bound to be misleading when death defines commemoration.

The past twenty years or so have seen a growing recognition that, 'the memory of a war can be as fruitful a field of investigation as its conduct or immediate impact.'[2] It was in 1992, for example, that Berg began publishing its series, 'The Legacy of the Great War', which now (under the Bloomsbury imprint) runs to over thirty-five volumes. Alex King's contribution to the series, *Memorials of the Great War in Britain: The Symbolism of Politics and Remembrance*, which appeared in 1998, provides a useful insight into the way in which the field was beginning to fragment. As well as exploring what he calls 'the war memorial business', King 'examines how the memorials were produced, what was said about them, how support for them was mobilized and behaviour around them regulated'.[3]

Unity and uniformity, difference and distinctiveness

There has been considerable interest, as one might expect, in the relationship between class and commemoration. Opinions diverge. Some, such as King, play down the power of class. War memorials, he suggests, 'were symbolic objects that transcended differences amongst participants through the practical activities and not the abstract ideas that were associated with them.'[4] Others put it more succinctly. 'Comradeship', it is said, 'extended to the dead. In the cemeteries created by the Imperial War Graves Commission, headstones were "uniform" to avoid class distinctions. Officers and men were buried alongside each other, to acknowledge the brotherhood that had grown up on French and Belgian soil.'[5] The standard design of the cemeteries, using standard components, confirmed that all of the lost generation were equally worthy of honour: the 'great and lowly, peer and peasant, rich and poor, learned and ignorant, raised to one supreme level in death by common sacrifice for a common cause'.[6]

It is right to stress the emphasis that the Imperial War Graves Commission (originally the Graves Registration Committee) placed on unity and uniformity. But this is not to say that its policy of communal commemoration went unchallenged.[7] There was influential opposition. Despite their sympathy for the public schools, Anthony Seldon and David Walsh make no attempt to conceal the sense of class separation and class superiority displayed by the families of certain officers. They show that in spite of official insistence that the war dead must be treated equally and should be buried near where they fell: 'Individual families, mostly from the wealthier classes, had lobbied hard for their own lost ones to be afforded special status, and some had succeeded in bringing their bodies home.' The result, Seldon and Walsh explain, was that the Imperial War Graves Commission received some ninety letters a week from relatives demanding the right of repatriation and/or the right to have a different style of headstone from that which the Commission wished to use for all those killed, irrespective of rank and background.[8]

Gerald's parents did not (so far as we know) lobby the Commission, and his headstone was identical to the hundreds of thousands others to be found in cemeteries across Belgium and northwest France. The inscription alone distinguished Gerald's grave from the three thousand that lay alongside it at the Aubigny Communal Cemetery Extension in the Pas de Calais:

> In Memory of Lieutenant Gerald Howard Smith MC
> 6th Bn. South Staffordshire Regiment who died on 29 March 1916 Age 36
> Son of Judge Howard Smith and Mrs. M.B. Howard Smith, of 11, Alexandra Mansions, London.
> Native of Wolverhampton.
> Remembered with Honour
> Aubigny Communal Cemetery Extension.[9]

But unity and uniformity had their limits. Even if the families of dead officers did not lobby for special status, the press reported the deaths of men like Gerald more frequently, more fully and more fulsomely than casualties lower down the military – and social – hierarchy. The *Midland Counties Express* was far from being the only newspaper to single out Gerald for particular mention. So, too, as one might expect, did local papers like the *Walsall Observer* and the *Birmingham Daily Mail*.[10] So, too, more surprisingly, did papers as far afield as the *Yorkshire Post* and the *Newcastle Daily Journal*.[11] There were common themes. The *Birmingham Gazette*, like the *Midland Counties Express*, wove together Gerald's class background, professional activities, military endeavours and sporting accomplishments into a patriotic narrative of sacrifice and loss. Its take on Gerald's death is clear from the heading it gave to its report: 'Officer-Athlete Dead':

> News reached Wolverhampton yesterday that Lieut. Gerald Howard-Smith, the well-known cricketer and athlete, son of Judge Howard Smith, has succumbed to the injuries he recently sustained on the western front.
> Lieut. Smith was a solicitor, and joined the local Territorials on the outbreak of war. He was wounded in the charge on the Hohenzollern Redoubt in the Loos Battle of October last, and it was in this neighbourhood that the fateful injuries were sustained. It was the third time he had been wounded.
> Deceased was a well-known cricketer, attached to the Wolverhampton Cricket Club, of which he was captain, and as a fast bowler his services were specially useful in bowling operations.[12]

Even if officers' families did not press for special recognition, their class position was sufficient to ensure that their sons, brothers and husbands were commemorated more widely and more permanently than the great majority of the 'lost generation'. In death, as in life, Gerald, his family and those like them were marked out by their class.

Gerald had been to prep school and public school (and taught briefly at two other prep schools), bodies that routinely commemorated the staff and old boys who had been killed during the course of the conflict.[13] School magazines recorded deaths as they occurred, and, well before the war was over, bereaved parents began pressing headmasters and governing bodies to recognise the sacrifices that their sons had made. The schools' most common response was to arrange for the erection of memorials listing the names of the fallen, sites, it has been pointed out, at which it was possible to grieve both individually and collectively.[14]

The *Temple Grove Magazine* reported Gerald's death in July 1916, by which time he was one of forty old boys to have been killed in action.[15] It explained the circumstances of his death and, as might be expected of such a publication, made particular mention of his sporting accomplishments. He 'became famous in Amateur Sport', it noted, 'both as a cricketer (fast bowler) and at clearing the bar'. It went on to provide details of some of his university successes: 'He won the high jump for Cambridge in the inter-varsity Sports three years in succession, jumping 5.10¼, 5.9¾, 5.10½' [1.77–1.79 metres].[16] The school later recorded his death more formally listing him, alongside eighty-six other old boys, on the *Temple Grove Roll of Honour* (a plaque that is now in the possession of a free school in Eastbourne, the town to which Temple Grove relocated in 1907).[17]

Eton, too, recorded Gerald's death. The *Eton College Chronicle*, like the *Temple Grove Magazine*, drew particular attention to his sporting achievements. However, its report was much more personal than that produced by his prep school. Published six weeks after Gerald was killed, it reprinted the 'notes' that had been sent to it by one of Gerald's friends. The resulting article made much of Gerald's high jumping style which, his friend claimed, revealed a great deal about his personality: 'No one who ever played an uphill game of either cricket or football on his side could fail to admire his indomitable spirit. His method of high jumping was characteristic of his life.'

> Despising the modern method of approaching the bar along a line almost parallel to it and then flinging the feet above the head, he jumped like a steeple-chase horse with a long straight run at right angles to the bar, and if he got his feet over he had not, like his rivals, to fear the danger of striking the bar with his shoulder-blades. What height he might have cleared if his proud spirit had allowed him to adopt the modern method, no one can say.

The report went on to stress Gerald's modesty, his physical courage and his bravery in the face of what turned out to be his fatal injuries. Repeating the story told by the *Midland Counties Express*, it was a fulsome tribute even by the standards of wartime school magazines. 'Instead of groaning with pain' from his blown off kneecap and his 'other grievous injuries', Gerald, the *Eton College Chronicle* explained, was carried to the field dressing station 'whistling Tipperary'. He could not be saved and just over a week later, 'his intrepid spirit found its glorious rest.'[18]

Gerald was remembered, too, albeit more impersonally, in the memorials that Eton erected after the war. The college had a lot to live up to: it had 'commemorated the Boer War with a building on a grandiose scale for 171 dead, so how to commemorate 1,157 dead posed problems of scale'.[19] It would cost the college £100,000, it was told in 1916, to pay for the memorial then being proposed. In the event, Eton commemorated its dead in a number of different ways: it erected memorials around the school grounds, it published a list of Old Etonian combatants and it installed commemorative panelling and tapestry in the school's upper chapel. The first of the four panels ('in a renaissance design of darkened oak, ebony and gold') had echoes of the education of St George, the fourth of the four presented British participation in the war as a crusade.[20]

The majority of Eton's memorials made no attempt to identify individuals. But some did, and two of them (both of which appeared in 1921) listed Gerald alongside the other old boys who had died during the course of the war. His name was one of more than 1,500 on a bronze plaque in the grounds[21] and one of those included, too, in the two hundred and thirty-three-page book, the *List of Etonians who Fought in the Great War, 1914–1919*:

> Smith, G. Howard, M.C., Lt. S. Staffordshire Regt., w.3 [wounded 3 times], m [mentioned in despatches]. France d.w. [died of his wounds] 29.3.16 S.A.D [housemaster Rev. S.A. Donaldson][22]

Gerald had connections with three other educational establishments: Trinity College, Cambridge, which he attended after Eton, and Stoke House and Northaw Place Preparatory Schools at which he taught briefly in 1906. It is not known what Stoke House did, but Trinity and Northaw Place both included Gerald in their commemorations of the war dead. Trinity laid a memorial on the floor of the college chapel in front of the high altar and installed on either side of it oak panels engraved with the names of the six hundred and eighteen Trinity fellows, students and staff – including Gerald – who died during the course of the war.[23] Northaw Place was careful to maintain the class distinctions that served prep schools so well: the plaque it erected distinguished between three groups 'who gave their lives in the Great War': old boys, masters and servants.[24]

Gerald's death was commemorated, too, by virtue of his membership of the sports clubs that he joined after moving to Wolverhampton. As might be expected, the South Staffordshire Golf Club knew the right thing to do. Within two weeks of news of Gerald's death reaching Wolverhampton, the committee passed a resolution of sympathy with his father, 'His Honour Judge Howard Smith' and instructed the club secretary 'to write him a suitable letter'.[25] Three years later, it included Gerald's name on the memorial tablet that it erected in the clubhouse. Although Wolverhampton Cricket Club was more mixed socially than the South Staffordshire Golf Club, it, too, boasted a strong middle- and upper middle-class presence. The memorial it erected in honour of the nine members of the club who gave their lives 'for their king and country in the great European war 1914–1919' listed nine officers: four captains, three lieutenants (including Gerald) and two second lieutenants.[26]

Gerald's parents were also in a position to shape the way in which their son was remembered. The rich, the powerful and those in positions of authority were able to finance, initiate or at least influence the forms of remembrance they thought appropriate. Some bereaved families founded bursaries, some funded school improvements, some erected much more substantial memorials. In Hampshire, to take but one well-known example, Mary Behrend and her husband not only built a chapel in memory of her dead brother, but commissioned the artist Stanley Spencer to produce a series of nineteen paintings depicting his wartime experiences in England and overseas. Recognised as Spencer's 'masterpiece', it was finally completed in 1932.[27]

Although Philip Howard-Smith and his wife were not in the same league financially as the Behrends, they were determined that their son should be remembered for the individual that he was. They had both the motivation and the means. Philip, it seems, was struck particularly hard by the death of his son. The two appeared to have got on very well: Gerald followed Philip into the law; they lived together in the same (admittedly spacious) family home; and they shared an interest in cricket, Philip umpiring and Gerald playing for Wolverhampton Cricket Club.[28] Fortunately, he and his wife were well able to afford the cost of commemorating their son. When Philip died in 1919, he left an estate of £12,659 – a sum that would have been sufficient to purchase, for example, twenty-five or so three-bedroom, semi-detached houses in and around Wolverhampton.[29]

The Howard-Smiths acted quickly and decisively when Gerald died. Nevertheless, there were formalities to attend to. However wealthy and well connected the bereaved might be, it was no easy matter to secure public, personalised commemoration for a member of one's family. It took Philip nearly three months and cost him just over £32 to get diocesan approval for the erection of a marble memorial tablet in Bushbury parish church, close to the family home.[30] He had to commission the design of the tablet, get it approved by the vicar, obtain a quotation for engraving it, agree to meet the cost, secure the consent of the vestry, submit a petition to the Diocese of Lichfield and pay the Diocesan Registry the fee it demanded.[31] The tablet, installed towards the end of 1916, was striking for its focus on Gerald's military career and, at least to modern eyes, for its focus on his father – and its failure to make any reference to his mother:

In Loving Memory of Gerald Howard Smith, M.C. Lieut. 6th Batt. South Staffordshire Regt. Eldest son of Judge Howard Smith, Who died 29th March 1916 At Aubigny in France of wounds received at Neuville St. Vaast.
Pro Patria. Pro Libertate

Representing and misrepresenting the lost generation

No memorial plaque, no matter how lovingly conceived, no matter how carefully constructed, could possibly encapsulate the length, layers and complexities of Gerald's – or anybody else's – life. Focusing as it did on Gerald's military service and omitting – pointedly or otherwise – any mention of his mother, the tablet that Philip installed in Bushbury parish church in 1916 was partial at best, misleading at worst. Although hinting at Gerald's background and character, it ignored completely the first thirty-four years of his life. One looks in vain for any reference to his formative years, his career choices, his sporting interests, let alone his inner life, his private concerns or his personal relationships with anybody beyond his immediate family. No memorial can ever capture the person – and certainly not when it is death that defines the memory.

There is a further difficulty. Gerald's memorial and the many others like it that were erected during and after the war of 1914–18 contribute to the picture that many of us have of the so-called 'lost generation'. The trouble is that these memorials encourage us to view the Victorian and Edwardian middle and upper middle classes not just through the prism of those who erected them but in the light of the industrial scale suffering and losses that we know took such a dreadful toll.[32] It is a perspective that can lead us, unless we are careful, into accepting late nineteenth- and early twentieth-century notions of social class and social hierarchy. It is easy to be seduced, albeit unthinkingly, into believing that while all First World War losses are to be regretted, there was something particularly tragic about the deaths of talented, privileged, young (or youngish) officers like Gerald who never had the chance to fulfil their potential.

This is dangerous ground. The lost generation is not a myth: it was the most privileged who suffered the heaviest losses in the trenches of the Western Front. But as J.M. Winter has pointed out, the legend of the 'lost generation' took on a life of its own in the years that followed: 'Remembering the slaughter of elites seemed to take precedence over recognising that such casualties were but a small fraction of total British war losses.'[33] One cannot but agree, one cannot but urge caution. It is no surprise, of course, that the biographer of Gerald Howard-Smith should think that his life was full of interest, his premature death a personal, family and perhaps even a wider tragedy. But the biographer's focus must not obscure the broader picture, must not be allowed to distort the way in which we use individual lives in seeking to understand the complexities, complications and power relationships of late Victorian and Edwardian Britain.[34]

Notes

1 *Midland Counties Express*, April 1, 1916. The story is repeated, with some modification, in W.R. Lyon, *The Elevens of Three Great Schools, 1805–1929: Being all Recorded Scores of Cricket Matches Played Between Winchester, Eton & Harrow, with Memories & Biographies of the Players* (Eton: Spottiswoode, Ballantine & Co., 1930), p. 337.

2 Catherine Moriarty, 'Review Article: The Material Culture of Great War Remembrance', *Journal of Contemporary History*, 34, 4, 1999, p. 655.
3 Alex King, *Memorials of the Great War in Britain: The Symbolism and Politics of Remembrance* (Oxford: Berg, 1998), dust jacket. See, for example, James M. Mayo, 'War Memorials as Political Memory', *Geographical Review*, 78, 1, 1988; K.S. Inglis, 'The Homecoming: The War Memorial Movement in Cambridge, England', *Journal of Contemporary History*, 27, 4, 1992.
4 Alex King cited in Gabriel Koureas, *Memory, Masculinity and National Identity in British Visual Culture, 1914–1930: A Study of 'Unconquerable Manhood'* (Aldershot: Ashgate, 2007), p. 20.
5 John Lewis-Stempel, *Six Weeks: The Short and Gallant Life of the British Officer in the First World War* (London: Orion, 2010), p. 314.
6 Cited in King, *Memorials*, p. 187.
7 King, *Memorials*, p. 197.
8 Anthony Seldon and David Walsh, *Public Schools and the Great War: The Generation Lost* (Barnsley: Pen & Sword, 2013), pp. 188–9. Also King, *Memorials*, p. 187; Koureas, *Memory*, pp. 45–7.
9 www.cwgc.org/find-war-dead/casualty/996506/SMITH,%20GERALD%20HOWARD [February 2015].
10 *Walsall Observer and South Staffordshire Chronicle*, April 1, 1916; *Birmingham Daily Post*, April 1, 1916. See, too, Staffordshire Regiment Museum, Book 59, Unattributed Press Cutting, October 23, 1915.
11 *Yorkshire Post*, April 4, 1916; *Newcastle Daily Journal*, April 3, 4, 1916.
12 *Birmingham Gazette*, April 1, 1916.
13 Vyvyen Brendon, *Prep School Children: A Class Apart over Two Centuries* (London: Continuum, 2009), p. 94.
14 Jay Winter, *Sites of Memory, Sites of Mourning: The Great War in European Cultural History* (Cambridge: Cambridge University Press, 1995), p. 79. Also Seldon and Walsh, *Public Schools*, p. 192.
15 Meston Batchelor, *Cradle of Empire: A Preparatory School through Nine Reigns* (Chichester: Phillimore, 1981), pp. 78–9.
16 East Sussex Record Office, Temple Grove School, TGS3/2/1, *Temple Grove Magazine*, July 1916, p. 4.
17 www.news.eastsussex.gov.uk/chairman/2015/02/09/gildredgehousefreeschool [March 2015]; TGS17/4/2, *Temple Grove Roll of Honour*.
18 *Eton College Chronicle*, May 11, 1916.
19 Seldon and Walsh, *Public Schools*, p. 196.
20 L.S.R. Byrne and E.L. Churchill, *Changing Eton: A Survey of Conditions based on the History of Eton since the Royal Commission of 1862–64* (London: Cape, 1937), pp. 184–7.
21 www.iwm.org.uk/memorials/item/memorial/41461 [March 2015].
22 *List of Etonians who Fought in the Great War, 1914–1919* (London: Eton College, 1921), p. 230.
23 www.trinitycollegechapel.com/about/memorials/memorials-index [March 2015].
24 Information from Anthony Whitaker.
25 South Staffordshire Golf Club, Minute Book, 1914–22, Minutes of Committee, April 15, 1916.
26 www.wolverhamptonwarmemorials.org.uk/index.php?page=page-1-6 [October 2014].
27 Seldon and Walsh, *Public Schools*, p. 202. See, too, pp. 194–203; Alexandra Churchill, *Blood and Thunder: The Boys of Eton College and the First World War* (Stroud: History Press, 2014), p. 370.
28 *Midland Counties Express*, May 17, 1919.

29 *Calendar of the Grants of Probate and Letters of Administration*, 1919, p. 356; G.J. Barnsby, *A History of Housing in Wolverhampton 1750 to 1975* (Wolverhampton: Integrated Publishing Services,N.D.), pp. 46–7.
30 It took until 1922 for a memorial to the forty-one local men (including Gerald) killed during the war to be installed in the church.
31 Lichfield Record Office, B/C/12/1/102, Diocese of Lichfield, Court Records, 1916, 1921.
32 J.A. Mangan, 'Lamentable Barbarians and Pitiful Sheep: Rhetoric of Protest and Pleasure in late Victorian and Edwardian "Oxbridge"', *Victorian Studies*, 34, 4, 1991, p. 473.
33 Winter, 'Lost Generation', p. 465.
34 See Koureas, *Memory*.

BIBLIOGRAPHY

Primary sources

Manuscript collections

Cambridge University Library
    Cambridge University Cricket Club
    Cambridge University Athletic Club
East Sussex Record Office
    Temple Grove School
Eton College Archives
    Donaldson House Notes
    Eton Society
    Field
    Mixed Wall Game
    Officer Training Corps
Lichfield Record Office
    Diocese of Lichfield
London University, Institute of Advanced Legal Studies
    Law Society examination records
National Archives
    First World War medal cards
Norfolk Record Office
    Stoke House School
South Staffordshire Golf Club
    Club records
Staffordshire Regiment Museum
    Battalion war diaries
    Press cuttings
Wolverhampton Archives
    Nock and Joseland sales material
    Recruiting committee

Official publications

Calendar of the Grants of Probate and Letters of Administration
Census of England and Wales

Newspapers, magazines, guides and gazettes

Birmingham Daily Post
Birmingham Gazette
Cambridge Chronicle
Cricket and Football Field
Daily Mail
Daily News
Eton Calendar
Eton Chronicle
Express and Star
Harvard Crimson
Kelly's Directory
London Gazette
Luton News
Midland Counties Express
Morning Post
New York Times
Outing
Pall Mall Gazette
Paton's List of Schools and Tutors (An Aid to Parents in the Selection of Schools)
Penny Illustrated
Play
Preparatory Schools Review
Slough, Eton and Windsor Observer
Sporting Chronicle
Standard
Temple Grove Magazine
Walsall Observer and South Staffordshire Observer
Wolverhampton Chronicle

Autobiographies

Foley, Lieut.-Col.Cyril P., *Autumn Foliage* (London: Methuen, 1935).
Graves, Robert, *Goodbye to All That* (London: Penguin, 2000).
Hill, M.D., *Eton and Elsewhere* (London: John Murray, 1928).
Leslie, Shane, *The End of a Chapter* (New York: Charles Scribner's Sons, 1916).

Contemporary and near contemporary studies

A Committee of Officers who Served with the Battalion, *The War History of the Sixth Battalion the South Staffordshire Regiment* (London: Heinemann, 1924).
Lyon, W.R., *The Elevens of Three Great Schools, 1805–1929: Being all Recorded Scores of Cricket Matches Played between Winchester, Eton & Harrow, with Memoirs & Biographies of the Players* (Eton: Spottiswoode, Ballantine & Co., 1930).
Priestley, R.E., *Breaking the Hindenberg Line: The Story of the 46th (North Midland) Division* (London: Fisher and Unwin, 1919).
Stirling, J., *The Territorial Divisions 1914–1918* (London: Dent, 1922).

Websites

www.cricketarchive.com
www.hellfirecorner.co.uk
www.1914-1918.invisionzone.com
www.wolverhamptonswar.wordpress.com/

Secondary sources

Books and articles

Batchelor, M., *Cradle of Empire: A Preparatory School through Nine Reigns* (Chichester: Phillimore, 1981).
Beckett, Ian W.F. and Keith Simpson (eds), *A Nation in Arms: A Social Study of the British Army in the First World War* (London: Tom Donovan, 1990).
Benson, John, *The Working Class in Britain, 1850–1939* (London: Longman, 1989).
Benson, John, *Prime Time: A History of the Middle Aged in Twentieth-Century Britain* (London: Longman, 1997).
Benson, John, *Affluence and Authority: A Social History of Twentieth-Century Britain* (London: Arnold, 2005).
Benson, John, 'Sport, Class and Place: Gerald Howard-Smith and Early Twentieth-Century Wolverhampton', *Midland History*, 37, 2, 2012, pp. 207–221.
Benson, John, 'Athletics, Class and Nation: The Oxford-Cambridge University Tour of Canada and the United States of America, 1901', *Sport in History*, 33, 1, 2013, pp. 1–18.
Benson, John, '"Get a Blue and You Will See Your Money Back Again": Staffing and Marketing the English Prep School, 1880–1912', *History of Education*, 43, 3, 2014, pp. 355–367.
Boliver, T., *South Staffordshire Golf Club 1892–1992* (Wolverhampton: South Staffordshire Golf Club, 1992).
Brendon, Vyvyen, *Prep School Children: A Class Apart over Two Centuries* (London: Continuum, 2009).
Byrne, L.S.R. and E.L. Churchill, *Changing Eton: A Survey of Conditions Based on the History of Eton since the Royal Commission of 1862–4* (London: Jonathan Cape, 1937).
Churchill, Alexandra, *Blood and Thunder: The Boys of Eton College and the First World War* (Stroud: History Press, 2014).
Cook, Tim, '"Literary Memorials": The Great War Regimental Histories, 1919–1939', *Journal of the Canadian Historical Association*, 13, 1, 2002, pp. 167–190.
DeGroot, Gerard J., *Blighty: British Society in the Era of the Great War* (London: Longman, 1996).
Deslandes, Paul R., *Oxbridge Men: British Masculinity and the Undergraduate Experience, 1850–1920* (Bloomington: Indiana University Press, 2005).
Frith, D. *The Golden Age of Cricket 1890–1914* (Ware: Omega Books, 1983).
Hamlett, Jane, *Material Relations: Domestic Interiors and Middle-Class Families in England, 1850–1910* (Manchester: Manchester University Press, 2010).
Hill, J., *Sport, Leisure and Culture in Twentieth-Century Britain* (Basingstoke: Palgrave, 2002).
Holmes, Richard, *Tommy: The British Soldier on the Western Front 1914–1918* (London: HarperCollins, 2004).

Holt, Richard, *Sport and the British: A Modern History* (Oxford: Oxford University Press, 1990).
Huggins, Mike, *The Victorians and Sport* (London: Hambledon, 2004).
Huggins, Mike and J.A. Mangan (eds), *Disreputable Pleasures: Less Virtuous Victorians at Play* (London: Frank Cass, 2004).
Inglis, K.S., 'The Homecoming: The War Memorial Movement in Cambridge, England', *Journal of Contemporary History*, 27, 4, 1992, pp. 583–605.
Joyce, Patrick, *The State of Freedom: A Social History of the British State since 1800* (Cambridge: Cambridge University Press, 2013).
King, Alex, *Memorials of the Great War in Britain: The Symbolism and Politics of Remembrance* (Oxford: Berg, 1998).
Koureas, Gabriel, *Memory, Masculinity and National Identity in British Visual Culture, 1914–1930: A Study of 'Unconquerable Manhood'* (Aldershot: Ashgate, 2007).
Lawrence, Jon, 'Class and Gender in the Making of Urban Toryism, 1880–1914', *English Historical Review*, 108, 428, 1993, pp. 629–652.
Leinster-Mackay, Donald, *The Rise of the English Prep School* (Lewes: Falmer Press, 1984).
Levett, Geoffrey, 'Sport and the Imperial City: Colonial Tours in Edwardian London', *London Journal*, 35, 1, 2010, pp. 39–57.
Light, Alison, *Mrs Woolf and the Servants* (London: Penguin, 2007).
Lowerson, John, 'Sport and the Victorian Sunday: The Beginnings of Middle-Class Apostasy', *International Journal of the History of Sport*, 1, 2, 1984, pp. 202–220.
Mangan, J.A., 'Lamentable Barbarians and Pitiful Sheep: Rhetoric of Protest and Pleasure in late Victorian and Edwardian "Oxbridge"', *Victorian Studies*, 34, 4, 1991, pp. 473–489.
Mason, Tony, *Association Football & English Society 1863–1915* (Brighton: Harvester, 1981).
Mason, Tony, *Sport in Britain* (London: Faber & Faber, 1988).
Mason, Tony and Eliza Riedi, *Sport and the Military: The British Armed Forces 1880–1960* (Cambridge: Cambridge University Press, 2010).
Mayo, M., 'War Memorials as Political Memory', *Geographical Review*, 78, 1, 1988, pp. 62–75.
Mitchinson, K.W., *The Territorial Force at War, 1914–1916* (London: Palgrave Macmillan, 2014).
Nauright, J. and T.J.L. Chandler (eds), *Making Men: Rugby and Masculine Identity* (London: Cass, 1999).
Peaple, Simon, *Mud, Blood and Determination: The History of the 46th (North Midland) Division in the Great War* (Solihull: Helion, 2015).
Perkin, Harold, *The Rise of Professional Society: England since 1880* (London: Routledge, 1989).
Porter, Dilwyn, 'Amateur Football in England, 1948–63: The Pegasus Phenomenon', *Contemporary British History*, 14, 2000, pp. 1–30.
Reader, W.J., *At Duty's Call: A Study in Obsolete Patriotism* (Manchester: Manchester University Press, 1988).
Seldon, Anthony and David Walsh, *Public Schools and the Great War: The Generation Lost* (Barnsley: Pen & Sword, 2013).
Sheffield, Gary, *Leadership in the Trenches: Officer–Man Relations, Morale and Discipline in the British Army in the Era of the First World War* (London: Palgrave, 2000).

Sheffield, Gary, *Forgotten Victory: The First World War: Myths and Realities* (London: Headline, 2001).
Sheffield, Gary, *The Chief: Douglas Haig and the British Army* (London: Aurum Press, 2011).
Sheffield, Gary, *Command and Morale: The British Army on the Western Front 1914–1918* (Barnsley: Pen & Sword, 2014).
Simkins, Peter, *Kitchener's Army: The Raising of the New Armies 1914–1916* (Barnsley: Pen & Sword, 2014).
Sugarman, David, 'Simple Images and Complex Realities: English Lawyers and their Relationship to Business and Politics, 1750–1950', *Law and History Review*, 11, 2, 1993, pp. 257–302.
Thompson, F.M.L., 'Social Control in Victorian Britain', *Economic History Review*, 34, 3, 1981, pp.189–208.
Thompson, F.M.L., *The Rise of Respectable Society: A Social History of Victorian Britain 1830–1900* (London: Fontana, 1988).
Thornton, Andrew, 'Recruiting for the Territorial Force in Staffordshire, August 1914– December 1915', *Journal of the Centre for First World War Studies*, 1, 2, 2004, pp. 1–30.
Tosh, John, *A Man's Place: Masculinity and the Middle Class Home in Victorian England* (London: Yale University Press, 2007).
Travers, Tim, *The Killing Ground: The British Army, the Western Front and the Experience of Modern War 1900–1918* (Barnsley: Pen & Sword, 1987).
Ugolini, Laura, *Men and Menswear: Sartorial Consumption in Britain 1880–1939* (Aldershot: Ashgate, 2007).
Ugolini, Laura, *Civvies: Middle-Class Men and the English Home Front, 1914–18* (Manchester: Manchester University Press, 2013).
Vamplew, Wray, 'Sharing Space: Inclusion, Exclusion and Accommodation at the British Golf Club before 1914', *Journal of Sport and Social Issues*, 34, 3, 2010, pp. 359–375.
Winter, J.M., *The Great War and the British People* (London: Macmillan, 1985).
Winter, Jay, *Sites of Memory, Sites of Mourning: The Great War in European Cultural History* (Cambridge: Cambridge University Press, 1995).
Winter, J.M., 'Britain's "Lost Generation" of the First World War', *Population Studies*, 31, 3, 1997, pp. 449–466.
Wright, S., *Waterfield's School: A Preparatory School in its Victorian Heyday* (Guildford: Heron Ghyll Press, 1994).

Unpublished works

Thornton, A., 'The Territorial Force in Staffordshire 1908–1915' (MPhil thesis, University of Birmingham, 2004).
Woods, Michael, '"Gas, Grenades and Grievances": The Attack on Hohenzollern Redoubt by 46th (North Midland) Division, 13 October 1915 (2015).

INDEX

Figures indexed in bold page numbering

adolescence 16, 23–5, 33, 76, 78
adulthood 4, 23, 78
Agar-Robartes, Gerald 23
Agar-Robartes, Thomas Charles Reginald 23
Age 3–4, 8, 11, 14, 24, 76, 78, 80, 100–4; *see also* childhood, adolescence, adulthood, middle age
amateurism 82, 84
Anglo-Indian families 5
Anglo-Irish families 8
aristocracy ix–x, 5, 98, 102
army 55, 98–9, 101, 104–6, 109, 121–2, 131; Bengal 5; hierarchy 125; policies 118; procedures 105; regular 102; territorial 90, 110, 116–31; volunteer 99–100, 103
Asquith, Raymond 25
Association of Headmasters of Preparatory Schools 10
Atherstone 58, 75–6
athletics 16–17, 19, 21, 32–40, 47, 56–7, 59–64
Atlee, Clement 64
Aubigny 142
Aubigny Communal Cemetery Extension 139

bachelorhood 78
Bailey, Clara 7
Barnes, Sydney 85
Battalion war diary 116
Battalions 102, 117, 123; 6th Battalion, South Staffordshire Regiment 87, 102–31, 116; arrival at the frontline 119–20; bombing parties 122–3, 126; training 18, 102–10, 115, 117–31; death toll 120; fatigue and anxiety 121
Bayliss, Samuel 88–9, 109
Beechmont School, Sevenoaks 68
Behrend, Mary 142
Bengal Army 5
Bennett, Judith M. xiii
billets 107, 120, 129
biography x–xiii; 'internal' xi–xii; 'external' xii–xiii
Bird, Alfred 87
Birmingham Daily Mail 139
Birmingham Gazette 139
Black Country 73–5, 89, 110
Blues 31–3, 44–6, 55–6, 61–5, 67–8, 85
bombs and bombing officers 122–3, 126
bowling and bowlers 21–2, 43, 61, 85, 139–40
Bradfield College, Berkshire 86
British Army 102, 130, 137; *see also* army
Burton-on-Trent 107–8
Bushbury parish church 142–3
Butterworth, George 25

Cambridge 16, 31–7, 40–7, 55–9, 61, 65, 74, 80–1, 84–5, 140–1
Cambridge Chronicle 31, 35, 43, 101
Cambridge University xvi, 31–47, 79, 84; difficulties of leaving 56–7, 60–3, 82; teams 34, 42, 44–5
Cambridge University Association Football Club 36
Cambridge University Athletic Club (CUAC) 33–4, 36–41, 44
Cambridge University Boat Club 36
Cambridge University Cricket Club (CUCC) 36, 40–1

152 Index

Cambridge University Rugby Union Football Club 36
Carnarvon, Countess of ix
casualties of war 97–8, 121, 123–4, 126, 139, 143
cemeteries 138–9
Chandler, T.L. 15
Charterhouse School 31, 33–5, 40, 44–6, 55–6, 58, 61–2, 64–6, 68, 77
Chesterfield xiv
childhood 4–9, 24–5, 33, 44, 76
chlorine gas 120–1
class, class awareness, class identity and class relationships 9, 24–5, 73–4, 110, 115, 117, 127–31,138–43; *see also* class superiority, cross-class cohesion and consensus
class superiority 110, 115, 127, 130, 138
classics, study and teaching of 3, 10–11, 15, 33
Collinson, Edwin Read 109
commanding officers 105, 108–9
commemoration 137–42; communal 138; personalised 142
commissions 102–6, 139, 142
comradeship 82, 137–8
contemporaries of Gerald 4, 7, 11–12, 22, 31, 44, 78, 83–4, 101, 103–5; Eton 24–5; Wolverhampton 79; Oxbridge 56; upper middle-class 32, 77
County Court Circuit 58, 75–6
Cresswell, Edward Arthur 109
cricket 11, 21–2, 33, 40–6, 55–8, 61–9, 84–7; county 40, 43, 84; Eton 21; first-class 42, 46, 56–7, 61–2; Harrow 4; Oxford and Cambridge 40–1, 43, 47; status and role of 40–1, 43, 45; umpires 18, 58, 88–9
cricket clubs 42, 90, 117; Cambridge University Cricket Club 36, 40–1; Gentlemen of Marylebone Cricket Club 85; London County Cricket Club 42; Marylebone Cricket Club 42, 46, 61–2, 74, 85–6; Staffordshire County Cricket Club 84–5; Wolverhampton Cricket Club 58, 81, 86–8, 97, 101, 105–6, 109, 117, 139, 141–2
cricket matches 11–12, 19, 22, 40–2, 44–6, 56, 60, 65, 84–6, 88–90
cross-class cohesion and consensus 126–7, 137
Crystal Palace 42

Daily Mail 22, 43–4, 46, 61, 68, 81
death 57, 73, 75, 116–17, 120–1, 124, 126, 128, 138–40, 142–3; demoralised by 124; premature 143; recorded 140; toll 120
DeGroot, Gerard J. 99, 104
dependence 69; domestic 76; financial 77
Deslandes, Paul R. 39, 77
Dickens, Charles 60
Dictionary of Labour Biography xi
discipline 87–8, 107, 128; *see also* military discipline
Donaldson, S.A. 16–18, 21, 23–4, 141
Downton Abbey ix, xiv
Duff, James 33

Eden, Anthony 115
Edgar, Rev. J.H. 9–10, 12, 14, 89
education 15, 59, 105, 141; commercial 15; prep school 9, 66–7; private 9, 15, 62, 65, 67; public school 15, 17, 56, 101, 103; university 55–6; *see also* schools
enlistment 100, 103–5, 110
Eton College xvi, 14–25, 32–3, 40, 42, 55, 64–5, 69, 80–1, 100–1, 140–1; Contingent 105; Field Eleven 21; Volunteer Battalion 18; Officers Training Corps 100–1; Eton Society ("Pop") 4, 16, 23; memorials at 141; and Temple Grove Preparatory School 14, 25, 77; and working-class sport 21, 59
Eton College Chronicle 15, 19–21, 59, 101, 140
Eton Ramblers 41–2, 62, 84, 89
Etonians, and Old Etonians 15–16, 20–1, 32, 59–60, 82, 97, 101, 105, 141
Evans, Richard J. xiii
Express and Star 86, 88, 102–3

families and family life 3–5, 7–9, 15, 24, 64–5, 76–7, 89–90, 100, 138–9, 142–3; Anglo-Indian 5; Anglo-Irish 8; bereaved 142; extended 8, 77, 126; upper middle-class 3–4, 24, 31, 58, 74, 77–8, 82, 98, 102–3, 116; wealthy 6, 36
Fenners 34–5, 40–1, 47
field dressing stations 140
Finnis, Arthur 89, 109
First World War 64, 68, 87, 97–110, 115–31, 137–43
Foley, Cyril Pelham 56

Index

football 11–12, 14, 19–21, 23, 59–61, 64, 68, 84, 101, 140; association 66; rugby 11–12, 15, 20–1, 40, 55
Foreman, Amanda ix
France 104, 107–8, 110, 115–30, 139, 141–2
Free Foresters 41–2, 61–2, 84–7, 89, 97, 118
Frior, Amy 7
Frith, David 57
frontline fighting 115, 118–20, 122, 127–30
Fry, C.B. 40

games 11–12, 19–22, 40–7, 59, 61–3, 68, 84, 86–7, 109; high level 44, 61, 84–6; rugby 11–12, 15, 20–1, 40, 55; soccer 21; ship's 125
games masters 33, 63
gentlemen and gentlemanliness 36, 40, 57, 60, 62, 79, 82–4, 88
Gentlemen of Marylebone Cricket Club 85
Gerald Howard-Smith xvii
Gerald Howard-Smith and a Trinity College Cricket XI, 1903 **45**
Gerald Howard-Smith and fellow officers of the 6th Battalion, South Staffordshire Regiment, three miles southeast of Ypres, March 1915 **119**
Gerald Howard-Smith and the Eton Field XI, 1898 **20**
Germans 119–20, 122, 124, 126
Godden, Olive 7
golf 83–4, 86–7, 97
graves 103; Aubigny Communal Cemetery Extension 139; of French and English soldiers 118
Graves Registration Committee 138
Graves, Robert 10, 103
Great War *see* First World War
Greek, study and teaching of 4, 10–11
Guinness, Edward 23

Haig, Douglas 55–6
Hamlett, Jane xiv, 78
Hanbury-Tracey, Charles 56
hand grenades 122–3, 126
Harrow School 4, 14–15, 22, 55–6, 100
headmasters 10, 12, 25, 55, 63, 65–6, 68, 102, 140
headstones 139
Heathcoat-Amory, Ludovic 23
Henderson, Walter 39, 61

Hill, Elizabeth 7
Hindley, Edward Obert 21
Hobhouse, Stephen 25
Hohenzollern Redoubt 123–4, 137, 139
Holmes, Richard 117, 122
Holt, Richard 33, 62, 82
Home Counties 57, 63, 69, 73, 81
Horn, Pamela ix
Horner, Arthur x
housemaids 5, 7–8 *see also* servants
housemasters 4, 16–17, 19, 68, 141
Howard-Smith, Gerald: background upbringing and circumstances 84, 100, 106, 139, 143; Cambridge Blue 68, 82, 97; childhood 4–14, 24, 33, 44, 76; death 81, 126, 130, 137, 139–42; Eton College 14–25, 32–3, 40, 42, 55, 64–5, 69, 80–1, 100–1, 140–1; frontline fighting 115, 118–20, 122, 127–30; grandparents 8, 15–16, 69; independence 69, 76, 78; injuries 120–1, 126, 128, 137, 139; leadership 18, 44, 82, 85, 98, 100–1, 122; military and religious commitment 19, 143; mythologizing of 137; parents 4, 24–5, 58–9, 139, 142; sporting performances 47, 62, 84; teaching career 65; Trinity College 16, 31–3, 37, 39–40, 42, 45, 60–1, 69, 141; undergraduate career 46
Howard-Smith, Judge Philip (Gerald's father) 4–9, 32, 57–8, 76, 79, 88, 142
Howard-Smith, Mary (Gerald's mother) 4–9, 25, 57–8, 76, 142
Howl, Clifford 89–90, 109
Huggins, Mike 46, 83
Hughes, Kathryn ix
Hunt, Tristram x

Imperial War Graves Commission 138

Jesus College, Cambridge 84–5

Kensington xvi, 4–9
Knowles, James Lees 37, 87
Koss, Stephen 5

Latin, study and teaching of 10–11, 80
law and lawyers 5, 8, 79–82, 89, 109; *see also* solicitors
Leader, Edward 61
Leamington Spa 74–5, 87, 90
Lees, James 37
Leinster-Mackay, Donald 11, 67

154 Index

letters home 10, 65–6, 121–2, 129–30, 138
Levett, Geoffrey 44
Lichfield 58, 75–6, 142
Lichfield Garrison 87
London Athletic Club (LAC) 35, 60–1, 74, 101
London clubs 8
London County Cricket Club 42
London Gazette 103, 105
Lord Lichfield 85–6, 102
"lost generation" xiii–xv 137–9, 143
Lowerson, John 84
Luton 107–8
Luton News 107–8

machine guns 123, 126, 129
Macmillan, Harold 115
magazines, guides and gazettes: *London Gazette* 103, 105; *Pall Mall Gazette* 5–6, 35; *Paton's List of Schools and Tutors* 67–8; *Temple Grove Magazine* 12, 140
Malvern College 41–2, 87, 89–90
Mangan, J.A. 31, 33, 46, 63
manhood and manliness 3–4,12, 15, 39, 76–9
Mansions, Alexandra 139
Manual of Domestic Economy 7
Markham, Violet xiv
marriage 77–8
Marseilles 124–5
Mason, Tony 36, 55
McKinley, William 38
Meakin, Bernard 84
memory 126, 137–9, 142–3
mercantile houses 60
middle age 76, 78, 82, 104
middle class 7, 13, 36, 73–4, 78, 83, 89, 101–3, 110; background 84; exclusivity 9; sociability 90; values 13
Middleditch, Bernard 84–5
Midland Counties Express 76, 137, 139–40
military 18, 31, 86, 100, 107, 124–5, 129–30, 137, 139; discipline 101, 106, 117; experience 105; historians 130; hospitals 127; life 18, 101, 110; operations 124; service 45, 98; tacticians 123; traditions 100; training 31, 59–60, 80, 89, 99, 101, 103, 106–8, 115–18, 127–8
Morgan, Kenneth x
Morning Post 4, 42

Moseley, Henry 25
Mourdant, Henry John 42

National Trust ix
Nepos, Cornelius 11
Neville, Jim 65
New York Times 38
Newcastle Daily Journal 139
newspapers: *Birmingham Daily Mail* 139; *Birmingham Gazette* 139; *Daily Mail* 22, 43–4, 46, 61, 68, 81; *Express and Star* 86, 88, 102–3; *Luton News* 107–8; *Midland Counties Express* 76, 137, 139–40; *Morning Post* 4, 42; *New York Times* 38; *Newcastle Daily Journal* 139; *Slough, Eton and Windsor Observer* 62; *Walsall Observer* 139; *Yorkshire Post* 139
Nordpeene 118, 128
North Midland Division 107, 123–4
North Staffordshire Regiment 122
Northaw Place Preparatory School 63–4, 67, 141
Nugent, George 36

Officer Training Corps 18
officers and officer class 18, 42, 87, 98, 103–10, 116, 118–22, 124–5, 127–30, 137–9, 142–3; Battalion 108, 129; committee of 87, 106, 130; deaths 139; junior 98; medical 74; potential 103; servants 109; territorial 131
Orwell, George 14
O'Shaughnessy, Mary Beaumont (Gerald's mother) 5–9, 14, 57–8, 76, 126
O'Shaughnessy, Richard (Gerald's maternal grandfather) 5
'other ranks' 18, 21, 87, 98, 108–9, 121–2, 124, 139
Oxbridge 31–3, 35, 39, 46, 55–6, 80
Oxbridge Blues 40, 55, 66, 68; *see also* Blues
Oxford and Cambridge 43, 45, 56; athletics clubs 37; athletics combined team's tour to Canada and the United States 36–9; athletics meeting at Queen's Club 37, 47; boat race 47; cricket 40–1, 43, 47; graduates 55; undergraduates 36
Oxford University 31, 33–5, 40, 44–6, 55–6, 58, 61–2, 64–6, 68, 77
Oxford University Athletic Club 33, 60
Oxfordshire Light Infantry 18

Index

Page, Edgar Wells 86, 89
Pall Mall Gazette 5–6, 35
parents 6, 9–10, 15–17, 24, 57–9, 63, 65, 67, 69, 76–7; burying sons 97; upper middle-class 3–4, 7; working-class 13
Parry, Edward Hagarty 64–5
Paton's List of Schools and Tutors 67–8
patriotism 12, 97–101, 103, 105, 107, 109, 115; and sacrifice 117, 119, 121, 123, 125, 127, 129; upper middle-class 99
Peace, Charles 10
Penny Cyclopaedia 4
Perkin, Harold 55
"Pop" (Eton Society) 4, 16, 23, 25, 32, 37, 42
power and power relationships ix–x, 15, 31, 66, 79, 138, 143; *see also* privilege
prep schools 3–4, 9–11, 14, 16, 24–5, 55, 63–8, 100, 139–40; class distinctions 141; curriculum 64; education 9, 66–7; facilities 67; masters 66; teaching 14, 62–3, 66, 68, 74
Prince Adolphus 12
Prince Albert 73
Prince Francis 12
Prince Ranjitsinhji 40
Princess Royal 12
private schools and private education 3, 9, 15, 25, 55, 62, 67
privilege ix–x, 4, 6, 7–8, 10–12, 14–16, 18, 20, 22–4, 31–2, 39, 42, 68, 90, 100–1, 105, 115 ; *see also* power and power relationships
public schools 3, 9–11, 13–15, 19–21, 39–40, 64, 82, 98, 100, 138–9; curriculum 15; games and sport 22, 33; education 15, 17, 56, 101, 103; *see also* headmasters
punting 66

Queen Victoria 12, 62, 73

Ramsden, Jack 17
Rees, Edmund Scott Gustave 81
Regiments 106, 127, 137; North Staffordshire 122; South Staffordshire 87, 102–10, 116–31, 139, 141–2; Suffolk 118
Roebuck, Peter 57
Roosevelt, Theodore 38
Royal Flying Corps 98
Royal Welch Fusiliers 103

Saffron Walden 108, 118, 137
school magazines 11–12, 65, 140
schoolboys 21, 33, 128; eighteen year-old 21; ex-public 36, 105; public 98, 100
schools 3–4, 9–21, 23–5, 32–3, 58–9, 63–9, 98, 101–2, 108, 140–1; Beechmont School 68; Bradfield College 86; Eton College 14–25, 32–3, 40, 42, 55, 64–5, 69, 80–1, 100–1, 140–1; Harrow 4, 14–15, 22, 55–6, 100; Northaw Place Preparatory School 63, 141; St Paul's School 5; Stoke House Preparatory School 64–5, 67–8, 141; Temple Grove Preparatory School 9–14, 16, 24–5, 32, 63, 65, 74, 100–1, 140; Tettenhall College 102; Tredennyke School 68; Wolverhampton Grammar School 102, 106
Seldon, Anthony 98–9, 138
servants 3, 5–8, 40, 58, 89, 109, 129, 141; liveried 8; *see also* housemaids
Shaluffa 125
Sheffield, Gary 56, 115
Simpson, Keith 103
Slough, Eton and Windsor Observer 62, 121
Smith, Sir William (Gerald's paternal grandfather) 4, 8
soccer 21, 40, 42, 55, 60
socialisation 3, 5, 7, 9, 11, 13–15, 17, 19, 21, 23; schools 3, 5, 7, 9, 11, 13, 15, 17, 19, 21; upper middle-class 4, 25
soldiers 13, 65, 122, 137
solicitors 79–81, 86, 89, 105, 109, 137, 139; *see also* law and lawyers
South Staffordshire Golf Club (SSGC) 83–4, 86, 97, 105, 109, 141
South Staffordshire Regiment 87, 102–10, 116–31, 139, 141–2
Spencer, Earl 31
Spencer, Stanley 142
sport, sportsmanship and sociability 4, 11–12, 14–22, 31–3, 35–41, 43–7, 55–8, 60–70, 81–90, 97, 100–108, 108, 141, 143
St Aubyn, Edward Geoffrey 32
St Paul's School 5
Staffordshire 42, 76, 84–6, 88, 90, 97, 101–3
Staffordshire County Cricket Club 84–5
Statham, Phoebe 7
status and standing ix–x, 5, 9, 31, 33, 35–7, 39, 62, 79–81, 85, 88, 138–9
Steedman, Carolyn xi

Stoke House Preparatory School 64–5, 67–8, 141
Stone, Florence 7
Strathcona, Lord 37–8
Stubbs, William 19
Suffolk Regiment 118
Sugarman, David 80
"Suicide Squad" 122
Sutton Coldfield 87–9

Taylor, A.J.P. xiv
teams and teammates 11–12, 15, 20–2, 32, 36–8, 43–6, 60–1, 65, 82–9, 82, 84–9, 105, 126
Temple Grove Magazine 12, 140
Temple Grove Preparatory School 9–14, 16, 24–5, 32, 63, 65, 74, 77, 100–1, 140
Temple Grove Roll of Honour 140
Territorial Force 102–3, 105, 108; commanders 103; units, divisions and regiments 87, 102, 105, 107, 117, 128–9
Tettenhall 74, 86–7, 89
Tettenhall College 102
Thomas Parker Company 81
Thompson, F.M.L. 3, 9, 13
Tomalin, Claire xi
Tosh, John 59, 76–7
Travellers' Club, London 102
Tredennyke School, Worcester 68
trenches and trench wafare 100, 107–8, 115, 119–24, 126, 128–9, 143
Trinity College, Cambridge 5, 8, 16, 31–3, 36–7, 39–40, 42, 45, 60–1, 141

Ugolini, Laura 76, 104
umpires 18, 58, 88–9
Underhill, James E. 79–81, 84, 104, 109
Underhill and Thorneycroft (later Underhill, Thorneycroft and Smith) 79–81, 84, 109

university ix–x, xiv, 3–4, 7, 9, 15–16, 19, 24–5, 31–7, 39–43, 45–7, 55–9, 62–3, 66, 69, 74, 77–8, 82, 84, 89, 98–105, 116, 131; sport 31–47

volunteers and volunteer army 18, 87, 98–105

Walsall Observer 139
Walsh, David 7, 25, 98–9, 138
Walsh, J.H. 7
War History of the Sixth Battalion the South Staffordshire Regiment 106, 109–10, 116, 118, 121, 124–6, 128–9
war memorials 138–43
Warre House 16–17
West Midlands 58, 73–6, 105
Western Front 99, 115, 117–31, 119–21, 126, 130, 139, 143
White, Robert 102
Wolverhampton xiv, 58–9, 73–90, 97, 101–10, 117, 129, 139, 141–2; solicitors 86, 105, 109; working class 73–4, 86
Wolverhampton Conservative Club 110, 129
Wolverhampton County Court 76
Wolverhampton Cricket Club 58, 81, 86–8, 97, 101, 105–6, 109, 117, 139, 141–2
Wolverhampton Grammar School 102, 106
women's history xi
working class 13, 21, 59, 73–4, 82, 86, 90, 104, 110
Wulverghem sector 119

Yorkshire Post 139
Ypres 119–21, 130